THE WRITER'S GUIDE TO MAGAZINE MARKETS: NONFICTION

Helen Rosengren Freedman and Karen Krieger

A PLUME BOOK
NEW AMERICAN LIBRARY
TIMES MIRROR
NEW YORK AND SCARBOROUGH, ONTARIO

Copyright © 1983 by Helen Rosengren Freedman and Karen
Krieger

PLUME TRADEMARK REG. U.S. PAT. OFF. AND FOREIGN COUNTRIES
REGISTERED TRADEMARK—MARCA REGISTRADA HECHO EN
WESTFORD, MASS., U.S.A.

SIGNET, SIGNET CLASSIC, MENTOR, PLUME, MERIDIAN
and NAL BOOKS are published *in the United States*
by The New American Library, Inc., 1633 Broadway, New York,
New York, 10019, *in Canada* by The New American Library of Canada Limited,
81 Mack Avenue, Scarborough, Ontario M1L 1M8

Library of Congress Cataloging in Publication Data:

Freedman, Helen Rosengren.
Writer's guide to magazine markets, nonfiction.

1. Authorship—Handbooks, manuals, etc.   2. American magazines
—Directories.   I. Krieger, Karen.   II. Title.
PN161.F73   1983   808'.02   83-13153
ISBN 0-452-25652-3

PRINTED IN THE UNITED STATES OF AMERICA

PROFESSIONAL WRITERS NEED INFORMATION AND MARKETING KNOWLEDGE

You may be just starting out, and wondering what your first move should be.

You may have been writing for years, but are still looking to expand your markets.

Whatever your status, this information-packed handbook will put you on the inside track to the most receptive magazine audience for your work.

THE WRITER'S GUIDE TO MAGAZINE MARKETS: NONFICTION

HELEN ROSENGREN FREEDMAN and KAREN KRIEGER have worked for numerous magazines as editors, and have been published in national magazines. They are also the authors of THE WRITER'S GUIDE TO MAGAZINE MARKETS: FICTION, available in a Plume edition.

To Howard,
    With love and thanks.
        Helen Rosengren Freedman

Contents

In acknowledgment:

The authors would like to thank all the magazine editors who gave so freely of their time to make this book possible.

THE WRITER'S GUIDE TO MAGAZINE MARKETS: NONFICTION

Introduction

To become a successful free-lancer all you have to do is hit the right magazine with the right idea at the right time.

Unfortunately it's not as easy as it sounds. The free-lancing business is tough and highly competitive. For every writer who receives a letter saying, "We like the sound of your idea. Let's discuss it some more," there are dozens, even hundreds, of other writers receiving letters that say, "Thank you for thinking of us, but unfortunately we cannot use your article at this time."

In order to succeed as a free-lancer, you need to write well and you need to sell what you write. No one can teach you how to write. But the rest of the formula for success involves some very practical considerations and *can* be learned. How much free-lance work is a magazine buying? What kinds of material is it buying? How do I approach a particular magazine? What are the chances the idea will be accepted? The answers are in this book. And a writer who acts without such information is simply setting himself up for rejection.

This book does not guarantee success. But it *does* contain a wealth of "bottom line," honest information about varying policies at magazines, different editors' personal preferences regarding the submissions process, and their tips for writers trying to break in.

To gather the information, we talked at length with the editors who handle unsolicited submissions, who make the "yes" or "no" decisions. In most cases the interviews were done in person; we talked to a few editors by phone and a few answered written questionnaires. In all cases we had to rely on the willingness of each of the editors to talk openly. Some were more willing to talk than others, believing the time spent might help the writer to more appropriately target his idea and reduce the never-ending pile of submissions on their own desks.

We chose the magazines listed because we consider them to be the best showcases for the article writer's work. All are consumer/newsstand publications. Most are "name" publications, distributed nationally. A published article appearing in any of them will provide an excellent start to the beginning writer's portfolio.

How to use the guide

The magazines are listed alphabetically. A cross-listing of magazines by category is included on pages 359–63. There you will find the women's magazines grouped together, the magazines that are looking for general-interest material, the sports magazines, etc.

Each listing begins with the address and phone number of the magazine, and the "**Source**"—the person who supplied the information in the listing. Unless otherwise indicated (under "How to Submit") this is the person to whom submissions should be sent.

"**In short**" sums up the free-lancer's chances—at a glance.

"**About the magazine**" gives a rundown of the market. It tells you: how often the magazine is published; how much of the magazine is free-lance–written; what the magazine's editorial content is; who reads the magazine; what the magazine's circulation and estimated total readership figures are.

"**Sample copy**": Most of the magazines listed are available on newsstands. For those that may be harder to locate, we have included details on ordering directly from the magazine. (If a difficult-to-find magazine does not have this listing, it means sample copies are not available and these will have to be located at your library.)

"**Areas open to free-lancers**": One of the most common complaints we heard from editors was the number of submissions they receive for areas in their magazines that are written by staffers. These areas are not generally easy to determine by studying mastheads, however. So with each listing we have given a rundown of the areas where free-lancers *may* submit. Don't risk an immediate rejection by assuming a certain area/department is open. If it is, it will be listed.

Basic information: How much the magazine pays for articles; whether they pay on acceptance of the finished manuscript or on publication of the article; extra fees they will pay for any expenses incurred; whether they will pay a kill fee on articles they decide not to publish; what rights they buy from the writer; roughly, the number of unsolicited submissions they're receiving weekly—how many other submissions is yours competing with? how long you will have to wait, approximately, for a reply to your submission; the magazine's lead time (time from editing to publication), and how far in advance they are planning issues.

"Free-lance possibilities": What are your *real* chances of being published at a particular magazine? A rundown is given of how much material is being written by free-lancers (as opposed to staff writers); the *kinds* of writers appearing in the magazine (how experienced are they?); how often new writers are appearing (as opposed to regular contributors); how often the magazine is using work by unpublished or little-published writers; what *kinds* of story ideas might work; subject areas the editors are *not* looking for; examples of published articles that originally came in over-the-transom; the most common reasons ideas—and writers—are being rejected; the amount of editing done, whether the writer is given the chance to do any necessary rewriting, whether galleys are shown to writers before publication.

"How to submit": How to approach the magazine the way *they* prefer. Will the magazine accept phone queries? Manuscript submissions? Photocopies? Multiple submissions? The editor's preferences on query letters are also given—how long they should be, what they should include, whether you should send clips and/or a list of writing credits.

"Rejections": Read this section before you get depressed by a form rejection, or elated by a personal reply. It tells you how the magazine rejects unsolicited material, and how to realistically read a rejection slip.

How to get an article published

In targeting your submission well, much depends on whether you have the story idea to begin with. If you do—if you know *what* you want to write about—the task is to find the magazines that will be most receptive to your idea.

If you don't have an actual article idea and just want to be published, one good strategy is to focus in on the kind of publications in which you might like to see your work appear. Alternatively, look through the guide to see which magazines are most open and then write a piece for one of those magazines. Try to be realistic. If you are a beginning writer, you should try magazines that are less well known, and probably pay less, but are somewhat open to writers with limited experience.

In either case, it is *essential* to *know* a magazine before you submit a proposal or manuscript. How can you do this? First, study the listings. Included in each, under "About the magazine," is a demographic breakdown of the readership. These facts and figures are important because one of the first steps in targeting a story idea is to ask: What kind of person reads this magazine and why would they be interested in *my* article?

Obviously, if a writer sends an article called "How to Deal with Office Politics" to a magazine that aims at housewives, he is looking for a rejection. Conversely, proposing "How to Deal with Your Children's Sibling Rivalry" for a working women's magazine is a similar waste of time.

Consider factors like style and content. These are important because most magazines have a distinctive style, and a writer increases his chances by writing *to* that style. As for content: If, while reading a magazine, you see an article similar in content to the one you want to propose, chances are that particular magazine won't be interested in your article for some time.

For further insight, you might go to the library to study some recent back issues. *Read* the articles, don't skim them. Look for style, content, and flavor. Studying the advertising slants can also tell you a lot about the audience.

QUERY VS. MANUSCRIPT: Assuming you have your story idea and the market in mind, should you submit a query or a manuscript? There are cases where a manuscript should be sent: Most magazines will not accept queries on humor, essays, personal-experience pieces—the kinds of articles that rely on writing style and skill more than the idea itself. In all other cases, the best strategy is to query first. Magazines rarely buy articles from the slush pile, preferring instead to have input on the article from its beginning.

Aside from the very limited chances of getting a completed manuscript published, there are other reasons why you should query before writing your article. One, you may never be able to sell the piece and recoup the time and energy spent on it. Secondly, in order to make a sale you may have to rewrite the piece (several times perhaps) to fit a specific market. The piece you wrote on child rearing and intended for *Parents* would probably have to be completely rewritten to sell to *Woman's Day*, even though these are both magazines read by mothers, aimed at families.

But there *are* times when a manuscript is preferred to a query: If you are little-published and want to approach a big magazine, a completed manuscript may be the best way to prove your writing talents. Many of the major magazines cannot afford to take chances on novice writers by giving them an assignment from a query; because of the effort involved on both sides, they may not even be willing to give a go-ahead on spec. Finally, a manuscript submission may be more appropriate when the subject matter of an article is so offbeat or unusual that it might be automatically rejected as a query.

PORTFOLIOS AND POSITIVE THINKING: There are a few magazines that keep a file of possible contributors; writers *can* send a résumé and clips, asking to be considered for assignments. Though it never hurts, don't necessarily expect a response from this kind of approach. The magazines that keep such files are as follows:

- *American Film*—Contact: Peter Biskind, editor. "If we're impressed with clips, we'll look for a story for the writer."
- *Attenzione*—Contact: Lois Spritzer, editor, who keeps a "Good Writers" file, and adds: "We go into it quite often." The emphasis is on *good* clips.

- *Continental*—looking for writers living in key geographical areas to do travel stories. Contact: "The Editor"—"just to let us know your background, where you are, and that you're available. We would like to keep as many good people on file as possible."
- *Cosmopolitan*—assignments given to very experienced writers. See listing for complete details.
- *Health*—keeps a "Writers" file. Says managing editor Joan Lippert: "We *do* refer to this file, especially if we have unusual geographic requirements for a story."
- *House & Garden*—looking for specialists. See listing for complete details.
- *House Beautiful*—Contact: Carol Cooper Garey, senior editor/copy.
- *Inc.*—Contact: George Gendron, executive editor. Currently the magazine is trying to establish a network of stringers in major metropolitan areas. The editors are looking for writers with demonstrative business sophistication and knowledge of the local business market.
- *Ladycom*—send bio and clips to Sheila J. Gibbons, editor: "It's worth doing this because I sometimes need writers in certain locales. I sometimes also make assignments if I'm impressed with clips. You should know the magazine, though."
- *Life*—keeps an author file. But chances are slim through it. "When it *is* useful to send us a résumé and clips is when you come at us later with a story idea and say: 'You have my clips. I sent them to you on such-and-such a date. . . .' " said a senior editor.
- *National Enquirer*—send bio and clips to "The Editor."
- *Ozark*—editor Laura Doss welcomes hearing from writers living in Ozark Airlines destination areas. She prefers to use writers living in the Midwest.
- *Psychology Today*—"really impressive" bios and clips will be kept on file, but Christopher Cory, managing editor, confides: "Our odds of remembering you that way are poor. Ideas and sound, crisp judgments are what we need."
- *Savvy*—*Very* open to this. Explains the editor, Wendy Reid Crisp: "We *want* to hear from top-notch writers. We discuss new writers, and their ideas and clips, at our weekly editorial

meetings. So tell us where you've been published and what your specialties are. Give us a *specific* field of specialization. I prefer women writers, but men may still apply."

- *Sport*—Contact: Neil Cohen, managing editor: "If they're good clips, chances are excellent. We may not assign a major piece first time out, but we'll give you a chance."
- *United*—associate editor Laura Manske keeps an "Active Authors" file. "I do keep queries and writing samples from good writers and I'll go to the file if I need to assign a story in different parts of the country."
- *Woman's Life*—editor-in-chief Yolanda Drake will review writer portfolios. Contact her first by letter, including samples.
- *Woman's World*—will give assignments to experienced writers. Contact Janel Bladow, news-features editor, who says: "We're probably one of the more open magazines around."
- *Young Miss*—says features/fiction editor Deborah Purcell: "We're quite happy to keep writers on file. Or if you live in, or visit, New York you can come in and see us. But we don't honestly go into the writer file very often. We pretty much consider it the writer's responsibility to come up with ideas, to remind us that he or she is still interested and available."

Successful writers talk about free-lancing

Free-lancing to magazines *is* tough. How have the successful writers done it, and what advice do they have to share? We talked with six writers, who gave generously of their time to talk about free-lancing and how to make it work:

- *Sylvia Auerbach:* personal finance specialist. Degree in economics. Worked as a secretary at trade magazines, then went to *The Library Journal* as an editorial assistant, later becoming managing editor. Wrote news bulletins at the Federal Reserve Bank, edited a *Reader's Digest* book on personal finance, continued to free-lance, mainly to business magazines, throughout. Author of *Your Money: How to Make It Stretch* (Doubleday, 1974), and *A Woman's Book of Money* (Doubleday, 1976). Articles on money and general subjects have appeared in *Playgirl, Bride's, American Home, Cosmopolitan, Harper's Bazaar, The New York Times, Signature,* and columns syndicated through Princeton Features. She has written a third book, *An Insider's Guide to Auctions,* while continuing to write articles, teach at various colleges, and lecture. "I think specializing is the best way to get started," she says.

- *Kathleen Brady:* general-interest writer. Began at Fairchild Publications, at *Footwear News,* as a summer job, and moved on to *Women's Wear Daily;* spent four years there as a reporter and feature writer. Features editor, *Harper's Bazaar.* New York correspondent, Australian Consolidated Press. Author: *Inside Out* (novel, Norton, 1979). Free-lancing since then, while working on two more books. Articles have appeared in *The Village Voice, Glamour, Town & Country, Working Woman, The Christian Science Monitor.* She comments: "Free-lancing is always 'Catch as catch can.' "

- *Claudia Dreifus:* general-interest, but emphasis on profiles and societal issues. Started in the sixties, doing profiles for the underground newspaper, *The East Village Other.* Has been free-lancing full-time since 1968, with articles appearing in *Newsday* (Sunday Magazine), *Redbook, Mademoiselle, Penthouse, Glamour, New York Daily News, New York Times Book Review, Family Circle, McCall's, Rolling Stone, Seventeen, Signature.* Has done several *Playboy* interviews. Author: *Seizing Our Bodies: The Politics of Women's Health* (Random House, 1978), *Woman's Fate* (Bantam, 1974), *Radical Lifestyles* (Lancer, 1971). She believes: "I honestly think editors are looking for good work and have a hard time finding it."

- *Mary Alice Kellogg:* general-interest writer. Began at *Newsweek,* as a researcher; moved on to correspondent, then associate editor. Free-lanced as well to newspaper Sunday supplements, *The Nation, Saturday Review.* Senior editor, *Parade.* Began a second stint at free-lancing full-time three years ago. Writes regularly for *TV Guide, Signature, Glamour,*

AdWeek, Harper's Bazaar, Seventeen. Contributes to *50 Plus, Penthouse, New York, Saturday Review, Woman's Day, Self.* Author: *Fast Track* (McGraw-Hill, 1978). "I work regularly for several markets but I'm always looking for more," she says. "I'm still hustling—every day."

• *Jesse Kornbluth:* general-interest writer. Worked during the summer as a journalism intern at *Manhattan East,* a community paper, while still in high school. The following summer worked as a copy boy in the ad department at *The New York Times.* Spent the following vacation in the research department at *Look;* first article published there at 19. Published *Notes from the New Underground* (Viking) his senior year in college. Out of college tried screen writing, then began free-lancing full-time. Articles have appeared in *New Times, Cosmopolitan, The New York Times, The Times Sunday Magazine, Glamour, Oui, Savvy, The Runner, American Lawyer.* Contributing editor: *New York, Metropolitan Home.* A Kornbluth credo: "The creativity goes in after the manuscript comes out of the typewriter."

• *Alan Markfield:* celebrity interviewer and photographer. Began as a desk assistant ("a gopher") at CBS News, New York, then moved to Cincinnati, finding a job with Scripps-Howard newspapers. Free-lanced part-time for detective magazines. Moved to Fairchild Publications, Cincinnati bureau. Came back to New York and worked for the *National Enquirer,* then based in New Jersey. Stayed with the *Enquirer* seven years— worked as articles editor, Los Angeles bureau chief, photo editor. Moved to Paris, free-lancing there 2½ years. Moved back to New York and free-lanced. A movie-set interview with Margaret Trudeau, which was syndicated throughout the world, fired an interest in syndication; began Reportage International, his own syndication company. Articles and photos now syndicated in 27 countries on a regular basis. He says: "The world is nothing more than a series of markets."

How to get started

"The best way to break into free-lancing is to have a steady job of some sort," advises Mary Alice Kellogg. "Then you can afford to get the rejections, to take the risks. I think it's suicidal—for someone who's never worked *in* publishing—to rely on free-lancing for a living." Agrees Claudia Dreifus: "I don't think you can type away in your attic five hours a day and make it as a successful free-lancer."

Supplementing your income can be done with a part-time job (if it's in publishing, so much the better, because that's where you'll make valuable contacts). An alternative may be a regular column of some sort on a local or community paper (although these usually do not pay too well, you *will* be building a portfolio). Or, keep your regular job and free-lance on the side—as all these writers did when getting started.

If you *must* plunge in, at least do some thinking and planning first, the writers advise. Mary Alice Kellogg failed at her first attempt at full-time free-lancing. "Mainly the problem was my attitude," she explains. "I wasn't being very methodical about it. I didn't really have a battle plan or a focus. I looked at free-lancing as something to get me through—not as the full-time commitment I now know it is. Psychologically I was more suited to working for someone else. I tried it for five months and became very frustrated. I was getting rejections and I was taking them personally. Eventually I just lost interest." With her second, now very successful attempt, she backed herself with six months' living expenses; she says now she would recommend a bankroll to last a year.

Claudia Dreifus adds: "When you're starting out you have to serve an apprenticeship. You have to be willing and you have to be very creative—to get a break, to get noticed. I think you have to work a couple of years for free. I did a lot of stories that didn't get published—for every success I had there were a lot of failures. There were editors who told me: 'I don't like the way you write.' But you have to be persistent. You have to be willing to work on spec, and you work through the rejections by writing pieces that you can redo and try selling elsewhere, even if it's just to your community newspaper. It's very important to develop your own voice and hope it works."

Adds Jesse Kornbluth: "You have to have a realistic assessment of who you are and what you can do." Mary Alice Kellogg concurs: "You have to start small, you have to be realistic about your goals. There are certain top markets that you shouldn't approach—until you've built up your clips."

The "reader story" departments in magazines were mentioned as good break-in areas, definitely worth trying. Kathleen Brady recommends starting out at newspapers. "Magazines have more time to fool around with a story and fool around they do. And the editors don't have the time to mess around with beginners. Newspapers are much more flexible."

Says Alan Markfield: "Sometimes you have to try and place your material in publications that don't pay a lot but will give you exposure. One of the reasons I'll still break a story in the [New York] *Daily News*—even though they'll pay me only $75 —is that people see it and there's likely to be spin-off from it. What the free-lancer has to concern himself with are: one, getting the material; two, knowing what to do with it; three, knowing who to send it to. As a free-lancer you have to have a steady stream of ideas. And because editors are constantly being disappointed—with writers who miss deadlines and the like—you have to make sure *you* don't disappoint them. And you've got to build a contact book! You never know when you're going to need someone as a contact."

Mary Alice Kellogg stresses the need to always have several projects going at once—to try and be working on articles and writing new queries while other proposals are circulating. Jesse Kornbluth agrees: "You have to be very much like a movie producer—always working on several projects." When first starting out as a full-time free-lancer, Kornbluth wrote essays for encyclopedias, Time/Life Books, and worked as a ghostwriter—in short, any assignment that paid and got him published. Even now, he says, "I'll write for just about anybody who asks me—if I want to do the piece."

Should the beginning writer try the wide general-interest market or narrow his focus into specialist writing? The consensus was for specialization. Even Claudia Dreifus, who has made her success as a general-interest writer, believes: "Now if I were trying to break in, I'd try and figure out what kind of writing is needed and what nobody else is doing, and I'd go and learn about that area if I didn't know it well enough. For instance, I think someone who could write for the layman about computers now could do well." Alan Markfield agrees: "We live in an age of specialization." But Mary Alice Kellogg also gives a bottom-line view: "Being a generalist suits my personality."

Getting ideas

How to constantly come up with new ideas for articles is not, unfortunately, something that can be learned in a writing class. It's a personal, instinctive process. But our writers gave these insights:

Jesse Kornbluth: "The inspiration comes from looking at your checking balance! As a full-time free-lancer, you're always in terrible trouble. That's why the motto of the free-lancer has to be: 'All the news before it happens.' To keep ahead, you may have to leave New York, or a major city, to get your stories."

Claudia Dreifus: "You have to be constantly thinking: What's going to be important six months from now? What are people going to be talking about six months from now?"

Alan Markfield: "Make sure you have a good newsstand near you!"

Mary Alice Kellogg: "I subscribe to 20 magazines. I read three newspapers a day. I make an effort to go out and do a lot of *different* things, to meet a lot of *different* people. I also think there's no such thing as a new idea. And write about what you know about—don't discount the value of your own exposure."

Making your approach

The two main factors discussed here: the importance of a good query letter, and the clips you enclose with your query.

"Always write provocative query letters," is Jesse Kornbluth's advice. "Life's too short to be dull!" "It's important to have backup statistics in your query," says Kathleen Brady. "Editors love them."

Says Mary Alice Kellogg: "The good query letter is never lazy. You have to let the editor know you have a handle on their market, readership. The idea has to be specific, focused in. There has to be a lot of research included. Editors are always going to ask: 'Why should I care?' You have to convince them. And if an idea is outrageous or off-the-beaten-track, editors will often prick up their ears."

Says Kathleen Brady: "The clips you send have to be well-written, grabby attention getters." Claudia Dreifus concurs: "I know a lot of editors who will take risks on a newcomer—but the clips have to be *interesting*."

How to be regarded as a professional

Sylvia Auerbach: "If you're not going to do the job to the best of your skills, you probably shouldn't do it at all."
Jesse Kornbluth: "Accept what you can do. If you hate an idea, don't do it. Or, if you don't like the editor's idea, have another of your own to suggest."
Mary Alice Kellogg: "You must be able, when you're asked, to do an assignment *fast*."
Sylvia Auerbach: "Having worked as both an editor and a writer, I think problems lie with both . . . editors who can be hasty giving out assignments and writers who don't come through. Who don't do enough research, who come up with old facts, who don't check their facts. And who hand in sloppy manuscripts."
Jesse Kornbluth: "Will I rewrite? Sure! Your commitment is to the *piece*.

"How *not* to appear professional is also to make it the editor's responsibility to give you a piece to do. Why not call Mom and ask for a handout? The last thing journalism is about is being handed things on a plate.

"And don't fight with editors. If you can't get along with an editor at a certain magazine, move on."
Alan Markfield: "Know when to say no. If you're working on assignments, your phone is ringing, and another editor calls you —say no. You have to know what your maximum capability is. Taking on more you'll do yourself more harm than good."

It's a business!

What makes one free-lancer successful and sets another floundering? Being committed to making it work, as all our writers pointed out, means treating your job as a *business*.

Said Alan Markfield: "You can't get so caught up with seeing your name in print you forget you have bills to pay." Added Kathleen Brady: "Getting the assignment is only a third of the battle."

Sylvia Auerbach, the money specialist, says that from her position at the editor's desk, she was astonished to see how many writers are careless about money and how many writers don't value their work highly enough. "They would hand in an assignment but never send an invoice. So I'd call them, also reminding them to include a social security number. Half the time they'd forget!

"And—once you've proven yourself—if you're not happy with the fee being offered with an assignment, you should ask for more money. If an editor calls you with an assignment, my advice is never to say yes immediately. Sit down and think about how much it's worth in time spent, and then one and a half times that because it always takes longer. This is not to say I've always valued my work appropriately, but you get to the stage where you must." For all her financial expertise, Auerbach recommends to writers the system she uses to keep track of her business: a simple notebook, divided into two parts—one detailing expenses laid out, the other fees coming in. She explains that this system not only keeps her records straight and tidy, it satisfies the tax man as well.

One of the banes of the free-lancer's existence is keeping track of payments. Most experienced writers won't work for magazines that pay on publication—a choice the beginning writer may not have. All agreed that if a magazine is paying on acceptance and the writer still hasn't received the check a month later (not an unusual situation at all), he should call the editor involved. Kathleen Brady adds an insight: "Usually they'll tell you it's still going through the accounting department. Which is so unfair because the accounting department always manages to pay the staff each week! So I ask the editor: '*Who* in the accounting department is handling my payment?' And I call them."

How to submit an article or idea

Unlike fiction, where the manuscript is what matters and cover letters often aren't even important, approaching a magazine with an article idea requires a selling strategy.

Most magazines have their "stable" of regular writers. Why should they assign an article to a free-lancer they don't know? The over-the-transom submissions that sell are the ones which cause the editor to sit up and take notice when he reads through the mail. What the editor is also looking for is the *professional* approach. He wants to see a neat, well-presented, thoughtful submission. Some guidelines follow:

PHONE QUERIES: Whether you're approaching a magazine with a query or a completed manuscript, the initial contact should be made in writing. A *few* editors will discuss article ideas on the phone—those willing to do so are listed in the "How to submit" section. But unless specified, phone queries are not accepted.

As one editor commented: "I would want to present your idea in writing at my editorial planning meeting; I'd want to make sure I have all the facts and that the angle of the story is clearly presented. What editor wants that kind of responsibility? And why should I have to take the time to sit down and transcribe *your* idea?" Commented another: "Some people can do a terrific sales job on the phone. Then you find out they can't write." Another reasoned: "I want to see that the writer has sat down and really thought through the idea, not just picked up the phone to run an idea past me."

"DEAR EDITOR . . .": Except where noted under "How to submit," it is always a good idea to send your manuscript to a specific editor, by name.

But before submitting, you should always call the magazine and make sure the particular editor is still on staff. And make sure you have the correct spelling of the editor's name and his title. Several editors made this kind of comment: "If a writer can't get my name right, why should I believe he will be able to do an accurate story?" It's a valid point.

PHOTOCOPIED SUBMISSIONS: A query should *never* be a photocopy; it should always be a typed, personal letter.

Many editors *will* accept photocopied manuscript submissions, however (some of them actually prefer not to have to take responsibility for the original). In these cases, a note is made in the "How to submit" section.

Photocopies are useful because submissions *do* get lost, and often. And originals are not *always* returned in the shape they were sent. Which calls for a retyping in order to submit the piece elsewhere.

At all other magazines, not listed as accepting photocopies, however, an original is what's preferred. The reason usually is because the editors at these magazines regard photocopied manuscripts as multiple submissions.

MULTIPLE/SIMULTANEOUS SUBMISSIONS: This means, simply, submitting your story—manuscript or query—to more than one magazine at the same time.

This is a process that has now become standard in book publishing, between agents and publishers. It is still largely frowned upon in the magazine business—editors often want exclusive offerings.

It can be an unfair practice at publications that have lengthy reply times. The writer has little recourse. The danger is that more than one publication will want to buy your article—and that's bound to cause problems. The "second choice" magazine may refuse to deal with you again. It's a choice the writer has to decide for himself.

Some magazines will accept multiple submissions—generally as long as the writer informs the editors at the time of submission. These magazines are noted as such under "How to submit." You do not have to tell the magazine where else you have also sent your submission.

THE QUERY/MANUSCRIPT: Editors' preferences on query letters vary. Some prefer short, simple queries, some long and detailed. Some prefer a businesslike approach, others a more chatty tone.

In general, however, it's fair to say that the writer should regard the query letter as he would a job application letter. If you are unknown at a magazine, you will be selling yourself—your idea and your writing skills—in the query letter. The editor will want to have four questions answered: What is the story idea? Is it right for my readers? Who is the writer? Can he carry it off?

The query letter is both your writing and marketing test. You must show that your idea is worthwhile and appropriate to the particular market, that you have thought it through from start to finish, and that you write well.

Many magazines hand out assignments on the strength of the query letter alone. If it takes a whole day (or more) to write, it will be time well spent.

A manuscript submission should always be typed on white 20-lb. bond paper. Your name should appear in the top left-hand corner of every page, and each page should be numbered in the top right-hand corner with a catchword followed by the page number. Example: For a manuscript about llamas, an appropriate paging system would be "llama . . . 1, llama . . . 2, etc." At least an inch of white space should be left at top and bottom of each page; the left-hand margin should be about 1½ inches wide, the right-hand margin about one inch.

The manuscript should also include a cover sheet—with your name, address, phone number (a number where you can be reached during the day is important) and a working title. All pages should be attached with a sturdy paper clip—not stapled.

On any submission—manuscript or query—there should never be typing mistakes, spelling errors, poor punctuation, coffee stains (etc.), crossouts. Colored typing paper and faint typewriter ribbons are also out. A messy submission is most often equated with a messy mind and lack of attention to detail. The state of your submission may very well mean the difference between acceptance and rejection.

CLIPS: Should you enclose samples of your published work with your article query? Editors' differing preferences are outlined in the "How to submit" section in each listing. But some general points should be noted:

• It is not necessary to include clips when you're submitting a manuscript. The purpose of clips is to prove your writing talents —the manuscript will do that much more succinctly. You may wish to tell an editor *where* you've been published. Include then, instead of clips, a list of your credits—the names of the magazines, article topics, issue dates.

• Never send original writing samples. Editors don't welcome the responsibility, and they can easily be lost. Out of courtesy— and to not hinder your sales pitch—photocopies should always be clear. Another reason for not sending originals: The editor may wish to keep them on file. In any case, you should never ask to have clips returned. Send photocopies and forget about them.

• How many clips to send, and what kind? Different editors have different policies. As a general rule, send one to three; never more than four. Select your *best* work—remember, you're selling yourself through your clips; and if possible, choose samples that are most similar to the story idea you're proposing. A clip about how to cook artichokes will be of little use to an editor who's considering sending you out to cover the Yankees in spring training. Unless your piece on artichokes is written with such panache it will stop the editor in his tracks.

• If you have a piece you're particulary proud of—but it ended up being hacked up for publication and your by-line is now an embarrassment—by all means send a copy of the original manuscript. Some editors even prefer this, particularly those who are suspicious of clips to start with.

• If you are little-published (your clips are skimpy or you're not particularly proud of them), and you're querying an editor at a big magazine, it might be better not to send clips at all. Let your query letter stand on its own, and wait till clips are requested. That way, an editor will have personally contacted you —you will have the chance to discuss your idea some more with someone who's no longer just a name. And if the editor finally declines on your idea—because of your clips—you can always take the opportunity to ask about working on spec.

SASE: The need for enclosing a self-addressed stamped envelope with your submission is not mentioned in every listing simply because it is so universal—a SASE should *always* be enclosed, whether you're sending a manuscript *or* a query.

Many magazines will not even respond without a SASE—in these cases the policy is mentioned in the listing.

Why should the writer worry about such things as SASEs? It's courteous; it's professional. Writers who don't send return postage was one of the most common complaints we heard from editors—it *annoys* them. And for the magazines, it all adds up. One magazine spent $100,000 last year for return postage of unsolicited material.

MAILING: If your submission is a query of a page or two, simply send it in a business-size envelope, or on your personal stationery, regular mail.

If you're sending a manuscript, or a query with clips included, a large envelope should be used. Send the submission first class. An envelope arriving third class won't encourage an editor to open it with any urgency.

How to make sure your submission has arrived? In trying to set up interviews for this book, we were stunned by the number of editors who claimed they had not received our introductory correspondence. We would highly recommend following either of these strategies to make *sure* your submission gets to its destination:

• Send it certified mail. This is cheap; a manuscript of six pages costs about 75 cents, plus regular postage. Certified mail ensures that someone at the magazine must sign on delivery. By paying an extra few cents and requesting "Restricted Delivery," the *addressee* must sign for the article.

• Enclose with your submission a return postcard (stamped of course). Make up your own, wording it something like: "We have received your query/manuscript. Signed . . ." These are being used more frequently and most editors welcome them. (If you don't receive the return postcard within a few weeks, a phone call to inquire would then be quite reasonable).

Making a living: money and rights

Successful free-lancing is not simply a matter of writing a good article and making a sale. So many other factors come into play: financial dealings, rights negotiations, sorting through contracts. Fewer and fewer agents are handling article sales these days; an agent is not necessary, but some guidelines are.

In order to protect himself and to get the best, fairest deal, the following areas should be discussed/made clear *before* the writer starts work on a project.

ASSIGNMENTS VS. ON SPEC: Is the article a definite assignment, or are you being expected to work on speculation? If this has not been made clear, ask the editor. At most magazines an *assigned* article guarantees the writer a specified payment, reimbursement for expenses incurred, and the guarantee of a kill fee payment if the magazine decides not to use the piece.

Writing *on spec* provides no such guarantees; payment is contingent on the magazine accepting the finished manuscript for publication. At the major magazines assignments generally are given only to experienced writers; on spec allows a less-experienced writer the opportunity to prove his abilities—without an investment on the magazine's part. And the untried writer will most probably—and probably should be most willing—to work on speculation to build up a portfolio. But the writer should always know where he stands.

PAYMENT: The editor should always mention payment in the initial discussion, and this amount should be stipulated whether you are being assigned or asked to work on spec. If the editor doesn't discuss payment, then the writer should. Article payments often aren't negotiable—although the writer with a lot of magazine experience has more bargaining power. In general, the less-experienced writer should accept the fee offered—unless he feels the project would not be worthwhile (in payment and credits) for the amount of work involved.

The writer should also know *when* payment will be made—

on acceptance of the manuscript or on publication of the article —and should be aware that payment "on acceptance" usually means "after it's been through the accounting department." This usually takes a couple of weeks, sometimes four or five (after a month you are within your rights to start calling and complaining).

PUBLICATION DATE: When is the article scheduled to appear? This should be asked, particularly if it is the magazine's policy to pay on publication. At some magazines publication can take a year or more, and the writer has to decide if it is worthwhile working on such an insecure basis. Most experienced writers refuse to work for magazines that pay on publication. Again, for the inexperienced writer it may be worthwhile—for the credit that will come eventually. It is a real gamble, however, to work on spec for a magazine that pays on publication. You may never see money or a by-line.

DEADLINES: The editor should mention a deadline date at the initial discussion. If not, ask. You do not want to be surprised two days before the article is expected and you weren't aware of it.

Also, if the deadline date presents a problem, the writer should always say so immediately. It is much better to have an extension *before* you start working, rather than at the last minute. Or worse, to miss a deadline. All editors work to tight schedules and missed deadlines *never* make a good impression.

LENGTH: The writer should always have an approximate word length before he starts working. You don't want to waste time writing pages that may be cut simply for space.

EXPENSES: These are described three different ways in the listings:
"Pays limited (or modest) expenses": Generally applies to small-budget magazines, which may pay only phone calls and perhaps mileage.
"Pays reasonable expenses": May pay extra expenses, like necessary travel costs and interview-related entertainment. May also pay mailing and photocopying costs.
"Pays all incidentals": The magazine will pay any article-related expenses.

With *all* categories, it is essential to discuss the matter of expenses *before* you start working.

The policy at some magazines is to limit expense money to a percentage of the article fee. Some magazines pay only limited expenses to first-time contributors and all incidentals to regular contributors. Some require receipts for all expenses submitted; others only if the expense is over a certain amount. But no editor will appreciate an expenses bill *after* the fact.

Also, expenses are paid only on assigned stories. When you approach any magazine with a completed manuscript, or when you ask/agree to do a piece on speculation, you cannot bill the magazine for any expenses incurred—unless the magazine offers them. Reimbursement of expenses is one of the "perks" of landing an assignment.

KILL FEES: It is now standard practice to pay a "kill fee" on assigned articles the magazine decides not to publish—either because of the quality of the finished manuscript, or because the magazine's editorial needs change. Kill fees range from 10% to 50%, the average being 20%. Most magazines have a standard kill fee; some will negotiate with the writer. The kill fee should be stipulated in the article contract or letter of agreement/assignment. If it's not (and with magazines that buy rights verbally, i.e. do not have a written contract), to cover oneself the writer should discuss the matter of a kill fee at the time of assignment and has every right to ask that a kill fee be stated in writing.

Again, the kill fee is one of the "perks" of landing an assignment. Doing articles on speculation does not entitle the writer to a kill fee payment.

RIGHTS: It is always to a writer's advantage to retain as many rights to a piece as possible. In each listing the magazine's policy concerning rights bought is stated. A writer in the early stages of a career (and even experienced writers at some major magazines) usually has to accept the magazine's policy. As it happens this is generally not a problem; most magazines only take one form or another of first rights, that is, the magazine has the right of first publication, and ownership of all remaining rights is held by the writer.

Rights can be bought verbally, by written contract, by letter or note of intent, or by check endorsement (cashing of the check means acceptance of terms. Negotiations must be made before cashing). A writer can, and should, insist on something in writing; if you sell an article to a magazine without a written agreement you are authorizing continued reprints of the piece in that magazine with no additional payment to you.

When the editor first discusses the article, ask what rights the magazine intends to buy. Make sure you understand what the terms mean. Check such points as exclusive vs. nonexclusive (can the writer resell elsewhere?).

When you sell first rights, check on the time length the magazine holds them after publication. How do you get the rights back: automatically or by written request? Is there a closeout period—for instance, if the magazine hasn't published your piece within two years, do you have the right to demand it back? When you resell a story, what percentage does the first publication get? Half? None? Are you obligated to give the first publication any credit in a reprint?

These are all legitimate questions for a writer to ask. Again, a beginning writer is not going to receive the best possible deal on all these issues, but he should still find out where he stands.

REWRITING: Time permitting, most magazines will allow the writer to rewrite his piece if this is needed. The editor is the person who decides *if* a rewrite is necessary; the writer's only recourse is to withdraw the piece from publication (not a good step unless a better publication is bidding for the piece). Rewrites *are* usual. But if a staff rewrite would not be acceptable, the writer should clear up this matter *before* he starts working.

The Magazines

AMERICAN BABY

575 Lexington Avenue
New York, NY 10022
(212) 752-0775

SOURCE: Phyllis Evans, managing editor

IN SHORT: All work done on spec, but new writers and ideas welcomed.

ABOUT THE MAGAZINE: Bi-monthly. Most articles are free-lance–written. *American Baby* is a magazine for expectant and new parents. Free six-month subscriptions are offered by direct mail; it's not available on the newsstand. Reader turnover is high. The editors regard their magazine as a service publication for the expectant or new mother at a time when she's eager to learn—and read—as much as possible. That's the main theme—coping with pregnancy and then with the new baby. But also covered are issues that are important to the woman's other needs: health, diet and nutrition, beauty and fashion. The magazine's goal is to "educate and inform these [new] parents about all issues relevant to them at this important time in their lives: medical and health issues; practical approaches to baby care; news about products and services for the baby; and sympathetic advice from experts and from other parents." *Controlled circulation:* One million. *Sample copy:* With 9x12 SASE and 70 cents postage. *Areas open to free-lancers:* Main features, "Family Finances," "Nutrition Report," and "My Own Experience" (this column is open to readers as well; payment is $100). *Rates:* Articles: $150–$300 (average article fee: $200–$250). *Payment:* On acceptance. *Expenses:* Some phone expenses only. *Kill fee:* Not applicable. *Rights:* Buys first North American rights, by written contract. (Because of high reader turnover, articles are repeated from time to time; author is paid half the original fee for reprints.) *Number of submissions received weekly:* 15–20. *Reply time to queries:* One week. *Advance dates:* Lead time is three months. Issues are planned six months to a year in advance.

FREE-LANCE POSSIBILITIES: Rates paid at *American Baby* are fairly modest ("$300 would be our top," Phyllis Evans says). And all work, whether you're a new writer or a seasoned one, must be done on spec. But there *are* compensations. Each issues carries six or seven articles. Some are done by medical/pediatric experts, but mostly they're written by free-lancers. And although the magazine does have its regular writers, they're always looking for new people to add to the regular ranks, and your ideas will be welcomed. Evans is very encouraging to new writers. "A lot of our regular writers came to us with one over-the-transom story idea," she says.

The magazine should be studied for the kind of topics required. Two recent articles were "Mealtime Manners," some helpful hints for feeding toddlers, and "The ABCs of Vitamins," a primer for the entire family. Also, recent articles have been written on subjects such as: job sharing; when to call the doctor; how to babyproof your home; and what to expect on labor day. Medical and health, baby care, coping techniques, psychological articles—all these are good areas for querying, particularly if you plan to talk to experts in the field for your information. But, because of the specialized nature of this magazine, go to a pediatrician for information and quotes, rather than a GP. Evans adds: "Writers can query me on any aspects of pregnancy and child care. But I would prefer free-lancers to stay away from heavy medical topics if possible. Psychology, though, is fine." No need for celebrity articles; when these are done, they're generally covered in-house. Also no market for humor here. But first-person/personal experience is good—for the "My Own Experience" column. "This column," Evans explains, "has to contain advice for other parents. It has to teach some kind of lesson. There has to be a bottom line to it."

Editing can be on the heavy side here—less so on articles written by professional writers (as opposed to mothers/parents writing of their experiences). Galleys are not shown to writers; neither are they informed of copy changes. "But we've never had any complaints," Evans says.

HOW TO SUBMIT: You can either submit your manuscript or send a written query to Phyllis Evans, who reviews all submissions and makes decisions on articles. Keep queries short; if you can include an opening paragraph, it's helpful. Your personal background details are not too important; neither are clips.

REJECTIONS: A standard rejection form is used for most submissions; personalized notes are sent only to those contributors with promise. If you receive a rejection, it will be for one of the following reasons: "We already have something planned on the topic you've suggested; it's not a good idea; we've received a lot of queries on the same topic; or you've given me too many typos and too much bad grammar in your manuscript or query—that will be almost an immediate rejection."

AMERICAN FILM

The American Film Institute
The John F. Kennedy Center for the Performing Arts
Washington, DC 20566
(202) 828-4050

SOURCE: Peter Biskind, editor

IN SHORT: Specialized market; wants offbeat ideas.

ABOUT THE MAGAZINE: Monthly (ten issues a year); 90% free-lance–written. Published under the auspices of the American Film Institute and distributed to its members nationally (also available on the newsstand), *American Film* covers the industry through profiles (of actors, directors), trend pieces, book reviews, and "think" pieces—articles about the impact of various social issues on the film industry. The magazine also covers TV, video, cable, and the new technology. Says Peter Biskind: "The magazine is read by a lot of people in the industry. But we try to cover both readership bases—industry and general interest." *Readership:* college-educated, young, urban, affluent. *Circulation:* 140,000 (includes 8000 newsstand sales). Estimated readership: 728,000. *Areas open to free-lancers:* All. *Rates:* Features: $500–$800. *Payment:* On publication. *Expenses:* Up to a $200 maximum. *Kill fee:* 20%. *Rights:* Buys all rights, by written contract. Negotiable. *Number of submissions received weekly:* 50. *Reply time to queries:* Two weeks. *Advance dates:* Lead time is three months. Issues are planned four to five months in advance.

FREE-LANCE POSSIBILITIES: Some of the free-lancers writing for *American Film* have an academic film background. This kind of credential can go a long way here, but it is by no means the only way into the magazine. About ten over-the-transom manuscripts and 20–25 queries materialize into features yearly; and often they are from general-interest writers who have managed to come up with a good, timely, or offbeat story idea. Says Peter Biskind: "We're not looking for big-name writers only. Basically, we're looking for good pieces."

Assuming that film writers and regular contributors are keeping tabs on *people* in the industry, possibly the best way for the free-lancer to break in is by querying with a trend or think piece.

Some published articles that came in over the transom were: blacks in soap operas (query); the making of trailers and previews (ms.); the opposition facing horror-film makers (query); the difficulties with prerecorded cassettes (ms.); and the historical inaccuracies to be found in "period" productions like *Reds, Ragtime, Brideshead Revisited* (ms.).

The magazine never publishes movie reviews. Also out is academic criticism and nostalgia pieces of the "I-live-next-door-to-a-famous-movie-star" kind. Ideas *must* have a timely/newsy peg. Profile chances are extremely slim here; these are assigned to known/regular writers and often turn up as the cover story. If you're not known at the magazine, you will need some kind of unique access to the subject. Important here are recognizable faces doing something current.

Assignment chances are good with good clips. With weak clips, the alternative approaches are these: send the manuscript; offer to work on spec; or suggest a short piece for a department like "Newsreel" (amusing, reportorial/anecdotal pieces, pegged to a timely event) or "Video" (new trends in the video industry, new technology, mini-profiles—all aimed at the consumer). "We're more likely to take a risk in these areas if the writer is someone who's not known to us," Biskind says. "Writers often start off with us this way."

He adds these general guidelines for submitting to the magazine: "It's a good idea to read *Variety*, which gives production schedules six months in advance. You can find out what's going on in the industry. And our pieces should be written to give information that doesn't sound naive to the industry, but is not too technical or trade-oriented for readers who aren't involved in the movie business."

Peter Biskind reviews all over-the-transom material and makes the final decision after promising submissions are discussed at the weekly editorial meeting. When rewriting needs to be done, he prefers to have the author, rather than an editor, do it. As for editing, Biskind says: "It depends on the manuscript, but we prefer not to edit heavily." Galleys are not shown, but writers are told about changes.

Biskind adds: "We *do* encourage free-lancers. It's an advantage to have a film background, but we do read all submissions and we treat them seriously." See "Portfolios and Positive Thinking," pages 7–9.

HOW TO SUBMIT: Mss. read (photocopies okay). Multiple submissions: "We don't like them but it doesn't mean they won't be considered." Query should include "the angle of the story and the proposed length. And you should give us some sense of why the piece is important, as well as some indication you can do the article. Give us contacts, or tell us how you would get contacts." Include clips (magazine samples are preferred over newspaper clips).

REJECTIONS: A standard rejection form is used. Personalized replies are sent "if we see something in the query or clips and we'd like to encourage the writer to try us again."

AMERICAN HEALTH

80 Fifth Avenue
New York, NY 10011
(212) 242-2460

SOURCE: T George Harris, editor

IN SHORT: Good free-lance possibilities for *news* stories in health and fitness.

ABOUT THE MAGAZINE: Bi-monthly. Mostly free-lance—written. The newest of the health/fitness magazines, with the most lavish graphics, *American Health*'s banner declares the magazine devoted to "Fitness of Body and Mind." Editor T George Harris elaborates: "It's a life-style magazine based on health. We're trying to provide useful material that is solid, scientifically and journalistically." There is an emphasis on physical fitness, as well as inner good health. *Readership:* 65% female, 35% male; high education and income levels; age: from the twenties on up. Harris describes the readers as "people with a desire to take life by the ears and go for it." *Circulation:* 400,000. *Areas open to free-lancers:* All. *Rates:* About 60 cents per published word. "It's best to start with short news items ($125–$250) or one- and two-page features of 500–1000 words ($300–$600)." *Payment:* On acceptance. *Expenses:* Pays all reasonable expenses. *Kill fee:* 25%. *Rights:* Buys first North American rights, by letter. *Reply time to queries:* Immediately to six weeks (depending on copy scheduling). *Advance dates:* Lead time is two months. Issues are planned about five months in advance.

FREE-LANCE POSSIBILITIES: *American Health* is nearly all free-lance—written. The staff is small and free-lancers are listed on the masthead when they become steady contributors. The editors are *very* open to ideas and welcome new writers; however, only about 10% of the over-the-transom ideas are working out. This *is* a market for the generalist, but really only if you have enough of an interest in health and fitness to be on top of news stories in the field. "A writer doesn't need to be stuck in a particular specialty, but you need to be grounded," Harris advises.

"What's toughest is trying to find writers who have a sense of the body, the spark of the kinetic, that translates into words. We're hunting for people who are aware of their bodies and can write about them with feeling." Harris cites the style of regular contributor John Jerome: "He did three articles on muscles and how they work. He writes in a way that enables the reader to feel the muscles moving."

Story ideas *must* be new and news; the information must be fresh and it must be worth reporting. "For instance, we know people need to know how to deal with the common cold. But if we don't have new information, then we won't run the story. There must be a new piece of information for us to pass on." Information can't be just speculation either; it has to have some kind of scientific basis and the writer is required to do the necessary research to back up the piece. "Often, writers might have the idea but not enough backup information.

"One writer can't report everything there is to be known on a particular subject. We don't expect the writer to go out and try to cover the whole field. We try to focus on tight, short text pieces and to do related information as a sidebar, at the same time giving as rich a body of information as possible. For the newcomer, it's best to approach us with a tightly focused news item, a short take. That's better than trying to start out with a broad text piece." (About 40–50 short takes are run each issue).

Generally writers work on assignment, not on spec. "When we get a promising article suggestion, the idea as it is seldom works for us. It's not a simple yes or no but a pretty active discussion that takes place between writer and editor." Copy is often fairly heavily edited to fit into size, style, and content requirements.

HOW TO SUBMIT: Queries, not manuscripts, are requested. No preferred length on queries. "We need enough information to be able to make a decision on the idea; it has to be focused enough to show that the writer has enough access to sources to do a good job." Include a writing résumé, and one or two clips.

REJECTIONS: Both standard forms and personalized notes are sent, the latter when the editors wish to encourage more submissions.

AMERICAN WAY

P.O. Box 61616
Dallas/Fort Worth Airport, TX 75261
(817) 355-1583

SOURCE: Walter A. Damtoft, editor and publisher

IN SHORT: Competitive market.

ABOUT THE MAGAZINE: Monthly; 95% free-lance—written. *American Way* is the in-flight magazine of American Airlines. Says Walter Damtoft: "Our goal is to provide information, entertainment, and diversion for passengers. We are interested in nearly any subject; a typical issue will have stories in eight or ten distinct fields. However, we rarely run articles about subjects involved in current controversy." The magazine is distributed in 40,000 airline seat pockets; surveys indicate a readership figure of between 1.3 and 1.6 million monthly. Among its readers, 68% are male; reader's median age is 46; 88% have graduated/attended college; 70% are professional/managerial; the median family income is $65,000. *Sample copy:* Free. *Areas open to free-lancers:* Everything except puzzles, books, bridge, food and dining. *Rates:* Short items: $100–$200. Features: payment begins at $400. *Payment:* On acceptance. *Expenses:* Pays reasonable expenses. *Kill fee:* Approximately 20%, but paid only by agreement to writers previously published in the magazine. *Rights:* Negotiable, specified in letter of agreement. *Number of submissions received weekly:* 100. *Reply time to queries:* Two to three weeks. *Advance dates:* Lead time is three months. Issues planned three months in advance.

FREE-LANCE POSSIBILITIES: Although 85–90% of articles published are the result of over-the-transom suggestions, most are by free-lancers who have written for the magazine before. Editor Walter Damtoft says: "It is easy to break into our magazine; simply give us a story idea that is compelling and interesting and then follow up with a thoroughly professional writing job." He also concedes that new writers break in only once or twice a year.

Unsolicited submissions are divided among the staff. "All items that survive the first read are then reviewed at twice-monthly staff meetings. If there is a favorable consensus, an assignment is usually then offered to the writer." That is, if the writer has good clips. "Otherwise," explains Damtoft, "if a first-time writer has no track record with national publications of some stature, we automatically ask them to submit on spec."

What *kinds* of ideas have the best chances? "We particularly like to know about developments in an area that are likely to have national ramifications: a new way of handling disruptive children, a new technique in energy conservation, a new way to help minority business persons get started. In other words, we like to be on top of the news as much as possible.

"Good humor is in extra short supply, but one of the best pieces we ever published came in over-the-transom: how the complete works of Shakespeare would be described in a program list for *TV Guide*. Another was an assemblage of letters between a magazine editor and a French priest, growing out of the editor's hunt for a photo of a truffle-hunting pig. Another was a recent article about a frontier dude-ranching experience in which the writer participated in one of the few surviving cattle drives."

The magazine prefers to return manuscripts to writers for any needed rewriting—"time permitting." Editing: "We put a premium on a variety of styles in our magazine and, on the average, edit only for clarity and style." Galleys are shown only if there has been extensive editing.

Once a story is published, "we might call on a writer again if a subject is in his particular geographic area. However, his or her best bet is to try to get a feel for our magazine and then keep a stream of ideas coming."

HOW TO SUBMIT: Send submissions to "Articles Editor." Completed manuscripts are accepted (legible photocopies okay), but queries are preferred. Simultaneous submissions are accepted if the writer informs the editor, "and is careful to protect any rights we might subsequently want to buy." Queries should be about one page. "To us a query letter is not much different from a backyard over-the-fence conversation that opens: 'Hey, I learned the most unusual thing today . . .' and then continues, conversationally, to give the details that make it interesting." Writers who have had no prior experience with the magazine should include clips. "With clips we're looking for signs of a professional at work, including evidence that the writer viewed

the subject from several perspectives and through several eyes."
Damtoft lists the mistakes contributors often make: "Telling us
why we *ought* to publish an article rather than providing a synopsis of elements that we find inherently interesting. We also
get a great many queries with misspellings and inaccuracies, and
those quickly go nowhere."

REJECTIONS: "We try to send as many personal notes as possible,
but our staff is small and we rarely have the time to go into the
reasons for a refusal in detail."

THE ATLANTIC

8 Arlington Street
Boston, MA 02116
(617) 536-9500

SOURCE: Maureen Foley, assistant to the editors

IN SHORT: Prestige market—difficult to sell.

ABOUT THE MAGAZINE: Monthly. Extensively free-lance–written. The magazine is known for its fiction, poetry, timely articles and essays. The editors give emphasis to political issues of national significance, as well as to culture and psychological/sociological subjects. *Readership:* 60% male, 40% female; median age 37; most readers have attended college, with over half graduating; middle income; 52% are in managerial/professional jobs. *Circulation:* 400,000. *Areas open to free-lancers:* All. *Rates:* $1500 minimum. *Payment:* On acceptance. *Expenses:* Pays all reasonable expenses. *Kill fee:* Negotiable. *Rights:* Buys first North American serial rights, by written contract. Rights retained by magazine while issue remains on newsstands; thereafter rights revert to author on request. *Number of submissions received weekly:* 80. *Reply time to queries:* Four to six weeks. *Advance dates:* Lead time is eight weeks. Issues are planned four to five months in advance.

FREE-LANCE POSSIBILITIES: *The Atlantic* is very open in that it reads all submissions and is always looking for ideas and new writers. But it is a limited market because the quality of the writing has to be extremely high. "Fine writing is what we're looking for in general," comments Maureen Foley. "In articles, we're always on the lookout for balanced, intelligent treatment of issues of national or international importance. We think of ourselves as a very considered magazine. We don't try to compete with the news magazines; we don't court news-breaking pieces. Instead, we tend to take a reflective stance—either backward of forward looking—on news issues. We're looking for pieces that say something surprising, that give some new viewpoint." *The Atlantic* rarely assigns pieces by authors it hasn't worked with; about 10% of manuscript submissions are of high enough caliber for a second, serious consideration. Because of the writing sophistication required, it's no surprise that almost all articles are written by experienced journalists and writers, or contributors with a particular area of expertise. "We're not necessarily impressed with how many clips a writer has, or if they're coming in through an agent. It's the manuscript that interests us. And we're willing to be surprised."

The following is a rundown of *The Atlantic's* three main areas: Reports & Comments: 3000–4000-word front-of-the-book articles; generally these are political comment pieces, which can include sociological issues. "We don't really run unoccasioned pieces here; there has to be a reason for the article, some kind of peg." The second section consists of main articles, an area with no specific guidelines. The final section is made up of reviews. These pieces are always assigned, and tend to be written by known contributors/writers. "Logistically, this is a difficult area for the free-lancer. If someone were able to get hold of, say, advance book galleys, and sent in a wonderful review, we would consider it. But we can't be very encouraging in this area."

Humor is a possibility, but the following areas aren't: interviews and profiles; commentary on local events that do not have national significance.

The amount of editing varies. Galleys are shown.

Maureen Foley sums up: "I would encourage writers, before they send us anything, to read four or five back issues and make an intelligent decision about their piece, asking: Is there anything like it in *The Atlantic?*"

HOW TO SUBMIT: Send all submissions to "The Editorial Department"; these will be distributed to appropriate editors. Photocopied manuscripts are okay. Multiple submissions: "We prefer not to get them, but we don't discount them." See "Rejections" below for information on query submissions.

REJECTIONS: Two reply forms are used. One is a polite form rejection; the other reply, used for queries, is a form note saying: "We would be happy to consider your piece," and asking the writer to forward the manuscript for consideration. This latter note is sent as a reply to any query "if there seems to be a shred of hope in the query." This reply signifies interest only (it is sent on most queries), and represents *no* commitment to buy.

ATTENZIONE

55 East 34th Street
New York, NY 10016
(212) 696-0633

SOURCE: Lois Spritzer, editor

IN SHORT: Open, but prefers established writers.

ABOUT THE MAGAZINE: English-language; published 11 times a year (July/August issues are combined); 60–70% free-lance–written. The magazine is aimed at Italian-Americans; it is distributed in the U.S. but has a "transatlantic scope." *Attenzione* covers people, places, and events of interest both in Italy and among the Italian-American community in the U.S. Included are articles on history, culture, nostalgia, politics, design and fashion. Fashion, travel, and food articles are generally run in each issue. *Readership:* male/female ratio fairly evenly split; 67% married; middle to upper income; median age is 51. Readers are described as up-scale and lovers of "the good life." *Circulation:* 130,000. Estimated readership: 750,000. *Sample copy:* $2.50. *Areas open to free-lancers:* Feature articles. ("Retrospect," "Events in Italy," "*Attenzione* Dines Out," and "Views & Reviews" are written by staff/contributing editors.) *Rates:* Columns: $400 minimum. Features: $600 minimum. *Payment:* On acceptance. *Expenses:* Pays all reasonable expenses. *Kill fee:* 25%. *Rights:* Buys first North American serial rights, by written contract. *Number of submissions received weekly:* 30. *Reply time to queries:* Eight weeks maximum (outright rejections receive "almost immediate" replies). *Advance dates:* Lead time is three months. Issues are planned six months in advance.

FREE-LANCE POSSIBILITIES: To answer the obvious question, you do not have to be Italian to write for *Attenzione*. There are, however, three requirements: You have to have an *appropriate* story idea, you have to understand the readership and the magazine itself, and your writing has to be of a high standard. "We're always concerned about the *writer*," Lois Spritzer says. "We pride ourselves on our writing standard. We will want to see clips."

A new writer breaks into *Attenzione* close to once an issue; it generally happens when the writer is, as the staff is, "attuned to things Italian." Certain areas are more probable than others. Spritzer explains: "To do fashion, you should know fashion. To do a food article, you should know about food writing—and you will always need to provide us with six recipes, which we test. Wine is less likely because we do have a regular wine writer, but it *is* open. Our celebrity profiles generally are done by good celebrity interviewers; there's a special knack to this and I would be very wary assigning a profile to a writer whose work I'm not familiar with.

"We try to run one think piece per issue. We've done a piece on breast cancer, and another on the other American who was missing in the film *Missing*—he happened to be Italian."

Travel is possible. But general-interest is probably the best area of all, and the only way to increase odds here is to study a few back issues to get a real feel for the magazine. Its scope is wide, though its audience is specialized. Lois Spritzer says: "The way I make decisions on stories is to put myself in the reader's place. Will Italian-Americans relate to this? Will it be interesting to them? A person can be obscure, of course, and still be interesting. We recently bought a piece from a writer in Italy who sent us a manuscript, with photos, on a young Italian artist who does whimsical sculptures in wood" (February '83).

Spritzer eventually sees all submissions; other editors may scan them first but they all end up on her desk. It could be worth asking to work on spec here if you don't have impressive clips; she may agree to it if a story has possibilities.

Editing varies. Rewriting is done by the author. Galleys are not shown. Future assignment chances are good once you are in here.

See "Portfolios and Positive Thinking," pages 7–9.

HOW TO SUBMIT: Mss. are read (photocopies okay), but queries are "definitely preferred." Include "as much detail as possible in the query; a couple of pages, if necessary, is fine." Include a résumé or brief rundown of your writing credits. Also include clips (magazine clips preferred, but newspapers/trades considered: "It's not *who* you've written for. It's the style, the quality of the writing, that we're looking for"). Lois Spritzer adds: "We're very favorably impressed when we see from the query that the writer has done his homework. We get a lot of letters, for instance, addressed to an editor who has long since left."

REJECTIONS: A standard rejection letter is sent most often. But personalized notes are sent to encourage more submissions, or to explain, perhaps, that only the timing might be off with the particular story suggestion.

BALLET NEWS

1865 Broadway
New York, NY 10023
(212) 582-7500

SOURCE: Karl Reuling, managing editor

IN SHORT: Possibilities only for dance/arts writers.

ABOUT THE MAGAZINE: Monthly. Mostly free-lance–written (but by regulars and stringers). Published by the Metropolitan Opera Guild, *Ballet News* is a young magazine (est. 1979). But despite its small circulation (about 40,000 subscribers), it has earned a prestigious reputation among cultural/arts magazines, covering ballet and dance in the U.S. and abroad. Readership is all ages, with the heaviest concentration between 25–44; a high percentage of readers are college grads, in professional occupations, of middle to upper income. They attend cultural events regularly; they do a lot of reading and they travel. Female readers outnumber males three to one. According to reader surveys, a large number of readers keep the magazine from month to month. *Areas open to free-lancers:* All features. ("Calendar," "Footnotes," reviews and "Reports" are written by staff/regular contributors.) *Rates:* Features: 11 cents published word. Reports and back-of-book pieces: 9 cents published word. *Payment:* On publication. *Expenses:* Pays reasonable expenses. *Kill fee:* Negotiable. *Rights:* Buys first North American serial rights—verbally (sometimes by confirming letter). *Number of submissions received:* Ten a month. *Reply time to queries:* "It could take a few months." *Advance dates:* Lead time is six weeks. Issues are planned at least three to four months in advance.

FREE-LANCE POSSIBILITIES: "Our aim," says Karl Reuling, "is to publish the best writing about dance, the best criticism and reviews—by the people best matched to the subject." Because this is a specialized market, one that requires a certain degree of background expertise, the writers who do manage to break in tend to be people with a dance/arts writing background. Reuling comments: "We're always on the lookout for fresh points of view, for new writing faces. But there aren't that many cases where someone unknown to us publishes a piece in *Ballet News.* Most of our pieces are assigned to our regular writers and stringers, or to new writers who have come to us through contacts. I'm always looking for the distinguished dance writers, the very best people."

If you aren't a dance specialist, your chances of being published in *Ballet News* are "very slim." For the general-interest writer, it is probably only worthwhile to approach *Ballet News* if you have a *terrific* idea and, if you don't possess high-caliber clips, you are willing to work on spec.

For the dance/arts writer, chances are better. Although the magazine has specialist stringers all over the country who supply local reviews and reports and are assigned needed local stories, there are still opportunities with a good idea, attached to clips which show your expertise in the field. Article possibilities may be something like the one dance writer Anita Finkel submitted, titled: "New York City—Ballet at Last." The piece told of her growing-up years in Los Angeles, of her move to New York and experience of City Ballet and of the difference in dance from West Coast to East. In the end the article could not be slotted in, but the quality of the writing aroused interest and it has led to assignments since.

Profiles of dancers, choreographers, and behind-the-scenes figures are a possibility for the dance writer. The magazine runs historical/reminiscence articles from time to time. The era of the romantic ballet, an article on the beginnings of the Swedish Ballet and its tour of the U.S. in the twenties are two ideas of this type. Also possible may be background pieces on specific ballets. Two recent examples: an article on "La Bayadère," another on the Houston Ballet's premiere of Frederick Ashton's "The Two Pigeons."

The magazine also runs articles on major regional companies, and highlights budding local companies—those with more than local significance. Both categories could be possibilities for a dance writer in a particular locality.

Most articles are written on assignment simply because the writers generally are known, and also because issues are planned around ballet events that are scheduled up to a year in advance. Editing varies. Galleys are shown on feature stories.

HOW TO SUBMIT: Completed manuscripts are read (photocopies okay), but queries are preferred. Try to keep the query under a page. Reuling comments: "People's time is short. Tell us your ideas quickly, as clearly and as succinctly as possible." Include clips, "but don't inundate us; send us samples that show range and variety of your dance writing." And remember: if you're not a dance specialist, sell yourself well!

REJECTIONS: Personal "thanks, but no" letters are sent. Encouraging notes are sent or phone calls made to writers the magazine would like to encourage.

BETTER HOMES AND GARDENS

Meredith Corporation
1716 Locust Street
Des Moines, IA 50336
(515) 284-3000

SOURCE: Margaret Daly, money management and features editor

IN SHORT: Very limited market; mostly staff-written.

ABOUT THE MAGAZINE: Monthly; 15–20% free-lance–written. *Better Homes and Gardens* is a magazine with strong service orientation, geared to home and family life. Emphasis is on home improvement projects, with gardening, cooking, and crafts. But the magazine also includes related subjects: education, cars, health, money management, travel, pets, etc. Information given is practical, timely, how-to. *Readership:* 73.5% female, 26.5% male; median age is 40; readers are middle income, with 30% in professional/managerial positions; 72% are married, most have children. *Circulation:* 8 million. *Estimated readership:* 34.2 million. *Areas open to free-lancers:* Money, health, education, travel, pets, cars, electronics, housing, decorating. *Rates:* Articles (600–1500 words): $500–$1000, and occasionally higher. *Payment:* On acceptance. *Expenses:* Pays reasonable expenses. *Kill fee:* About $150. May be negotiable. *Rights:* Buys all rights, by written contract. Rarely negotiable. *Number of submissions received weekly:* 20–30. *Reply time to queries:* Three to four weeks (sometimes sooner; outright rejections generally receive immediate replies). *Advance dates:* Lead time is six to seven months. Issues are planned about a year in advance, with flexibility on text pieces.

FREE-LANCE POSSIBILITIES: Although the editors say they are always looking for new writers, this is basically a staff-written magazine. Free-lance pieces tend to be done by regulars, or by writers with particular expertise. Although a few newcomers break in each year, only about one in 50 submissions is likely to be successful.

Says Margaret Daly: "One of the most common mistakes is when writers don't gear their queries to our style, content, and audience. For example, we never do celebrity profiles, yet we get queries for them; we rarely, if ever, do personal narratives."

If an unsolicited query *is* pulled, an assignment will not be made automatically. Writers new to the magazine *may* be asked to work on spec. And if an article cannot be scheduled within the near future, the editors are likely to pass on it. Writers are sometimes kept on file when *they* look promising but the query is not quite right. Once into the magazine, future assignments may be offered.

When a rewrite is required, the manuscript is returned to the writer. If this attempt is unsuccessful, a kill fee is paid. Editing tends to be heavy, and manuscripts are checked for accuracy with a number of sources.

HOW TO SUBMIT: Send submissions to the departmental editor listed on the masthead. Completed manuscripts are accepted, but queries are preferred. Include title of proposed article and three to four sentences outlining content. Include clips, "especially if you're new to us." Newspapers, trades, and small magazine clips are okay; "We're looking for good writing: research, style, organization, a 'fit' to *Better Homes and Gardens*."

REJECTIONS: The decision to send either a form rejection or a personalized note is made by each departmental editor.

BON APPETIT

5900 Wilshire Boulevard
Los Angeles, CA 90036
(213) 937-1025

SOURCE: Laurie G. Buckle, assistant editor

IN SHORT: Market for specialists only.

ABOUT THE MAGAZINE: Monthly; 80% free-lance–written. *Bon Appetit* is a food/entertaining magazine. *Circulation:* 1.3 million. *Estimated readership:* 3 million. *Areas open to free-lancers:* All features. *Rates:* Pays "medium to top rates." *Payment:* On acceptance. *Rights:* Buys all rights, by written contract. Not negotiable. *Number of submissions received weekly:* 25–30. *Reply time to queries:* Three to four weeks. *Advance dates:* Issues are planned up to a year in advance.

FREE-LANCE POSSIBILITIES: This is not a market for the general-interest writer. Most features highlight food and recipes, and a writer must be a food specialist and able to submit original recipes (which the magazine always tests first). The July '82 issue, for instance, carried four main features: "New Pasta Salads," "Cooking Class—Step by Step to the Perfect Barbecue," "The Ultimate Dessert," and "Romantic Caribbean Dinner." New writers break in here infrequently; there's a contingent of regular, established food and travel specialists, both feature writers and columnists. New people coming in do so mostly through a travel or back-of-the-book piece—and they're specialists in the field.

Says Laurie Buckle: "Rejected writers, generally, are not reading the magazine. They're suggesting stories we have recently covered, or they're suggesting ideas that are clearly not right for us—subjects like humor. A good, thorough knowledge of the magazine—our style, format, and content—is a necessary prerequisite for any writer considering submitting a proposal."

HOW TO SUBMIT: Manuscripts are accepted (originals preferred over photocopies), but queries are preferred. Short queries are best, "outlining the focus and including a list of recipes (original and unpublished) with brief descriptions." Including food-related clips is helpful.

REJECTIONS: All contributors receive a personally typed letter, but it's usually standard-reply wording—unless an editor wishes to encourage more submissions.

BRIDE'S

Condé Nast Publications
350 Madison Avenue
New York, NY 10017
(212) 880-8800

SOURCE: Andrea Feld, copy and features editor

IN SHORT: Very open to writers and ideas; good opportunities.

ABOUT THE MAGAZINE: Bi-monthly. *Bride's* is a magazine concerned with bridal fashion and beauty, but articles also cover wedding planning and etiquette, honeymoons, relationships and marriage, health and sex, finances, home management and decorating. The magazine also includes reviews of books, films, and TV shows concerning relationships. Articles should be written in a friendly style: "to encourage the bride and groom to be successful in their quest for happily married life." The average age of the bride-to-be is around 22; 60% of the readers have attended or graduated from college, and it's estimated the average reader will buy between three and six issues of the magazine during her engagement. *Circulation:* 350,000. *Areas open to free-lancers:* Everything except fashion and beauty, decorating, etiquette. *Rates:* Articles: $300–$600. "Something New" pays $25 for reader ideas. "Love" column pays $25 for reader love poems, songs. *Payment:* On acceptance. *Expenses:* Some phone calls, photocopying, and mailing, but must be cleared first. *Kill fee:* 20%. *Rights:* Buys all rights, by check endorsement. *Number of submissions received weekly:* 30. *Reply time to queries:* Six to eight weeks. *Advance dates:* Lead time is four months. Issues are planned eight months in advance. Submit seasonal material at least 6 months in advance.

FREE-LANCE POSSIBILITIES: *Bride's* pays decently, encourages, and welcomes new writers, pays on acceptance, and constantly needs material. "There really is a lot of opportunity at *Bride's* for the free-lancer," says Andrea Feld. "Writing for the bride might seem specialized, but we really do cover a lot of topics, and because of our reader turnover we constantly have to update and revise stories. We're happy to consider completed manuscripts and quite often get material that we can edit right into the magazine. And we do give over-the-transom queries a lot of time."

What more can a free-lancer ask? There are really no catches here, with one exception: All writers new to the magazine must do the first piece on spec, and *all* writers must submit an outline or the first few pages of the proposed article before going ahead with the piece.

Of the 30-odd queries received weekly, however, only about three work out successfully, so the challenge is to come up with the right idea. For which Feld offers these tips: "Our readers want really good advice on planning their wedding and adjusting to their marriage relationship. We want queries on issues affecting the husband-wife relationship. We also like first-person emotional pieces—on topics like getting along with one's in-laws. And familiar, anecdotal, slice-of-life pieces are always good—on becoming a stepparent, or coping with prewedding jitters."

The following is a list of topics that are covered in the magazine over the course of each year: birth control, second marriage, in-laws, careers (limited coverage), religion, friends, sex, babies, stepparenting, fighting, romance, communication skills, money, housework, background differences, expectations and the reality of marriage, individuality within marriage, fidelity, what makes marriage work, preparing for marriage (counseling, etc.), and coping with the unexpected in marriage.

Other possible topics include interreligious marriages, couples who work together, older brides, second-time brides, and reaffirmation ceremonies. Interracial marriage stories are not a good bet: "We would like to tackle this subject but it's just too narrow to appeal to most of our readers."

All article information should be aimed at the bride ("you"— second person singular), rather than the bride and groom as a couple, and article tone should always be warm and supportive.

"We don't need any queries on wedding etiquette or wedding customs. And we don't need many queries for career articles; to our reader that's not what is of prime importance. We also don't need queries in areas like stocking a medicine cabinet or setting up your home (these articles are staff-written), or investing in gold and diamonds (our readers keep these for sentimental reasons). We don't want service/news information pieces. And we don't want very religious pieces or experiences, unless they're worked into a general feature."

There *are* possibilities for small pieces in the "Something New" section, and for fractional pieces—one, two or three columns in length.

Travel is mostly written in-house and by regular writers (including "Trip Tips"). The only real possibility is with a 1000–1500-word filler along the lines of: honeymoon trousseaus for sun honeymoons, snow honeymoons, or driving honeymoons; budgeting for a wedding trip; honeymoon planning; last-minute honeymoons. Even with a similar idea chances aren't great; only one or two fillers used yearly are written by writers new to the magazine. Says travel editor Marcia Vickery: "Forget anything that makes fun of honeymooners; personal experiences readers cannot relate to (backpacking in Bolivia, for example); and pieces in which the destination is too specific. (We would not use a piece specifically on a Boston hotel; we would want a roundup of Boston's ten most luxurious honeymoon suites, ten great American cities, or something on driving through New England). Possibilities could also be roundup pieces on particular types of honeymoons (houseboating, exotic places to be married, etc.). These must be well researched, complete, and include information on costs, how to get in touch with the hotel or tourist board, as well as rundowns on restaurants, sightseeing, and staying places."

HOW TO SUBMIT: Phone queries are not encouraged. "I'll always talk to a writer, but I'll still ask them to put their query in writing," Feld says.

Queries can be of any length: "The key is that they should be really well written," Feld stresses. "Mainly we want to see that the writer has read the magazine and has indicated how they would tackle the story." In the way of personal background information, it's helpful to add any "unique experience that's relevant to the query. Anything that adds credibility." It's not necessary to include clips with the query, but it is helpful. Newspaper and trade clips okay.

A footnote: "Often queries are too generalized. And sometimes the writer will say something like: 'This was a piece that was just rejected at *Redbook*.' I don't think any editor wants to feel they're second choice!"

REJECTIONS: A standard form is usually used. "But if the idea's right on target but it's already in the magazine or in the works, we'll type a note on the reply letter, explaining this to the writer and encouraging her/him to try us again."

BUSINESSWEEK

McGraw-Hill Building
1221 Avenue of the Americas
New York, NY 10020
(212) 997-2511

BusinessWeek is completely staff-written; no free-lance contributions are accepted.

CALIFORNIA

P.O. Box 69990
Los Angeles, CA 90069
(213) 273-7516

SOURCE: The editor interviewed here preferred not to be named.

IN SHORT: Regional stories only; fairly limited feature possibilities.

ABOUT THE MAGAZINE: Monthly. Over 60% staff-written, and increasing. *California* is a regional magazine. *Readership:* median age is 41; 81% attended/graduated college; 57% are in professional/managerial positions. The readers are interested in cultural events and outdoor activities. *Circulation:* 250,000 subscribers. *Estimated readership:* 285,000. *Sample copy:* $1.75 to Lindee Cox, Subscriber Service Coordinator; $3.50 for back issues. *Areas open to free-lancers:* Everything except regular-contributor columns (movies, music, books, restaurants, wine, politics, business, etc.). *Rates:* "California People": up to $100. "California Reporter": up to $200. Features: up to $2500. *Payment:* On acceptance. *Expenses:* Up to 20% of article fee. *Kill fee:* 20%. *Rights:* Buys first North American rights, by written contract. *Number of submissions received weekly:* 75. *Reply time to queries:* Generally within a month, often sooner. *Advance dates:* Lead time is anywhere from six months to a week. Issues are planned three or four months in advance.

FREE-LANCE POSSIBILITIES: The editor interviewed rated free-lance chances at *California* as "very slim." She explained: "Over 60% of the magazine is staff-written, and we'd like to raise that percentage. But though most of our ideas are staff-generated and written, we are always looking for newsworthy stories and new voices. We would advise writers to keep trying us; we don't want to overlook the next Hemingway."

She cited the following articles as examples of over-the-transom submissions that *did* work out: "It's A Wonderful Life," a profile of Leon Schwab; and "Portrait of the Artist as a Mass Murderer," a feature on the Zodiac murders. About seven features are run monthly and include profiles, investigative pieces, general-interest, and consumer articles—with a California as well as Los Angeles/Hollywood/San Francisco emphasis.

The one area where there *are* possibilities is "California Reporter." "This is the best foot in the door. About 40% of it comes in from the outside. There *is* some hope in this area." Articles run about 800–1200 words and can best be described as mini-features—less news-angled, more general-interest, behind-the-news pieces. The August '82 issue, for instance, included these "Reporter" pieces: an article on the high cost of campaigning for political office; another on Butterball, a manatee living at the Steinhart Aquarium in San Francisco; a report on California's "Talk-radio" network; a day over the Pacific with the navy's antisubmarine patrol; a report on the problems that have arisen with San Francisco's crackdown on parking violations; a story on mural art to be found in bars in Baja, Mexico.

The mistakes contributors make here? "Most often the writer hasn't *read* the magazine; they'll submit fiction, for instance, when we've never run fiction. We publish no poetry, history; rarely do we publish satire. Or the writer submits a query on something we've recently covered; we don't have enough issues in a year to cover a subject more than once. And taking a look at the magazine masthead is helpful, to avoid spelling mistakes in editors' names." The editor also adds that the magazine does not use previously published articles.

Any necessary rewriting is done by the writer. Of general editing: "Our standards are high. This means very careful editing, which often tends toward extensive. But we work *very* closely with the writer, pulling the words from *him*." Galleys are shown.

HOW TO SUBMIT: Manuscripts are considered, but queries are much preferred. There are no length requirements on queries. Include clips: "Clips are much more helpful than résumés." (Newspaper and small magazine clips are okay: "We're interested in quality of writing, not publication status.")

REJECTIONS: A personalized reply is sent to all contributors.

COMPLETE WOMAN

19 East Bellevue Place
Chicago, IL 60611
(312) 266-8680

Bi-monthly. Covers health and beauty, decorating and food, self-help/psychological articles, careers, relationships. Uses original material and a lot of reprints. Declined to participate. Editor: Bonnie L. Krueger.

CONSUMER REPORTS

Consumers Union
256 Washington Street
Mount Vernon, NY 10550
(914) 667-9400

SOURCE: Irwin Landau, editorial director
Eileen Denver, managing editor

IN SHORT: Unsolicited submissions are discouraged.

ABOUT THE MAGAZINE: Monthly. *Consumer Reports* is a publication of Consumers Union of United States. It is available by subscription and has limited newsstand distribution. No advertising is accepted. The magazine consists of reports on products, everything from aspirin to vacuum cleaners, and on services, from choosing a lawyer to buying insurance. This is an independent organization working for the consumer; all goods, appliances, and services are bought, tested, and then rated for performance, durability, value for money, etc. The main group of readers ranges from 35–45; education and income levels are high. *Circulation:* 3 million. *Rates:* Shorts: $100. Features (3000–5000 words): $1000–$3000. *Payment:* Half on acceptance, half on publication. *Expenses:* Pays reasonable expenses. *Kill fee:* 50%. *Rights:* Buys all rights, by written contract. Not negotiable. *Reply time to queries:* Two weeks. *Advance dates:* Lead time is two months. Issues are planned at least three months in advance.

FREE-LANCE POSSIBILITIES: *Consumer Reports* is almost entirely staff-written. Says Eileen Denver: "We do use some outside material, usually in the areas of economics and finance, and rarely, health and nutrition. But it will be only one or two pieces a year, and they're always assigned to people we know, who tend to be former staff members. To approach us, you must be a specialist in a particular field; if you've done some important research work or have published a book in a specialist area, we might consider a query. But generally we must discourage free-lance submissions; in the past seven years, for instance, we haven't used anything that's come in over-the-transom."

Only queries are considered. A standard form rejection is used, with encouragement added in rare instances.

CONTINENTAL

East/West Network
5900 Wilshire Boulevard
Suite 800
Los Angeles, CA 90036
(213) 937-5810

SOURCE: The editor here preferred not to be named.

IN SHORT: A market for experienced writers.

ABOUT THE MAGAZINE: Monthly; 80% free-lance—written. *Continental* is the in-flight magazine of Continental Airlines, which is business-oriented editorially. The readers are 60% male, 40% female; most are between the ages of 35 to 50; most are in professional/managerial positions. *Circulation:* 80,000. *Estimated readership:* 400,000. *Sample copy:* $2. *Areas open to free-lancers:* Everything except: "Grapevine," "Bottom Line," "Options." *Rates:* Features: $400–$500; columns $250–350. *Payment:* On publication. *Expenses:* Pays reasonable expenses to $50 maximum. *Kill fee:* 25%. *Rights:* Buys first North American rights, by written contract. *Number of submissions received weekly:* 12. *Reply time to queries:* Three weeks. *Advance dates:* Lead time is three months. Issues are planned four months in advance.

FREE-LANCE POSSIBILITIES: *Continental* mainly publishes seasoned writers. When beginning writers do break in, it's generally through some kind of contact or recommendation, or because they are working in a particular field or on a particular project from which they can bring a certain amout of expertise. Otherwise, writers who are low on good clips will probably find this market a struggle. Everything will depend on the idea. If it's something the editors really want and if it will fit into the editorial schedule, they *may* take a chance—after researching the writer's background and ability through their own contacts, and after the writer has submitted a "detailed synopsis" of the idea.

Writers do not work on spec here. The magazine will either assign or decline the idea depending on the writer, the idea, and the synopsis presented.

Some area guidelines: One travel story is run monthly; the

subject is determined by the airline. "But we do go back to the same locations once or twice a year," the editor commented, adding: "It's hard for us to find different writers to give us a new angle on a location." Writers strategically placed geographically are needed (see "Portfolios and Positive Thinking," pages 7–9).

General-interest is a possible area. Features *are* geared to the business traveler and the magazine likes to run one fairly heavy concept piece per issue. Examples: the boom in banking in Florida; the revitalization of urban waterfronts; the decline in American productivity (this piece was about the writings of two professors at Harvard).

Profiles almost always focus on people in business, and there are two requirements: they have to be people at the top of their profession, or else people who are rapidly moving up to the top. In other words, success stories about people with some recognition value. Says the editor: "It's always good to let us know about interesting people doing constructive things. They don't have to be top-notch people; they can be ordinary people doing something extraordinary in their spare time. But their activities and ideas should be intriguing."

Health/medical articles are being done less and less, but new scientific developments are a possibility if they're intriguing. The magazine isn't interested in straight psychological pieces, but they might look at a piece that presents a big, new development in the field.

Editing varies here. The writer is required to do any rewriting needed. Galleys are not shown, but writers are given "a general impression of how we're going to run the piece."

HOW TO SUBMIT: Send completed ms. (photocopies okay) or query. Multiple submissions are okay. No preferences on query length, but you should include a rundown of writing experience/credits. Clips are not necessary at query stage.

REJECTIONS: The form of rejection "depends on the writer. If it's someone I don't know and the idea is wrong for us, they'll receive a standard rejection. If it's someone I know, or the idea is sound but we can't use it, then I'll reply personally."

COSMOPOLITAN

The Hearst Corporation
224 West 57th Street
New York, NY 10019
(212) 262-5700

SOURCE: Roberta Ashley, executive editor

IN SHORT: Open, but very competitive market.

ABOUT THE MAGAZINE: Monthly. All articles are free-lance—written. *Cosmopolitan* is a magazine for young women, 18–35. Emphasis is on male/female relationships, health and beauty, and sexuality. Says Roberta Ashley: "Our goal is to help our reader have a better life." *Circulation:* 2.8 million nationally. *Estimated readership:* 25 million in the U.S. alone; there are ten foreign editions. *Areas open to free-lancers:* Everything except regular columns listed under "Departments." *Rates:* Shorter features (3000 words): $500–$750. Longer features (5000 words): $1500. Higher payments for established writers. *Payment:* On acceptance. *Expenses:* All reasonable expenses. *Kill fee:* 10%. *Rights:* Buys all rights, by confirming letter. Not negotiable. (Selected copy goes to the ten foreign editions). *Number of submissions received weekly:* "Hundreds." *Reply time to queries:* One to two weeks. *Advance dates:* Lead time is three months. Issues are planned up to eight months in advance.

FREE-LANCE POSSIBILITIES: All *Cosmopolitan*'s articles are free-lance—written, mostly by writers known at the magazine. "But that's not because we prefer it that way," Roberta Ashley insists. "It's because it's very difficult for writers to come in off the street; they tend to think of the obvious ideas." Only about one in 200 over-the-transom submissions works out. But Ashley stresses: "This is totally a free-lance market; there's a constant need for good new writers."

Ashley's advice to writers trying to break in is to send a query, with clips included. Time and effort should be put into the query: "Query letters are not easy to do. So many people send bland, uninteresting queries." If the query hits and if you're a writer with a track record at leading magazines, you'll almost certainly get an assignment. If your credits are limited to newspapers and/or small magazines, you may be asked to work on spec (unless your clips include articles of the length, depth, and scope of *Cosmopolitan*'s). Basically, to land an assignment from an idea that appeals, you have to demonstrate—either with clips, or in discussion with Ashley—that you can handle the piece. ("If an idea seems close, if the query is nicely written, and the clips look interesting, then I'll have the writer come in or I'll talk to them on the phone.") If you're unpublished, or barely published, then Ashley's advice is to approach the magazine with a manuscript. Otherwise you could run the risk of a rejection due to a limited track record.

Mention should be made here of a "policy" that has become part of the magazine's reputation: Editors allow free-lancers to come into the magazine's offices and choose articles to do from the dozens that are reportedly stored up just for the purpose. In fact, there *is* a book of ideas. The catch is that writers have to be highly qualified (with clips from the leading magazines) to get a look at the book. Ashley will only set up an appointment if the writer and clips fall into these categories: "It has to be someone whose work we know, someone whose work we are anxious to acquire, or someone who has worked for us—successfully—before. And as well as sending clips, these writers should also send some ideas."

Here's what-not-to-do in approaching *Cosmopolitan:* "Don't send us a query that says: 'How about doing something on Washington?' That's not an idea; that's a city. Don't send us ideas that should be in men's magazines—a sports story, for instance. We do profiles only on celebrities, not unknown people. We don't run stories on local oddities; material must have national appeal. We reject a lot of submissions because thoughts are not organized properly; there's no structure. Or there's no creativity or imagination. You must polish your writing skills before you can write for us.

"The biggest problem is that writers haven't studied the mazagine well enough. Yet in a way it *is* a formularized magazine. We're consistent. Our desire is to get the reader through the night. Get hold of the last 12 issues and study them. There is a test for your idea—the article should be aimed at a 25-year-old working woman and that woman as an individual. She may be a mother, but we're interested in her as a woman, not as a mother. What interests this kind of woman—that's what will interest us. She's not interested in retirement stories then. And she's not interested in the problems of the older woman going back into the working world."

The following published articles came in over-the-transom from writers unknown to the editors: "A writer in Houston, someone who wasn't well known, had covered a crime story; she sent us the manuscript and we bought it. Another writer in Seattle sent us a wonderfully humorous piece about her early days wrestling with contraception. It was hysterically funny; we bought it immediately."

Well-written humor is a good area for the free-lancer. Others are: psychological pieces; interesting fact pieces (e.g. the caterers of Beverly Hills who do all the big parties, the difficulties of getting celebrities to appear in TV commercials); emotional problems (e.g. dealing with jealousy, possessiveness); man/woman problems (e.g. how to tell if your lover is unfaithful, sexual boredom). Medical pieces are a possibility—"on any kind of health problem that would interest our readers." You do not *have* to be a specialized health writer, although Ashley cautions: "You shouldn't propose any article that's going to be too hard, too technical." Beauty is open: "A free-lancer could approach us with something like 'New Breakthroughs in Dentistry' or a first-person account of struggling with, say, hairiness." Travel is not a great area for the free-lancer. "If you think it's a really good idea, then by all means propose it. But what we won't do is pay for a writer to go somewhere, or to use our name."

The magazine generally runs a couple of celebrity profiles in each issue, but these are probably the hardest way in. Says Ashley: "It's very dicey to take an unknown writer who might waste Henry Kissinger's time. Generally our profiles are done by writers who have demonstrated their skills to us. We use them very often as rewards for writers who have been out there laboring in the vineyards for us. . . ." The only way a new writer *could* break in with a profile is through some kind of close contact with an impossible-to-get celebrity. A celebrity roundup article is a little easier. "We'll give a go-ahead there if the roundup idea is a good one, and you're able to demonstrate an ability to get to these celebrities. They're not easy to do; you have to have access to these people."

Roberta Ashley sees all over-the-transom submissions; possibilities are then discussed with managing editor Guy Flatley and editor Helen Gurley Brown.

Rewriting is not done by staff editors. "We do a lot of polishing —line editing—but we never put anything through the typewriter again. If a rewrite is needed, we'll give the manuscript back to the author. As long as a writer is willing to rewrite, and the article is 50–60% there, then I'll work with her as long as she's willing to." Galleys are shown to all authors.

HOW TO SUBMIT: Send the manuscript or query to Roberta Ashley (she prefers originals over photocopies, and asks that manuscripts not be typed on erasable bond). Keep queries to a page if possible, and include clips with the query.

REJECTIONS: A standard form is sent on over-the-transom submissions.

DANCE MAGAZINE

1180 Avenue of the Americas
New York, NY 10036
(212) 921-9300

SOURCE: Richard Philp, managing editor

IN SHORT: Specialized market, but open to general-interest writers.

ABOUT THE MAGAZINE: Monthly. Richard Philp says of his magazine: "It's one which takes the broadest possible view of dance and dance-related activities going on today." Readers range in age, but a high percentage are in the 20–35 age group. Most readers are female. Philp pegs the audience as "well educated, interested in the arts in general, and sophisticated and knowledgeable in terms of dance." *Circulation:* 60,000 subscribers. *Estimated readership:* 200,000. *Sample copy:* Free. *Areas open to free-lancers:* Everything except reviews. *Rates:* Reports: $50–$75. Features: Usual fee for new writers is $200, but can pay up to $350. *Payment:* On publication. *Expenses:* All reasonable expenses. *Kill fee:* 50%. *Rights:* In most cases buys all rights, by written contract. *Number of submissions received weekly:* 15–20. *Reply time to queries:* Up to three months. *Advance dates:* Lead time is two months. Issues are planned five months to a year in advance.

FREE-LANCE POSSIBILITIES: You do not have to be a dance specialist to write for *Dance Magazine.* It certainly helps if you have dance/arts clips to show, but if your idea is right and you write well, you may have a chance here, although if you're unknown to the magazine, you will be asked to work on spec. Says Richard Philp: "The important thing is good writing. But we have a great many inquiries and willing writers." So the way into *Dance Magazine* is either with an especially interesting feature subject, or an away-from-the-mainstream idea. Another possibility is the small regional spot item. Although there are stringers throughout the country and abroad, "that doesn't mean the stringers are going to cover everything. There *is* opportunity out there for feature ideas, and for writers who submit small items, on spec." Of the 1000-odd submissions received yearly, only about six work out.

Writers unknown to the editors have broken in with ideas like these: the state of dance in West Germany (Richard Sikes, May '82), and T'ai Chi (Charlotte Honda-Smith, Feb. '82). Nina Alovert, who wrote a piece on Baryshnikov in the April '82 issue, originally submitted the manuscript with photos she had taken.

When suggestions from free-lancers fail, it's often because of timing. "Very often the queries don't relate to our immediate needs. Often, too, the writer hasn't tailored his query or manuscript to our needs." Although the magazine covers a fairly wide sphere, the articles must have current appeal. Many are connected to the year's dance calendar; that is, they may link in with a company season or result from a recently noticed rising young soloist. "If your suggestions are about upcoming events, though, remember to make your query well in advance. Allow enough lead time!" A well-timed query may save some valuable time and energy.

Philp adds: "So often people send us messy manuscripts and queries. To me that indicates messy thinking. I have neither the time nor the patience to rethink a piece for a writer."

HOW TO SUBMIT: Phone queries are okay. Manuscripts are read (no photocopies), but one-page queries are preferred; include the point and the peaks/highlights of the proposed article; sell the editors on why the piece is important *now;* and state your qualifications for writing on the proposed subject. It's also helpful to include a rough idea of article length; most features run 2000 words, but they *can* run longer. Include clips too—preferably dance/arts samples—and state photo availability if possible.

REJECTIONS: No standard forms are used; personalized responses are sent to all contributors.

DAYTIMERS AND REAL LIFE

D.S. Magazines, Inc.
7060 Hollywood Boulevard
Suite 800
Hollywood, CA 90028
(213) 467-3111

SOURCE: Diane Dalbey, editor

IN SHORT: Open, but not looking for new writers.

ABOUT THE MAGAZINE: Monthly; 30–40% free-lance–written. *Daytimers and Real Life* is a magazine for daytime TV viewers, recently expanded to include TV, movies, music, and real-life drama; the magazine covers TV and other performers and their attitudes and activities both on and off camera. It also covers some behind-the-scenes production elements. *Readership:* Primarily women, with some younger readers. High readership among college students. Readers tend to be middle income. *Circulation:* 400,000. *Areas open to free-lancers:* Everything except "Dayteline," "Speakout," "One Man's Opinion," "Primetime Patter," and "Health & Beauty." *Rates:* $100–$150. *Payment:* On acceptance. *Expenses:* Pays reasonable expenses. *Kill fee:* One-quarter to one-third. *Rights:* Buys all rights, by check endorsement. Negotiable. *Number of submissions received weekly:* Three. *Reply time to queries:* Four weeks. *Advance dates:* Lead time is 2–2½ months. Issues are planned three months in advance.

FREE-LANCE POSSIBILITIES: Editor Diane Dalbey rates unknown free-lancers' chances here (if you're an unknown writer in the entertainment field) as "slim." She explains: "We have a good group of staff and free-lance writers at present who fill our needs fairly well." A newcomer appears in the magazine only about six times a year.

Only 10% of the article ideas come in over-the-transom. But Dalbey adds: "We're always open to queries from free-lancers—with samples. It's risky to assign stories to writers who don't send samples (published or unpublished)."

Dalbey sees all unsolicited submissions and makes assignment/rejection decisions alone, or after discussion with the managing editor Arthur Stern. An assignment will be made "*if we* need the story and aren't already committed for the next issue or two." Writers usually aren't asked to work on spec, although this can happen if the writer has weak clips.

Profiles and short interviews with daytime TV stars are possibilities, but chances for the outsider are better in these two areas: issues (involving TV shows/personalities) and real-life drama (concerning TV stars). Queries are discouraged for "What My Acting Craft Means to Me." These are too inside the acting profession to interest our middle-American readers."

Don'ts: "Poor grammar, syntax, style, no point of view or angle. Hand-written queries. A lot of contributors obviously aren't familiar with *Daytimers*."

Rewriting is done by the writer, if time allows. Galleys are not shown.

One final note from Dalbey: "I always appreciate continuous idea pitching once you've been published in the magazine. That's how I work with our current regular free-lancers."

HOW TO SUBMIT: Completed mss. are read (photocopies are discouraged). Queries: "Try to contain your idea in one to three succinct paragraphs." Include a "résumé or some information about your writing background, and two or three *related* writing samples." (Writer will be asked to show clips before an assignment is given.) A SASE is important here.

REJECTIONS: All contributors receive personalized replies.

DISCOVER

Time & Life Building
Rockefeller Center
New York, NY 10020
(212) 586-1212

"The Newsmagazine of Science." Monthly. Mostly staff-written. Free-lance pieces are solicited from known, usually specialized, writers.

DUN'S BUSINESS MONTH

875 Third Avenue
New York, NY 10022
(212) 605-9400

SOURCE: Clem Morgello, editor

IN SHORT: A very difficult sell, even for business writers.

ABOUT THE MAGAZINE: Monthly. Mostly staff-written. Previously published as *Dun's Review, Dun's Business Month* is a business magazine for upper-echelon *corporate* (as opposed to general business) executives. Distribution is controlled; it's available by subscription and has limited newsstand distribution. Median reader age: 52. Ninety-five percent of the readers are male. Average personal income of readers is around $99,000. *Circulation:* 284,000, nationally. *Sample copy:* $2.25. *Areas open to free-lancers:* Articles, except for "The Business Month" and "The Managers," which are staff-written. *Rates:* $300–$1,000 (depending on length and complexity of article). *Payment:* On acceptance. *Expenses:* Pays modest expenses. *Kill fee:* $200. *Rights:* Buys all rights, by confirming letter. Negotiable. *Number of submissions received weekly:* 10–12. *Reply time to queries:* Two to four weeks. *Advance dates:* Lead time is two months. Issues are planned at least one month in advance.

FREE-LANCE POSSIBILITIES: *Dun's Business Month* differs from the other business magazines in that its audience is made up of top-level corporate executives who are looking for top-level business news and information. The magazine runs 10–12 free-lanced features yearly. These are written by regular or known free-lancers. However, most of these writers originally came to the magazine over-the-transom. So there *are* opportunities, but the odds aren't great. Says Clem Morgello: "We don't limit the type of material free-lancers can do for us. We write for a sophisticated audience, but that doesn't mean a nonbusiness writer can't do a story for us. But truthfully, it doesn't happen very often. Because of the sophistication of our audience, and because free-lancers are in competition with our staff writers, you really need business writing experience to both write for our audience and to know where the news is. You have to know the literature, as an academic would say."

Even if you're a business writer, *Dun's* is not an easy sell. A piece by a new writer appears only about once a year. The key, of course, is to come up with an idea staffers won't be covering. "There are two main mistakes free-lancers make. They don't know who our audience is, and they don't know what has been published previously," Morgello says. "Often, for instance, we'll be offered material designed for consumers. That's not our audience. Another common mistake is not realizing this is a magazine with a two-month lead time. While everything must have a news angle, it can't be written as a news story."

Apart from general business topics, the magazine does run profiles. These generally highlight a particular executive within the context of a company profile. The piece on Kenneth M. Miller, chief executive of Penril Corp. (August '82) is a good profile example to study.

Writers generally work on assignment; they are asked to work on spec only if the story is somewhat uncertain.

Editing varies. If a rewrite is needed and there's time, the manuscript will be sent back to the author; otherwise it will be done by staff. But rewrites are rare. Authors are shown galleys and are informed if cuts are made.

HOW TO SUBMIT: Mss. are read (photocopied mss. are okay), but queries are preferred. Queries should be short—"a couple of paragraphs." Include a rundown of your business-writing expertise. Don't sent clips with the query; these will be requested if there's interest in the idea.

REJECTIONS: A standard rejection form is used here for all unsuitable submissions.

DYNAMIC YEARS

215 Long Beach Boulevard
Long Beach, CA 90802
(213) 432-5781

SOURCE: Carol Powers, editor

IN SHORT: Very open; good possibilities.

ABOUT THE MAGAZINE: Bi-monthly; 80% free-lance—written. This
is a publication of Action for Independent Maturity, a division
of the American Association of Retired Persons. The magazine
goes only to AIM members; it's not available on the newsstand.
Dynamic Years is written for "working Americans in their middle years." It's a general-interest publication that helps readers
plan for retirement while showing them how to live their middle-aged years to the fullest. Readers are in the 40–60 age group.
Covered are: human-interest stories, travel, retirement planning,
leisure-time activities, health, financial planning, how-to, and
life-style issues. *Circulation:* 258,000, nationally. *Sample copy:*
Free. *Areas open to free-lancers:* Everything except "As We See
It" and "News Worth Filing." *Rates:* Features: $750 and up;
shorts: $150 and up. *Payment:* On acceptance. *Expenses:* Pays
all reasonable expenses. *Kill fee:* 25%. *Rights:* Buys first North
American rights, by assignment or acceptance letter. *Number of
submissions received weekly:* 50. *Reply time to queries:* Two to
four weeks. *Advance dates:* Lead time is four months. Issues are
planned six months in advance.

FREE-LANCE POSSIBILITIES: Editor Carol Powers describes *Dynamic Years* as an "excellent market for free-lancers." Of the
free-lance—written material, only about half is done by writers
known at the magazine. Not only are there openings for free-
lancers, the range of possibilities is also wide.
  "Dynamic Americans," the regular feature that highlights 40–
60-year-olds excelling in interesting or unusual areas, is probably the most open section; short pieces in the 150-word range
are always needed, and most of these profiles come from over-
the-transom suggestions. "Changing Gears," which also consists
of short profiles, is a regular feature on people changing careers/
interests in their midyears; it also reports on unusual events of
interest. "Changing Gears" is similarly wide open to over-the-

transom suggestions. "The Voice of Experience"—first-person reader essays, which can be humorous—is a forum for readers and writers alike; it's another good area for the previously unpublished writer.

New angles are always needed for retirement-planning stories; human-interest stories and midlife-issue discussions are always sought. There's also a constant need for financial articles, but here the writer must either have business/finance expertise or else be able to interview experts in the field. Relevant celebrity profiles are also welcomed. Other possible areas: career/job issues; how-to service pieces; articles on alternative/interesting life-styles for middle-aged readers; sports/health/fitness. The key is: general interst for 40–60-year-olds, *nationally.*

Assignments are given to writers known to the editors, and to unknown writers with good clips. Otherwise, a writer is asked to work on spec—for the first story.

HOW TO SUBMIT: Mss. are read (photocopied mss. are okay), but queries are preferred. Preference is for short queries; personal details aren't necessary, and specialist qualifications should be given only if relevant. Include clips with your query if you're unknown at the magazine (preferably not trade magazine samples).

REJECTIONS: A standard rejection form is used; personalized notes are sent to contributors on the right track.

EBONY

Johnson Publishing
820 South Michigan Avenue
Chicago, IL 60605
(312) 322-9252

SOURCE: Charles L. Sanders, managing editor

IN SHORT: Little free-lance material is used; very limited chances over-the-transom.

ABOUT THE MAGAZINE: Monthly. The magazine is 10–15% free-lance–written at most. A black-oriented general-interest magazine, *Ebony* covers personalities (unknown and well known), current trends, and stories of historical significance. *Readership:* Fairly evenly split male/female, and across-the-board in age group, income, occupations, and life-style. *Circulation:* 1,450,000. *Estimated readership:* 6.5 million. *Areas open to free-lancers:* Everything except "Fashions," "Foods," "Backstage," and "Speaking of People" (will accept suggestions for this department; however, does not pay for them). *Rates:* $200–$1000 plus. *Payment:* About 30 days after publication. *Expenses:* Pays reasonable expenses. *Kill fee:* Not usually paid. *Rights:* Generally buys all rights, by letter of agreement. Negotiable. *Number of submissions received weekly:* 25–30. *Reply time to queries:* Two to four weeks (will not discuss queries, acceptance, or rejection by phone). *Advance dates:* Lead time is 2½ months. Issues are planned about three months in advance.

FREE-LANCE POSSIBILITIES: Managing editor Charles L. Sanders describes chances here as "very slim." *Ebony* mainly publishes experienced, tested writers—a newcomer will appear only once or twice a year. Says Sanders: "Lawsuits are so common these days that we are very careful about writers' facts. We usually steer clear of 'new' writers whom we just don't know. We have a full staff and about half a dozen free-lancers we use regularly."

For an unknown writer to break in here, his story idea must be very desirable and the writer must have good backup clips. Clips should be sent with queries; they're asked for before any assignments are made. Without good clips, the writer may be asked to work on spec, time permitting. What's more likely is that the editors will simply offer to pay for the story idea and then have one of their staffers cover it.

For experienced writers, the subject scope is wide. The November '82 issue, for instance, carried this range: interviews with Gladys Knight, tennis player Yannick Noah, actor Roger Mosley; "Black Dynasty"—a piece on a Texas family and its oil and cattle empire; another on licensed toys; a report on New York City's honoring of the long-running jazz musical *One Mo' Time;* a piece on an Alabama man who lost 280 pounds; a report on a six-year-old golf champ in California; an article posing the question: "Should you marry someone with children?"; a report on black cops and the strides they're making; another on black actors on TV soap operas. When asked about areas where queries are not wanted, Sanders replied: "Poetry; short stories; articles about 'A nice Negro lady I knew when I was a child.' "

Editing can be heavy here. "If there's enough time, I'll send the manuscript back to the author. Otherwise we'll make cuts and then show the writer either the edited manuscript or galleys."

HOW TO SUBMIT: Completed manuscripts are accepted (photocopies okay), but queries are preferred. Multiple submissions are accepted on both queries and manuscripts. Short queries consisting of just a few paragraphs preferred. Include résumé/writing background and clips. Newspaper clips are okay; "we simply want to see style and skill."

REJECTIONS: Personalized replies are sent. Says Charles Sanders: "We try to individualize our replies. Sometimes I'll also suggest another publication the writer might try."

ESQUIRE

Two Park Avenue
New York, NY 10016
(212) 561-8100

SOURCE: The editor interviewed here preferred not to be named.

IN SHORT: Very competitive market; very limited possibilities.

ABOUT THE MAGAZINE: Monthly; 80–90% free-lance–written. *Esquire* is classified as a men's magazine; in fact, 43% of the readers are women and it is a general-interest publication, covering a wide range of topics from politics to sports, current affairs, social trends, design and fashion, and so on. Half the readers are aged 25–44; 45% of all readers are college grads. *Circulation:* 650,000. *Estimated readership:* 3.4 million. *Areas open to free-lancers:* All articles (not columns). *Rates:* $500–$2500 (mainly depending on length). *Payment:* On acceptance. *Expenses:* Pays all incidentals. *Kill fee:* $150–$300. *Rights:* Buys first North American, by written contract. Plus anthology rights and limited periodical resale rights (lasting two months after publication and guaranteeing author 50% of fees). *Number of submissions received weekly:* 100–200. *Reply time to queries:* Four weeks maximum. *Advance dates:* Lead time is 3½ months. Issues are planned 4½ months in advance.

FREE-LANCE POSSIBILITIES: *Esquire has* published first-time writers, and one of its policies, under the fairly recent new management, is an openness to new, young writers. But most contributors have written for the magazine before or else they are known to *Esquire* editors. A first-time writer's by-line will be seen here only a few times a year; often these are actually people working on books, whose work is coming in through an agent. For the unpublished writer coming in cold, chances are slim.

An example of an unknown writer who broke in is Chip Elliott. A Midwest writer, he wrote a letter to the editor pleading his case for carrying a gun. The editors were so impressed with his writing style and the way he presented his argument, they asked him to try expanding the concept into a full-length article. It appeared as the cover story in the September '81 issue. This instance is far from being a usual one, but it *did* happen.

Despite the few submissions bought, *all* are read. The first step is to get past the editorial assistants. Anything with promise moves on to one of several editors. These editors pull possibilities and go to bat for them.

There is no set rule on assignments; each case is different. No assignments are ever given without the editors seeing clips. Writers without good clips can either send in a manuscript or else ask to work on spec.

If a rewrite is needed, the writer does it. From then on staff editors "do whatever editing is needed; the extent of the editing varies from article to article." But the writer sees galleys before publication.

What *won't* work at *Esquire?* Sexually explicit material (this is a literary men's magazine!); straight Q. & A. interviews (profiles are never done this way); news stories that are too timely for the long lead time; suggestions for profiles on people who have either been done to death or whose timeliness has passed; trend pieces "everyone else is covering."

Remember: If you're unknown at *Esquire,* your idea *has* to be a fairly unique one. Said the editor interviewed: "The obvious ideas just won't work." Studying several issues will give you a better idea of what does work. With humor, essays, and opinion pieces, you must send the manuscript, not a query; chances in these areas are slimmer than in general articles.

HOW TO SUBMIT: Send all submissions to Phillip Moffitt, editor. Manuscripts are read (photocopies okay), but queries are preferred. Queries should be on the short side; no more than a page or two. Said the editor interviewed: "The length isn't as important as expressing the idea clearly and convincing us that this is a piece that should be in *Esquire.*" Include one or two clips, preferably samples that are similar in content or style to the piece you are proposing.

REJECTIONS: The editorial assistants (the first screeners) send standard slips for most rejected submissions. Editors send either a standard slip or else a more personalized note. The form of reply all depends on how much time the editor has that week; a personalized reply should only be taken as a sign of encouragement if the editor has taken the time to make constructive comments.

ESSENCE

Essence Communications, Inc.
1500 Broadway
New York, NY 10036
(212) 730-4260

SOURCE: Audrey Edwards, executive editor

IN SHORT: Possibilities for experienced writers.

ABOUT THE MAGAZINE: Monthly; 90% free-lance–written. *Essence* describes itself as "The Magazine for Today's Black Woman." The magazine's audience includes everyone from the typist to the professional woman. It's part a health and beauty magazine, part a service magazine—covering health, relationships, work, parenting, and life-style issues. Readers range in age from 18–34; the average age is around 27. Most readers have had some college or vocational training; most are in traditional jobs. About 75% of the readers are parents; a high percentage are single mothers. Interestingly, about 34% of the readers are men. *Circulation:* 700,000. *Estimated readership:* 2.3 million. *Areas open to free-lancers:* Service features about health, career, travel, and entertainment; "Speak!" *Rates:* Articles: $500–$1500. (Top payments to big-name writers.) "Main Events": $300–$400. "Essence Women": $100–$150. *Payment:* On acceptance. *Expenses:* Pays reasonable expenses. *Kill fee:* 25%. *Rights:* Except for name writers and those who have come through agents, *Essence* generally buys all rights, by written contract. However, these revert to the author 90 days after publication (but only on written request). *Number of submissions received weekly:* 120. *Reply time to queries:* Four to six weeks. *Advance dates:* Lead time is three months. Issues planned at least six months in advance.

FREE-LANCE POSSIBILITIES: About 90% of all published articles are staff-generated and assigned to regular writers. The regular writers are often the contributing editors listed on the masthead; other writers published here are well credentialed, come through agents, or are found by *Essence* editors through their work in other magazines.

However, the unsolicited pile is taken seriously, and it *is* possible to break in with a main feature. Laura Randolph's piece in the September '80 issue, "Dealing with a Cheap Man," came in originally as a query; she has gone on to write another piece for the magazine. Breaking in is probably easier, though, through a travel piece, a "Main Events," or an "Essence Women" profile. Tips for each:

For a travel piece, find an unusual slant, "perhaps something like: 'Here's a place where the American dollar goes further,' or 'You may not be aware of this, but half the people in this country are black like you are.' "

For "Main Events": "What your query letter should do is make a case why a particular story would be good for *Essence*." New writers do not break in here very often; the best possibility may be a celebrity profile for which you have *unique* access (otherwise this kind of piece would never be assigned if you're unknown).

For "Essence Women": "We're interested in reading about women from all over. A mistake that a lot of New York writers make, in particular, is sending us an idea that has local flavor. We have to gear all our stories to a national audience." This section (along with "Working World") is mostly free-lance—written, often by writers previously unknown to the editors.

Name writers are the ones who will get assignments at *Essence;* generally, new writers will be asked to work on spec— unless you have terrific clips, or in the case of a celebrity profile, you have access to people the magazine hasn't been able to reach.

Also worth noting: "Some writers send us ten 'Main Events' profile possibilities, all at once. I would much prefer to get one good idea. And it's very important, for *Essence,* to be aware of the audience. We're specialized by race. That sounds easy. But it really isn't; you have to convince us why your particular story works for black women."

Editing varies. Generally the manuscript is given back to the writer if a rewrite is needed, and the writer is given two chances to perfect the piece. Galleys are shown on request.

HOW TO SUBMIT: Send submissions to either Audrey Edwards or Susan Taylor, editor-in-chief (who together make the decisions on articles). Completed mss. are read (photocopies okay), but queries are preferred. Include with your story idea details of your writing experience and "tell us what particular strength or asset you might bring to the story." Clips are not required. Says

Audrey Edwards: "I really have mixed feelings about clips. Certainly don't deluge us with them; just send one or two, particularly if there are any that are similar in subject or feeling to the idea you're suggesting. When I look at clips I'm looking at the way the writer has executed stories, and if they have a magazine style. A lot of writers are newspaper reporters and that kind of writing can be very different. It's *how* you write, not so much where you've been published. But clips can also be examples of very heavily edited work. So your query letter will be the most important thing you send us."

REJECTIONS: Standard form rejection letters are generally sent to those contributors who are unknown to the editors. If the contributor is a writer known from previous work, or through reputation, or if it's someone the editors would like to encourage, a personal note will be sent.

THE EXECUTIVE FEMALE

NAFE
120 East 56th Street
#1440
New York, NY 10022
(212) 371-0740

SOURCE: Susan Strecker, managing editor/vice-president of publications

IN SHORT: Open, but fairly limited possibilities.

ABOUT THE MAGAZINE: Begun as a newsletter, *The Executive Female* is now a glossy bi-monthly, serving the 60,000-plus members of The National Association for Female Executives. The magazine is not available on newsstands. This publication concentrates on financial and career management for executive women. All articles are business-related, and many of them written by business specialists; there are no food, fashion, or home articles included. NAFE membership falls into the 25–40 age group. Most members/readers have attended college and a high percentage are married women working full-time. *Sample copy:* $1.50. *Areas open to free-lancers:* All sections and columns except "Financial Counselor" and "Career Counselor." *Rates:* $50–$300. Average article fee: $200–$250. *Payment:* On publication. *Expenses:* Pays long-distance phone calls. *Kill fee:* None. *Rights:* Buys first North American serial rights, by general release letter. *Number of submissions received weekly:* 30. *Reply time to queries:* Varies from "a few weeks to three or four months if we're really busy." *Advance dates:* Lead time is six weeks. Issues are planned two to four months in advance.

FREE-LANCE POSSIBILITIES: There are, at varying times, about three free-lancers who write fairly regularly for this magazine. Susan Strecker says: "I'd love to have more writers." But the bind is a financial one; this is a restricted-distribution magazine and the budget is low. In an average issue, of the six feature articles included, five have come from business specialists (for which they are paid an honorarium). Susan Strecker explains: "The problem with taking on any more free-lancers is that I can't give out any more assignments." But she also adds: "I would never discourage queries from free-lancers. It never hurts to send us a query and you just never know."

The good news: Although article rates are fairly low, work is done on an assignment basis. No writer has yet been asked to work on spec, and no kill fee policy has yet been required.

Although possibilities here are very limited, here are a few guidelines if you have studied the magazine, and think you might have something: "Often writers send me ideas that are too basic, too mundane, or too negative—focusing on sexual harassment, for example. We want ideas that give a somewhat different slant. I think some writers think: 'Oh, a women's magazine. Let's tell them how to set goals or how to manage their money.' But we're pretty focused and we've already done all that. What we want is a new angle. And an idea that hasn't been done in every other women's magazine."

Like most of the working women's magazines, this one has close to its fill of stories on successful women in New York. Articles on people outside New York and pieces with national appeal have better chances. Strecker adds: "Even though we're a women's publication, we don't always like to have articles that are geared strictly to women. Particularly with business and economic issues, we don't need women's articles but general ones. As female executives we need men in business and they need us; we need to work together. And that includes submissions to the magazine as well—we accept articles equally from male and female writers!"

There is no great need for money articles or profiles, unless it's a very new angle in the case of a financial piece (it also helps if the writer has some kind of financial expertise). In the case of a profile, the only possibility is one that focuses on a woman who's really forging the way or else is successful in an area that's very untraditional. In all articles, information must be aimed at career advancement; articles must "talk" to the readers.

As for the long reply time to queries, you can call after a few weeks, but Susan Strecker cautions: "Unfortunately a phone call probably won't help. Sometimes I simply *can't* get to the queries. I send replies as soon as I can."

Galleys are rarely shown, but if major changes are made, the writer is informed of them.

HOW TO SUBMIT: Written queries are preferred over manuscripts, but both will be read. Sending clips is not a requirement, although Susan Strecker adds: "For a writer who's unknown to me, sending one or two clips is probably helpful." Newspaper and trade clips are okay. "Where a writer has been published is not going to influence me that much, but I'd like to make sure the writer has the ability to tackle the story."

What to include in the query? "I want enough information to have a feeling of the tone of the article, and also some kind of idea how the writer might cover the topic in a wider perspective. I don't want a query letter that's too cheery, too intimate. That's not to say I want something formal, but a Pollyanna style puts me off. And if there's no strong lead-in, if you don't attract my attention straight off, that really lessens your chances. Tell me briefly or forget it. I stop reading by the end of page one!"

REJECTIONS: A standard form is used. But personalized replies are sent "if it's a writer I've dealt with before. Or if a writer is suggesting a story we already have in progress. Or if the idea is on target, and I'd like to hear from the writer again."

(AMTRAK) EXPRESS

East/West Network
34 East 51st Street
New York, NY 10022
(212) 888-5900

SOURCE: James A. Frank, editor

IN SHORT: Welcomes new writers and ideas.

ABOUT THE MAGAZINE: Monthly; 90% free-lance–written. *Express* is the on-board magazine of Amtrak and is distributed on trains nationally. It is published by East/West Network, in-flight magazine publishers. Like an in-flight magazine, *Express* is general interest, with emphasis on photography and graphics. It does not do magazine reprints. Says Jim Frank: "We're trying to create a magazine that isn't just what people see everywhere else. We want to give the train traveler stories, of a wide general interest, that have a novel and perhaps a little offbeat approach." As well as general articles, the magazine also runs columns from time to time covering books, health, money, career, and sports. *Readership:* A high percentage of businesspeople; slightly more male readers; well educated; "up-scale." *Circulation:* 150,000. *Estimated readership:* 750,000. *Sample copy:* $2. *Areas open to freelancers:* Everything except "Calendar." *Rates:* $350–$750. *Payment:* On acceptance. *Expenses:* Pays reasonable expenses. *Kill fee:* 25%. *Rights:* Buys first North American rights, by letter of agreement. *Number of submissions received weekly:* 20–25. *Reply time:* One to two weeks. *Advance dates:* Lead time is eight to ten weeks. Issues planned three to four months in advance.

FREE-LANCE POSSIBILITIES: *Express* is basically a free-lanced magazine. The staff is very small and there are no regular contributing editors. A new writer is apt to break in with a feature every other issue. Jim Frank is encouraging about free-lance opportunities and he also talks enthusiastically about working with writers. "Chances are good here," he says. "I really like to find and use new people. I'm absolutely anxious to get more talented people into the magazine."

Some guidelines: Frank would like to see more queries for business-related articles—pieces that discuss business and industry as opposed to personal investment (the latter area is a difficult one for the unknown writer; known business writers generally handle these stories). Of the business story he says: "This is a very important and growing field."

Science can be a good area, even for the general-interest writer, "as long as you're a writer who can understand the science facts and can explain them to a general public."

General-interest is probably the area with the most possibilities. An over-the-transom submission that managed to fit the *Express* bill was a piece on the National Aquarium in Baltimore. Frank explains: "This was good because the aquarium is new and it's a little offbeat; we tend to think aquariums just house fish, but there's a lot more to this one."

There are two areas where most queries are received: profiles and travel. As it happens, these are also the two areas that receive the most rejections. Frank elaborates: "Profiles *can* be a good idea. I personally like profiles, but only if they're about fascinating people who are doing something fascinating. Just because someone is an actor in a new TV series does not make him interesting to me. Show-business and sports figures tend to be done to death elsewhere. We're interested in people who aren't covered in magazines like *People* or *Us*. The person doesn't have to be famous, but there has to be a reason *why* I'd like to read about them." A recent profile example: Daniel Boorstin, the librarian of Congress. "In that profile we talked about the Library of Congress, what is it and what does Boorstin do?"

Travel, on the other hand, is not a good area for the free-lancer —simply because it is the rail company that decides which place to feature in an *Express* issue. Health/medical can be a possible area, but specialist writers are preferred here. "At least," Frank says, "I'm going to have to be very careful about assigning here if I don't know the writer."

What won't work? "We get a lot of train-trip reminiscences or travelogs. We don't do an awful lot of these; when we do they *have* to be really good. And I get a lot of ideas that are rip-offs from other magazines; some people even send a clip from another magazine, using it as a selling point as to why *they* should now do the story for us!"

Rarely are writers asked to work on spec. Frank sees all over-the-transom submissions; he will make a decision on a particular idea after reviewing clips and talking to the writer by phone. He will request the piece on spec only if clips are weak. "You don't *have* to have major magazine clips. I want to be able to see, though, that you can write and have enough qualifications to be able to handle the story."

Editing varies. "I would never reedit till a piece is unrecognizable." Rewriting is done by the author. Galleys are shown only in the case of health, personal finance, or technical articles. "But I will talk to writers about any changes I would like to make," Frank says.

A final note: "If you can get into the magazine, and if you're good, I'm going to want to use you again. This happens all the time."

HOW TO SUBMIT: Mss. are read (photocopies okay), but queries are much preferred. Simultaneous submissions accepted—if Frank is informed. No length preferences on queries, "but give me not just the idea but also tell me how you would plan to tackle the story; what angle you'd use." Include a list of writing credits; also include clips.

REJECTIONS: A standard form rejection is used mostly; personalized notes are sent to encourage more submissions.

FAMILY CIRCLE

488 Madison Avenue
New York, NY 10022
(212) 593-8000

SOURCE: Margaret Jaworski, articles editor

IN SHORT: Open, but very competitive market.

ABOUT THE MAGAZINE: Every three weeks. About 70% free-lance–written. "We're a women's consumer magazine; we present new ideas for today's woman—do-able, affordable projects and ideas for improving the quality of her life without drastically reducing the quantity of her savings." The magazine is sold in supermarkets and on newsstands. A strong emphasis is put on recipes, needlework and crafts, and service articles centering on home and family. *Readership:* Most readers are between 30–40; 69% are married, most with children; 32% have attended/graduated college; most readers live in middle-income households. *Circulation:* 8.4 million. *Estimated readership:* 22 million. *Areas open to free-lancers:* All. *Rates:* Articles (2500 words): $1500 and up. *Payment:* On acceptance. *Expenses:* Pays reasonable expenses. *Kill fee:* 20%. *Rights:* Rights bought vary, but all transactions include a written contract. *Number of submissions received weekly:* 1500. *Reply time to queries:* 8–12 weeks. *Advance dates:* Lead time is three to four months.

FREE-LANCE POSSIBILITIES: Articles editor Margaret Jaworski says, "A writer with a terrific idea and a good working knowledge of our magazine and our audience has a good chance of breaking in." But competition is strong here. About 1500 over-the-transom submissions are received weekly. And keep in mind that the magazine already has a group of known free-lance writers who are regularly assigned stories.

But Jaworski encourages perseverance. "The best way to break in is to come up with innovative, timely, and exciting ideas. The writer should have access to large and varied sources of information and must be able to use those sources to produce the ideas. The writer must ask: Why would 22 million readers of *Family Circle* want to read this story, and what can I tell them that hasn't already been told?"

Possible areas: "Stories of human experience whereby the subject has learned something and therefore the reader will learn from it also." The editors also look for articles that tie in a social issue with a personal experience, such as "The Agonizing Decision of Debra Sorensen" (April 6, '82), in which doctors give a young woman only 24 hours to decide whether or not to let her severely deformed newborn baby live or die. This story explores the question of euthanasia in a personal and sensitive way.

"We are always interested in new services, either individual or community, which can help our readers or which our readers can implement in their own lives—for example, the 'Fighting Back' article about crime, with a sidebar on how to start a neighborhood watch program on your block" (September 22, '81).

Because of the bulk of unsolicited material received, a submission can be read by one of several associate or assistant editors, or by a free-lance reader. Clips are sometimes requested. Writers are asked to work on spec "if we are unfamiliar with the writer and his work, or if we feel the subject matter needs expansion before we can assign—in which case we ask to read a rough draft."

Any necessary rewriting is done by the author. The extent of editing varies. Galleys are not generally shown.

HOW TO SUBMIT: Completed manuscripts are read (legible photocopies okay), but queries are preferred. "The query letter should be a succinct, clearly written description of the article proposed and why this particular writer should write it. Often query letters are vague, uninformative, and misdirected. The writer should be specific about what he wants to write, why he should write it, and include what sources he plans to use/interview. Also what, if any, information has already been written on the subject." Clips are accepted, but not required: "Clips sent with a query letter should be pertinent to that query; they should also have subject matter similar to that which is contained in *Family Circle*, style similar to our editorial style, and they should be current and relative."

REJECTIONS: Both standard forms and personalized replies are used. Margaret Jaworski adds: "A query may be rejected for several reasons: bad timing, already assigned or not right for our publication. But the writer should continue to search out new ideas and submit them, as those ideas rejected are not necessarily 'bad ideas,' just not acceptable at the time of querying."

FAMILY CIRCLE GREAT IDEAS

488 Madison Avenue
New York, NY 10022
(212) 593-8000

SOURCE: Karen L. Saks, managing editor

IN SHORT: Mostly staff-written. Specialized market; very limited possibilities.

ABOUT THE MAGAZINE: Published nine times a year (not in May, September, December); 10% free-lance–written. Special publications from *Family Circle*, with their own editorial staff and requirements. Issue titles vary, but these remain constant: "How To Be Pretty and Trim," "Decorating Made Easy," "Fashions and Crafts," "Christmas Helps." Changing titles have included: "Great Ground Meat Recipes," "201 Kitchen Ideas," "Easy Summer Meals," "Gardening and Houseplants." The magazine is distributed mainly in supermarkets, some drugstore chains, and a few newsstands. *Readership:* median age 32; 75% of readers are married; half are working; middle income. Circulation averages around 500,000; the exception is the issue called "Christmas Helps," a best-seller, with one million plus sales. *Sample copy:* Not available. *Rates:* $200–$500. *Payment:* On acceptance. *Expenses:* None. *Kill fee:* Negotiable. *Rights:* Buys first North American serial rights, by letter of agreement. *Number of submissions received weekly:* 10–15. *Reply time to queries:* Two weeks. *Advance dates:* Lead time is two months. Issues are planned four to five months in advance.

FREE-LANCE POSSIBILITIES: *Family Circle Great Ideas* buys only about three or four articles per year over-the-transom. The reason: The material is a hefty 90% staff-written and the free-lancers used here are known and tested and are, for the most part, specialists—in food, decorating, nutrition, health and beauty.

Says Karen Saks: "We really can't encourage free-lance submissions. The only area we're interested in from outside contributors is actual craft ideas—you should send a slide of what you've made—or decorating/home improvement projects. Chances are really slim. And if the idea *is* perfectly targeted, I'll buy it only if it's something we haven't thought of." Saks recently bought a piece on how to refinish furniture; it came in unsolicited. She also bought an over-the-transom piece on collectibles. But this happens rarely.

She does offer these guidelines: "We're all service—how-to. So in the decorating area, for instance, we're not interested in a piece on the new elements in high tech or an interview with a trendy designer. I'd rather see a piece on 'How I Changed My Old Tea Chest into a Coffee Table.' What we want are easy, inexpensive projects. This is why our readers buy the decorating titles; they're not involved in huge, expensive, remodeling projects. They buy the food titles for the recipes; the beauty books for commonsense approaches to health, beauty, nutrition, and exercise. And they buy the crafts titles to actually make the items.

"A lot of free-lancers tend to think we're the same as *Family Circle*. We're not. Or they send us ideas for columns that don't even exist."

If an idea *is* accepted, whether you'll work on assignment or on spec will depend on your clips; these should be included with the query.

Galleys are shown.

HOW TO SUBMIT: Mss. are read (photocopies okay), but queries are preferred. Simultaneous submissions are okay, but the magazines do not use reprints. No preferences with queries, but include clips.

REJECTIONS: A standard rejection form is sometimes used. Personalized replies are sent "if someone has sent in an idea we're already doing; I want to make it clear that they were on target. Or, when a manuscript is good, but not right for us, I'll tell the writer so and may even suggest where else it might be worth sending it."

FIELD & STREAM

CBS Publications
1515 Broadway
New York, NY 10036
(212) 719-6000

SOURCE: Duncan Barnes, editor

IN SHORT: Good market for hunting, fishing, outdoors articles.

ABOUT THE MAGAZINE: Monthly. At least 50% free-lance–written. Billed as "America's number one sportsman's magazine," *Field & Stream* is for outdoors aficionados—in particular, hunters and fishermen. The magazine covers hunting and fishing (and allied activities like camping, nature, backpacking, photography, equipment) and related issues—conservation being a major one. Most readers are male and of middle income; the highest percentage of readers live in either rural or suburban areas. *Circulation:* 2 million. Estimated readership is nearly 9 million. Each issue also contains an eight-page bonus regional section—"Your Local Outdoors"—covering the Far West, West, Midwest, Northeast, and the South. And there are four annuals: Fishing, Bass Fishing, Hunting, and Deer Hunting. *Areas open to freelancers:* All articles (all columns listed under "Departments" are staff-written). *Rates:* "How-It's-Done" (500–1000 words): $250. Articles (1000–2500 words): $500–$1000 plus. "Your Local Outdoors" copy/photo packages: $450. Annuals copy/photo packages: $500. *Payment:* On acceptance. *Expenses:* Pays reasonable expenses (only on assigned articles). *Kill fee:* Negotiable. *Rights:* General articles: buys first world rights, by written contract. "Your Local Outdoors": buys first North American rights, by written contract. Annuals: buys first North American rights, by check endorsement. *Number of submissions received weekly:* 50 queries, 50–60 manuscripts. *Reply time to queries:* General articles: "We try to move queries quickly, to reply within a matter of weeks, not months." "Your Local Outdoors": within four weeks on queries; within eight weeks on manuscripts. Annuals: two months. *Advance dates:* General articles: Lead time is two months. Issues planned four months in advance. "Your Local Outdoors": see "How to Submit." Annuals: see "Free-lance Possibilities."

FREE-LANCE POSSIBILITIES: Assignments are only occasionally given at *Field & Stream*. You should be familiar with the magazine's style and content; writers interested in hunting and fishing definitely have the advantage when it comes to developing appropriate article ideas.

Field & Stream is an excellent market for free-lancers willing to submit on spec. Most articles are free-lanced, and many are the result of unsolicited queries. "The magazine is always looking for good writing; we never have enough."

What's important is to submit a targeted query (are you sure your idea is appropriate?), and if it's a seasonal story, to time the query. It's bad timing, for instance, to submit a hunting story during the hunting season. Check the advance dates first.

Coming up with an appropriate story idea is the real challenge. "There's a certain structure to our articles; it's not a great mystery. You just need to study the magazine carefully and read the articles to get a sense of the *Field & Stream* style. If you can, pick up the larger April or May issues."

None of the "Departments" is open to free-lancers, but all articles are. Keep in mind the following points: Local stories are fine, but make sure they're relevant to a nationwide audience. Humor is welcomed, but it has to relate to hunting and fishing. There is a constant need for articles on deer and turkey hunting. Small-game-bird hunting material is welcomed. Freshwater fishing articles (bass, trout, walleyes, pike, etc.) are also needed. But saltwater fishing is well covered by the resident fishing editors. Feature ideas with an offbeat slant may be good for back-of-the-magazine slots. A past example: the Japanese art of fish printing.

There is very little need for "where-to-go." Except for the regional sections, these are mostly staff-written. So are the conservation articles. There's also no need for pieces on what it's like to live with a husband who's a hunter, etc. The women who read the magazine also fish and hunt.

The "How-It's-Done" section could well be the easiest way to break in. "We want to give the readers ideas they might not have thought of; the more ingenious, the better." Length can be anywhere from one column to 1000 words. "How-It's Done" pieces have included: hypothermia, woodsmen's medicine, how to find morrel mushrooms, how to build an ice-fishing sled, how to make a little stove out of a tuna can, how to make a camp cookbox.

The "Guest Shot" column is a market for "mood pieces." Humor or nostalgia could fit in here. "Often these are pieces that turn on an incident, a feeling, a description—something with particular meaning in terms of the outdoors. The 'why' of it all, that would be too slight for a main feature but just right for an essay."

Three articles called "Your Local Outdoors" are run monthly in each of the five regional sections; length is from 1000–2000 words. The emphasis is on fishing and hunting (where-to and how-to) for each particular region. Article information should be *timely* and service-oriented: sparking interest and then explaining where-to, including such information as travel and accommodation possibilities, area hunting/fishing laws, costs of licenses, etc. Timing is crucial; most articles in this section are fishing-oriented January through August; from September through December the emphasis is on hunting. Steer clear of the "me and Joe" style and avoid action leads. Profiles and pieces on conservation and ecology are not needed. Articles should be informative and written in a journalistic style; personal touches are fine, but the personal "my trip" piece isn't.

Field & Stream has four special annual issues. The four annuals and timing requirements are as follows:

- Hunting Annual—covering the game animals and varmints of North America. Published in August. Queries should be submitted by the previous December 1, at the latest (expect a reply by February 1 at the latest).
- Deer Hunting Annual—covering the whitetail, mule, and blacktail deer of North America. Published in September. Submit queries by December 1; expect a reply by Feburary 1.
- Fishing Annual—deals with freshwater and saltwater fishing in North America. Published in January or February. Submit queries by April 15 (replies by June 15).
- Bass Fishing Annual—covering only black bass (largemouth, spotted, and smallmouth bass), white bass, and inland striped bass. Published in March. Submit by April 15 (replies by June 15).

Note: When submitting a piece for one of the annuals, send queries only. Manuscripts will be returned, unread.

The aim is to reach as large a readership as possible, so too-localized stories won't work. This includes the specific where-to-go piece. Articles (all done on spec) run from 2000–2500 words maximum. Writers must also supply photographs (see following section). *Photography:* The magazine publishes a detailed, helpful photographic tip sheet. It's advisable to send for this (include a stamped business-size envelope) in advance of your query. Decisions are often made according to quality and/or availability of accompanying photos; the tip sheet will help you understand what's required. Poor photography is one of the most common reasons queries and manuscripts are rejected at *Field & Stream.* Copy and photos are often bought as a package; photography *must* be of high quality. For a general feature, color is preferred (slides only, not prints); for the regional sections only black-and-white is used (8x10 prints required); for the annuals, both color and b/w are used.

When sending color, write your name on every slide. Include a separate caption sheet, with caption information corresponding with numbered slides. For black-and-white, send contact sheet or prints. A caption sheet is required. If you're sending prints, glue a label with your name and address to the back of each.

For both regionals and annuals, photos are required at the time of query. Action photos are the key for regionals; both color and b/w are used for annuals, but if not practical, go for b/w.

HOW TO SUBMIT: All manuscripts will be read, although queries are preferred, except on humor, mood, or nostalgia. "Explain briefly why your article is going to be different from any other we've printed, why it's a good idea, and why it would be valuable to our readers. Short queries are best. We want to see intelligent queries that are cleverly worded; in our case cutesiness is not sensible. If you've been published before, tell us where. Include personal background information if it's pertinent, if it would help give us a sense that you'd be able to write the story. And if you've never written for us before, include some kind of writing sample; since we rarely assign, one clip would be plenty."

What are some of the mistakes writers make in submitting to *Field & Stream?* "They write by hand. They'll tell us, 'I don't know anything about writing, but I have an article for you. . . .' Or they'll be hostile: 'I've noticed your magazine never runs anything worth reading. . . .' They'll get hold of an old issue and write to the editor who was here 20 years ago. Or they'll submit a query that's too long and too detailed. Such mistakes will not help your case."

For the regional articles, written queries are preferred over manuscripts. Submit all queries to Glenn L. Sapir, regional editorial director. There is a five-month lead time here; queries may be sent as early as 18 months before an issue date. And don't forget a SASE!

For the annual issues, send written queries only. Unsolicited manuscripts are returned, *unread.* Include with your query the proposed title of your article.

REJECTIONS: Standard forms are used. Personalized replies are sent to regular contributors, or to encourage more submissions.

50 PLUS

850 Third Avenue
New York, NY 10022
(212) 593-2100

SOURCE: Mark Reiter, managing editor

IN SHORT: Market now more open to free-lancers.

ABOUT THE MAGAZINE: Monthly; 50% free-lance—written. *50 Plus* is a magazine aimed at the over-50 reader. It is available only by subscription. The editorial focus is heaviest on health, personal finance, and leisure. *Readership:* the male/female ratio is about 50/50; 60% of readers work and 40% are retired. These are people who like to travel, who are interested in personal finance, who indulge in gardening and leisure-time pursuits. *Circulation:* 275,000. *Estimated readership:* At least one million. *Sample copy:* $1.50. *Areas open to free-lancers:* All articles. *Rates:* $500–$1000. *Payment:* On acceptance. *Expenses:* All incidentals. *Kill fee:* Negotiable. *Rights:* Buys first North American rights, verbally. *Number of submissions received weekly:* 100. *Reply time to queries:* Up to a month. *Advance dates:* Lead time is two months. Issues planned four months in advance.

FREE-LANCE POSSIBILITIES: In the past, *50 Plus* has used very little free-lance material. But there has been a recent push toward searching out and using *good* material from reliable free-lance writers; there's a constant need for solid ideas and good writing. Says Mark Reiter: "We're very open to ideas and to giving writers a chance. But we get a lot of unexciting suggestions and we've had a number of experiences with writers whose work has fallen short of our standards." You'll get an assignment here if you have decent clips to show; otherwise you will be asked to work on spec. But even if you work on spec, rates are decent, payment is on acceptance, and it will get you an "in."

It's important to note here that the magazine no longer accepts unsolicited manuscripts. Queries only should be sent, always with a SASE.

Best bets: profiles and articles on people who have started second careers in midlife. The subject's personal annual budget is usually included in a piece like this. The editors are also looking for over-50 fitness pieces: "jock" profiles; celebrity profiles—people who are timely yet not overexposed; travel—focusing on a particular place rather than a piece written travelog-style; pieces on where to retire. For specialist writers there are possibilities in health and medical stories for over-50s; and personal finance features.

Reiter comments: "Often queries don't work for us because free-lancers want to do stories on people they consider interesting, who really are quite ordinary. It's a very tricky business to magnify an uncelebrated person's achievement into something worthy of national attention. It requires considerable journalistic finesse, unless of course the 'ordinary person' has some unique talent or service that may inspire our readers in *specific* ways to improve their lives. For example, we recently ran a story on an executive who quit corporate life for a second career as a shoemaker. Potentially, it's a mundane subject, but we think it's useful because shoe repair is a dying craft with good opportunities for handy men and women.

"Another mistake writers make is in approaching us with overused retirement-story ideas; they believe they're the first person to think up a general theme on retirement. We're constantly looking for a news or service angle to all our stories."

Generally writers are not shown galleys. Exceptions may be made for medical stories or controversial/technical pieces.

HOW TO SUBMIT: Queries only are accepted. Include the subject, your focus and approach, and a brief outline (about ten lines). Include two clips; the editors always ask to see clips before they will agree to an assignment. Replies are made only to queries with SASE.

REJECTIONS: Standard rejection form used. "If a writer comes in over-the-transom and really impresses us, we'll call them."

FOOD & WINE

1120 Avenue of the Americas
New York, NY 10036
(212) 386-5600 (new number—should be checked first)

SOURCE: Warren Picower, managing editor

IN SHORT: Open, but writers with food/wine/dining expertise have best chances.

ABOUT THE MAGAZINE: Monthly; 40–60% staff-written. A magazine of food, wine, and good living, *Food & Wine* is published by The International Review of Food & Wine Associates, an affiliate of American Express Publishing Corporation. Warren Picower describes the magazine: "We're all about dining and entertaining at home and in restaurants—locally, about the country, and abroad—and all the accoutrements that relate to this, whether it's food processors or mail-order chiles. We're very service-oriented. While we speak to the romance of the subject, we also want our readers to use the magazine. We expect our readers will make a dish from one or more of our recipes, pick up a tip for entertaining, learn something about a restaurant." *Readership:* male/female ratio is fairly even; median age is 43; 53% are college grads; high income; 61% are in professional/managerial positions and 22% are in top management. *Circulation:* 500,000. *Estimated readership:* 2.1 million. *Areas open to free-lancers:* Articles, "The Restaurant Column," "Wine Etcetera," and "What's New." *Rates:* Range from $50 for an item to up to $1800 for a major feature. Average fee for article (1200–1500 words) with four to six accompanying recipes is $800–$1200. *Payment:* On acceptance. *Expenses:* Pays all incidentals. *Kill fee:* 25%. *Rights:* Buys first-time world rights, by letter of agreement. *Number of submissions received weekly:* 40. *Reply time to queries:* Two to four weeks. *Advance dates:* Lead time is three months. Theme and seasonal issues are planned over a year in advance.

FREE-LANCE POSSIBILITIES: Over the course of a year about ten full-length features appearing in *Food & Wine* result from ideas sent over-the-transom. The writers will be new to the magazine and may be previously unknown. But managing editor Warren

Picower is encouraging only with reservations: "We have criteria for who and what is appropriate for us. We're not necessarily looking for famous people, name writers. But we aim to be interesting, helpful, and stimulating through advice on dining, entertaining, or cooking which carries a little more weight because the writers have professional qualifications in the subject area.

"While we welcome and use free-lance submissions (and knowing someone on staff doesn't necessarily help here), 40–60% of our articles are done in-house. The voice of authority and expertise ultimately is our own. The rest of the features tend to be done by people who are in the field or fully knowledgeable of it, and we do expect a professional level of knowledge. We want people who understand the subject from a professional point of view, because we don't intend to be naive in print. We'll consider people just starting out in the field, but we always ask: What does this person *know* about the subject, and are they ready yet to write for our magazine?"

Of departments, while "The Restaurant Column" and "Wine Etcetera" are open to free-lancers, Picower rates the situation here as "a very, very long shot. We're likely to buy only one or two items a year for these columns from the outside."

A much better area is "What's New," a department he describes as offering "a good way to get into the magazine, to establish a relationship." Items here are short—from three sentences to 200 words; about 15 items are run monthly. Guidelines: "This column is about people, places, and products. It does not report on anything after the fact and items must have service value—the opportunity for the reader to buy, taste, read, use, see, or go somewhere."

Most food articles also feature recipes, presenting either people or a location ("Riviera Dining," "A Leisurely Summer Lunch in the Italian Wine Country"); a collection of recipes with a theme ("Cool Combinations: Make-Ahead Vegetable Recipes," "Preserving the Fruits of Summer"); or concentrate on a particular food (e.g. ginger, leeks, hot peppers. The piece on leeks came in over-the-transom; hot peppers came in from a first-timer). Food-related queries should include a list of proposed recipes. "If we're interested we'll ask for two recipes to test. If they work out, we'll make the assignment. All recipes appearing in the magazine are tested in our food kitchen, and there's often a certain amount of refinement of them. We always ask for the two recipes first, even from people who have written for us before."

Although there is a wine staff on the magazine, beverage articles are considered from free-lancers, and ideas *are* considered from writers not specializing in the field. A manuscript was once received on a writer's "love affair with red wines." Says Warren Picower: "We bought it on the spot." But generally the same level of knowledge and expertise is needed in wine as it is in food.

Location/restaurant stories must involve an appealing place readers *may* visit with an eye to restauranting. "We'll do, say, the best regional restaurants in Rome. Or Barcelona, with its Catalan life-style and culinary traditions. But we are less likely, say, to do Istanbul as a restaurant story. We can't assume many readers are going to travel to Turkey just for its restaurants. Instead we're more likely to look for Turkish recipes that could be adapted to the American kitchen, and do that kind of story."

"Where a lot of people make a mistake in approaching us is by calling up and saying they're off to Helsinki. That's no reason, though, for us to do a story on Helsinki. That's not an article idea. We have to be sold that this would be a culinary story we would want. Similarly, when someone calls up and says 'Asparagus,' I'll say: 'What about it?' We like a *context* for what's being suggested."

Article meetings are held twice monthly. All articles are assigned; writers do not work on spec here because the recipe-testing policy entails a certain amount of commitment. Says Warren Picower: "We'll give assignments to people we don't know if we are impressed by the query letter. A well-written query definitely helps."

Editing varies. "If we have to edit heavily, there's a problem. It's less likely we're going to rush to work with that writer again." Galleys are sent to all writers. "If there are extensive changes, and if there's time, we generally discuss them with the writer beforehand on the phone, so they won't be surprised when they see the galleys."

HOW TO SUBMIT: Manuscripts are read, but queries are preferred. Says Warren Picower: "Contributors can really do themselves a disservice by sending a completed manuscript; they don't know what our angle might be, if we're interested in the subject. We prefer a very specific query letter. It should be as short or as long as it needs; I would consider a page and a half a long query. The query should tell us the approach and, if recipes are involved, should include a list of them. Just looking at our magazine will tell you the staff really cares about the product, so we're not interested in uncaring submissions from free-lancers. Remember: You're asking for a writing assignment. If the query is over-written, it's just as bad as if we were left guessing. We don't want all form and no substance."

REJECTIONS: Both standard forms and personal notes are sent. A personal note is usually sent, out of courtesy, to professional writers.

FORBES

60 Fifth Avenue
New York, NY 10011
(212) 620-2200

A business magazine published monthly, *Forbes* is almost entirely staff-written; free-lance pieces are magazine-assigned.

FORTUNE

Time & Life Building
Rockefeller Center
New York, NY 10020
(212) 586-1212

Fortune is a staff-written magazine; occasional free-lance pieces
are done on assignment by field specialists.

GENTLEMEN'S QUARTERLY

Condé Nast Publications
350 Madison Avenue
New York, NY 10017
(212) 880-8800

SOURCE: Philip Smith, managing editor
Luther Sperberg, associate managing editor

IN SHORT: Limited space, but good possibilities.

ABOUT THE MAGAZINE: Monthly; 50% free-lance–written. *Gentlemen's Quarterly* is a men's life-style magazine covering fashion, grooming, exercise and fitness, business, relationships, health, and the arts. It is aimed at young, well-educated males. Most readers are in the 18–34 age group; they are mostly single, college-educated, and "upwardly mobile"—both socially and in business. Says Philip Smith: "For the man of the eighties, *GQ* is the source he picks up." Interestingly, about one-third of readers are women; all copy, however, is slanted to male readers. *Circulation:* 550,000. *Estimated readership:* 3 million. *Areas open to free-lancers:* Articles, and the following departments: "Lifelines," "Looking Good," "Health," "Money," "Living," "Destinations," "Viewpoint," and personality profiles. *Rates:* Articles (1500–2500 words): $350 for first piece. *Payment:* On publication. *Expenses:* To $50. *Kill fee:* $200. *Rights:* Generally buys all rights, by check endorsement. Negotiable. *Number of submissions received weekly:* 15–25. *Reply time to queries:* Three weeks. *Advance dates:* Lead time is 3½ months. Issues are planned five months in advance.

FREE-LANCE POSSIBILITIES: *GQ* is an intelligent, impressive showcase and its editors are very encouraging to free-lancers. Philip Smith and Luther Sperberg see all submissions. They stress: "If you get a rejection, that certainly doesn't mean you should stop trying us. If the idea is right and if you exhibit good writing skills in your query letter, we'll be willing to give you a go." All work is done on assignment. Much of the free-lance material used monthly is written by people who are completely new to the magazine. And among *GQ*'s regular writers, most broke in initially as unknowns.

There is not a *lot* of space available for outside copy; much of the editorial space goes to fashion coverage and regular columns. But here is a rundown of the areas open to free-lancers:

"Lifelines" reports on trends in personal self-help and discusses coping-in-business strategies. "Looking Good" covers physical fitness, grooming, diet, and nutrition. "Health" discusses pertinent-to-the-readership medical issues. "Money" explores relevant financial issues and topics. "Living" can cover topics as varied as what kind of apartment insurance to buy and how to choose a personal business manager. "Destinations" supplies travel advice, singling out the activities, restaurants, and clubs that would be of interest to readers, while at the same time including information readers can't get elsewhere. "Viewpoints" covers the arts and welcomes "fresh and original ideas —an unusual person or movement, an overlooked building, town, dance company. Anything that would provide a new insight, while avoiding the overly esoteric."

The editors would like to see more queries on: grooming, physical fitness, personality/celebrity profiles, investment, and psychological topics (e.g. men/women relationships). Forget fashion; there are about 12 people at the magazine covering that area.

Editing varies. Galleys are not shown.

HOW TO SUBMIT: Manuscripts are considered (no photocopies), but queries are preferred. Luther Sperberg offers these guidelines: "Your query letter should do three things. It has to explain the article idea succinctly (one page max.). It must spell out your qualifications as a writer and as a person qualified to write the proposed article. And your very best writing should be on exhibit; through your letter *you're* on exhibit." It's not a requirement to send clips, but if your writing experience is limited, sending along *one* clip may be "a way of preventing our dismissing you out of hand." (Remember: Assignments are the norm here, not work on speculation.) Newspaper and small magazine clips are okay. If you have no clips, try with a query anyway; the editors have been known to call prospective contributors to discuss possibilities. Some don'ts: Don't handwrite the query. Don't send photocopied queries. And don't propose yourself as an article subject!

REJECTIONS: Standard forms are used, to which a personal note of encouragement may be added.

GEO

Knapp Communications
600 Madison Avenue
New York, NY 10022
(212) 223-0001

SOURCE: David Maxey, managing editor

IN SHORT: Difficult to sell.

ABOUT THE MAGAZINE: Monthly. Most features written by free-lancers. A lavishly illustrated general magazine. Says David Maxey: "We're a general magazine with a particular interest in the arts, sciences, individual human beings, adventure . . . and we have a generally optimistic view of the world." *Readership:* 52% female, 48% male; the median age of readers is 41; over half are college educated; the readers' median income is $67,500; 59% of all readers are in professional/managerial positions. *Circulation:* 225,000. *Estimated readership:* 815,000. *Areas open to free-lancers:* Everything except: "Geosphere." *Rates:* Around $1 per published word, average. *Payment:* On acceptance. *Expenses:* Pays reasonable expenses. *Kill fee:* Approximately 25%. *Rights:* Buys first world rights, reverting to author 18 months after acceptance, or if sooner, three months after publication. *Number of submissions received weekly:* 25. *Reply time to queries:* About four weeks. *Advance dates:* Lead time is two months. Issues are planned three to four months in advance.

FREE-LANCE POSSIBILITIES: There is only one area that is not open to free-lancers, "Geosphere." In an average issue, this leaves around nine major features of which eight, at least, are written by free-lancers. But just what are the chances of getting published in *Geo* if you're unknown to the editors by contact or reputation? "I would be mildly optimistic only," David Maxey answers. Newcomers *do* break in with features, although not in every issue. But Maxey adds: "What will work is the well-written query letter." And if that takes pages, it can be worth the trouble, as Nancy Lyon found out. Her six-page query for a personal story on life on Inishbofin, a tiny island off the Irish coast, landed her an assignment.

Clips alone will not get you in the door. "There are some

writers who are so well credentialed they don't think they have to write a good query," Maxey says, adding: "I can't emphasize too strongly, though, how important that query letter is. What we want is a good idea that's right for us, fire-in-the-belly to go with it, and a well-written, well-presented query letter."

Assignments are the norm at *Geo*. "We don't ask writers to work on spec because we don't believe that's fair." If you're unknown to *Geo* editors, you will be asked to show clips, but it's the strength of the query letter that will be the deciding factor.

There's no formula to the kinds of pieces *Geo* favors; 1982's issues carried the following selections: "Coyotes Triumphant" (how this cagey animal continues to thrive despite efforts to stem its population); "The Night Stalkers" (a celebration of owls); "Good News from Angkor Wat" (the survival of the famous Cambodian temples); "Catch a Rising Star" (ballet's new stars); "Always on the Left" (a school for butlers in London); and "The First U.S. Women in Space."

"GEO Conversation," a Q. & A. profile, is run monthly. "They're a varied group," David Maxey comments. The subjects profiled are well known and accomplished. In 1982 subjects included: Francis Crick, the Nobel laureate, who at age 60 switched from molecular biology to brain research (this "Conversation" was suggested by a free-lancer; the writer had been published in *Geo* before, however); William Conway, general director of the New York Zoological Society, talking about wildlife management; and Clare Boothe Luce. Profile subjects are generally staff-generated, but the area *is* open to outside suggestions.

For all articles, these points should be kept in mind: "*Geo* is not a news magazine; so don't send us story queries that have a news peg. Don't call (or write) and say something like: 'I'm going to China tomorrow afternoon; can I do something for you?' That's a travel plan; that's not an idea at all. And don't approach us with: 'I just want to talk with you for a few minutes.'" The onus is on the writer *only* to handle the copy side of the article; *Geo* prefers to use its own photographers.

Editing: "The optimistic view is that your article, once assigned, is not going to need rewriting. We don't have a rewrite desk; we do care about individual voice."

To sum up: *Geo* writers are general-interest for the most part; they're rarely specialists. But they're approaching the magazine with knowledge gained through advance research. Says David Maxey: "It's as hard as hell to get a *Geo* assignment. But it *is* possible. It just doesn't happen often because we have a great many people writing to us who obviously haven't really looked at the magazine."

HOW TO SUBMIT: Completed mss. are read (photocopies okay), but queries are definitely preferred. David Maxey says: "We'll read a manuscript, but it would be a real long shot. If a piece exists as a manuscript, my feeling is that it's been elsewhere."

Some query-letter tips: "Your query should tell us something we didn't know about previously. We're very strong on the element of surprise. We love stories that cover a topic people think they know all about—and then we surprise them. So, if that's the case, say so high up in your query.

"Dont send us ten one-paragraph ideas. Send us one well-developed idea. And if you can't hook us in the first paragraph of your query, chances are you wouldn't be able to hook a *Geo* reader in the first paragraph of an article."

REJECTIONS: A standard form letter is used mostly; personalized notes are sent to encourage more submissions.

GLAMOUR

Condé Nast Publications
350 Madison Avenue
New York, NY 10017
(212) 880-8800

SOURCE: Janet Chan, articles editor

IN SHORT: Very open; looking for article ideas.

ABOUT THE MAGAZINE: Monthly; 95% free-lance–written. Says
Janet Chan: "We're a magazine with a dual purpose: beauty and
fashion, as well as service, covering almost every aspect relevant
to young women—education, jobs, relationships, sex, mother-
hood, health and medical issues. We publish articles that in
some way will help, or interest young women." *Readership:* 18–
34, with a median age of 27; 61% have graduated or attended
college; 48% are married; 86% have a full- or part-time job. *Circulation:* Over 2 million. *Estimated readership:* Over 6 million.
Areas open to free-lancers: Articles, "Viewpoint," "His/Hers,"
"Medical Report." Beauty, fashion, food, the "At Home" section,
travel, entertainment, and the other regular columns are all staff-
written. The "How to Do Anything Better Guide" is basically
staff-written, and Susan Gordon, editor of that section, says:
"There are about eight writers working on that section at different times. It's meant to be staff-generated and staff-written.
We're not looking for ideas from free-lancers." *Rates:* "Viewpoint": $400. "His/Hers": $800. Articles: $1,000–$2000 and up.
Payment: On acceptance. *Expenses:* Pays agreed upon expenses.
Kill fee: 20%. *Rights:* Generally buys first North American
rights, by written contract. *Number of submissions received
weekly:* Approximately 100. *Reply time to queries:* "Within a
few weeks." *Advance dates:* Lead time is three months. Issues
are planned about three to five months in advance.

FREE-LANCE POSSIBILITIES: *Glamour* is a well-established, prestige market. But it's surprisingly possible to break in with a main
feature; approximately 12 main articles are run monthly, and
most months a newcomer's by-line will appear. In addition, the
"Viewpoint" opinion column, which invites reader submissions,
is written primarily by writers new to the magazine. Says Janet
Chan: "We do use certain writers regularly for articles because

they're reliable and we know we can count on them. But we'd like to be able to count on more! Our regular writers keep appearing in the magazine because they're regular with ideas." Currently, about 70% of article ideas are generated in-house—"but we don't want it to be that way. We'd love to see more ideas from free-lancers. We prefer to assign stories. We only ask writers to work on spec if we're not familiar with them and don't have a sense of the strength of their writing—either through clips or an impressive proposal."

A really good query letter backing up an appealing idea is what's needed. For example, Barbara Wilcox, a California free-lancer, wrote "Psychological Rape" in the October '82 issue; her assignment was based on "an intriguing, provocative proposal," says Chan. Clips help, but the proposal counts. "I would never make a decision based solely on clips."

Subject scope is wide. *Glamour* looks for ideas "with a sense of freshness, a reason for running it now. A news peg is helpful." What won't help? "This may sound exceedingly trivial, but salutations to an editor who has long departed the magazine are annoying. And you can tell immediately the writers who haven't studied the magazine. It's insulting to get queries that just wouldn't be right for *Glamour*—something like a parents' guide to living with a teenager who has a drug problem, for instance."

Editing varies. Copies of the edited manuscript are shown to writers before publication.

HOW TO SUBMIT: Phone queries are discouraged, except if the story is urgent in terms of timing. Completed manuscripts are read (originals preferred over photocopies), but detailed proposals are preferred. "The query is very important; in effect it's a portfolio," says Janet Chan. Her advice: "Tell us your whole idea. Some writers think they should tease an editor. They'll query with a question, such as 'What's the best way to break off a relationship?' But they won't give the answer in the query! You have to give an editor a sense of what you want to say in your article, where you would take it, and the people you would interview for your information. Make your query letter as detailed as possible." Including clips is "helpful." Reply time can be slow here, because of the number of queries received weekly.

REJECTIONS: Both standard forms and personalized notes are sent. The latter is likely "when it's a writer we've worked with before, or whose work we know, or when we think a more detailed explanation would be helpful to the writer."

GOLF

Times Mirror Magazines
380 Madison Avenue
New York, NY 10017
(212) 687-3000

SOURCE: George Peper, editor

IN SHORT: Limited possibilities, even for golf writers trying to break in.

ABOUT THE MAGAZINE: Monthly; one-third free-lance—written. *Golf* is a magazine for golf enthusiasts. Its editorial aim is "to help our readers play golf better and enjoy it more." A good third of the magazine is devoted to instructional articles; it's instruction, in fact, that sells the magazine. For additional material, the editors strive for information that will enable the reader to keep abreast of what's happening in the golf world. Subscribers are 90% male; the average reader age is 45; 60% belong to private golf clubs. It's an educated, up-scale, sophisticated audience. *Circulation:* 725,000. *Estimated readership:* 2.2 million. *Areas open to free-lancers:* Features, and the following columns: "Golf Reports," "Hotline," and "The Strangest of Games." *Rates:* Features: $250–$750. "Golf Reports": $50–$75. *Payment:* On acceptance. *Expenses:* Pays reasonable expenses. *Kill fee:* 25%. *Rights:* Buys first North American serial rights, by written contract. *Number of submissions received weekly:* 25. *Reply time to queries:* Ten days—two weeks. *Advance dates:* Lead time is three months. Issues are planned four months in advance.

FREE-LANCE POSSIBILITIES: Unless you're a writer who knows the golf world fairly well, chances of getting published here are limited. One-third of the magazine is devoted to instructional articles (not open to free-lancers); one-third of the copy is written by the magazine staff and contributing editors. The remaining one-third is written by free-lancers, but these are writers who are known to *Golf*'s editors; they have either been published in the magazine before or are members of the fraternity of golf writers throughout the country who are known by reputation. A good 90% of these free-lancers are keen golfers themselves. They know the game, they know the people on the circuit, they have the contacts. It doesn't leave much room for the general-interest writer who doesn't play golf or know too much about the game. And it's hard to come up with article ideas that aren't being covered already by *Golf*'s regular writers.

Of the 100-odd queries received monthly at *Golf*, only about five will be accepted. And fewer than five manuscripts a year will be bought. It's not easy here, but if you're determined, George Peper offers this encouragement: "We're always looking for a good golf writer who not only turns a phrase well but who also knows the game."

Two of the best places for free-lancers are "Hotline," which consists of late-breaking items and news of practical value, and "The Strangest of Games," which is a small (one-paragraph) report of a strange or remarkable event in golf history or play; reader submissions are also invited here. Two-hundred-word pieces may have a chance in "Golf Reports" if they're reports on offbeat characters or shorts of interest. One new writer made a study of Jack Nicklaus's performance and had the piece published in "Golf Reports." Another broke in with a small, offbeat piece on swan decoys being used to thwart troublesome geese at a local club.

A profile is a very hard nut to crack; forget the big-name pros and try if you must with a lesser-known player *Golf*'s editors may be thinking about with interest. If you have the contacts and the timing's right, a profile may be your way in. Consider the big-name pros only in this respect: an offbeat slant for "Golf Reports," or as George Peper puts it: "Give us a fresh angle on an 'old' guy." He explains further: "Chances are we've done a profile on someone like Jack Nicklaus already. I would really encourage a writer who's interested in doing a profile—or any other kind of feature—to go to the library and study the last two years of our magazine just to make sure we haven't covered the subject." He adds: "Don't try us with something we have already done." As for behind-the-scenes profiles, the magazine does run pieces on people like Dave Pelz (scientist turned putting guru to the pros) from time to time. But a word of advice: "If these personalities are unusual enough, fine. But if they don't have a name, they had better have a pretty good story—preferably related to improving one's game."

Chances are, if your idea is acceptable you'll be asked to do the piece on spec. But take some comfort in statistics: At least 75% of on-spec pieces end up being published in the magazine.

The magazine does tend to edit heavily. Galleys are not shown but writers are told of any major changes.

One last word from George Peper: "Send me a critique of the magazine each month. Spot every typo. Tell me when our statistics missed something. Tell me when our competition beats us. Tell me how we can improve the magazine. I'll notice you."

HOW TO SUBMIT: Mss. are as welcomed as queries (preferably no photocopied mss.), and clips not required. What's wanted in a query is a good idea, well presented: "If someone writes us a good letter with a good idea that's well conceived, we can generally tell how good a writer he is. I'm not concerned so much with clips or personal details; what interests me is how sharp the person is in addressing me and the needs of the magazine."

An additional tip: "It's a mistake to present us with a sloppy query, a letter that doesn't inspire confidence in a person's professionalism."

REJECTIONS: Standard forms are used. A personalized reply is sent "if I know the writer and/or it's something it pains us to reject."

GOLF DIGEST

495 Westport Avenue
Norwalk, CT 06856
(203) 847-5811

SOURCE: Dwayne Netland, senior editor

IN SHORT: Specialist market. Limited possibilities.

ABOUT THE MAGAZINE: Monthly; 25% free-lance—written. *Golf Digest* is a magazine for golf enthusiasts. Readership is 95% male; median age is 52; almost half are college grads; income level is high. *Circulation:* 1,025,000. *Estimated readership:* 2.5 million. *Areas open to free-lancers:* Everything except instruction. *Rates:* "The Digest": $75–$100. "People in Golf": $250. Features: $1000–$1500. *Payment:* On acceptance. *Expenses:* Pays all incidentals. *Kill fee:* 25%. *Rights:* Buys all rights, by written contract. Not negotiable. *Number of submissions received weekly:* 25. *Reply time to queries:* Immediate. *Advance dates:* Lead time is two months. Issues are planned five to six months in advance.

FREE-LANCE POSSIBILITIES: From 20 to 25 features written by free-lancers appear in *Golf Digest* yearly. Probably six of these are written by newcomers. But this is a tough market if you're not a specialist in the field. Says Dwayne Netland: "You don't *have* to be a golfer to write for us. But you have to know the game and you have to know the audience. Golf writing is tough; it's a field that doesn't support a lot of free-lancers. We have two or three people writing 'regularly' for us, but that means probably only once a year. We have ten staff editors, eight of whom write. So while we're open-minded and while we do watch the unsolicited submissions carefully, there just isn't a lot of space for the free-lancer."

Chances, slim though they are, are better here with a query. Netland comments that in the past eight years only one major manuscript has been bought over-the-transom—a piece on Johnny Miller.

All instruction is written by staff/contributing editors. And Dwayne Netland comments: "A writer unknown to us is not going to get in with a profile on someone like Jack Nicklaus. If you're thinking profiles, you'll have to go for the offbeat. Profiles are tough to break in with, but we're always looking for fresh, new angles."

Netland advises trying for a short, rather than a feature. "Service items like tipping, or packing, or how to select a resort—we're always interested in these kinds of items. 'People in Golf' could also be a possibility for short, behind-the-scenes pieces. Like the piece we did on a service that rents out golf clubs at airports. And 'Places to Play' is a good area for a short piece; a query on a *new* resort would get pretty close attention."

Netland advises sending clips with queries: "We always look at clips. If they're good we may look for a story in that writer's area—possibly starting him off with a smaller piece. It can be a way in."

Writers untried at *Golf Digest* will be asked to work on spec.

What *won't* work at *Golf Digest?* "A lot of writers approach us with stories we've done ourselves—recently. We get a lot of verse, which we run rarely. Generally the personal recollection piece doesn't work; it may be interesting to the writer, but is it to golfers throughout the country? And a lot of submissions are attempts at humor. Golf humor is probably one of the hardest to pull off. And often the standard of submissions just isn't high enough."

Galleys are not shown, but the writer *is* told of changes made.

HOW TO SUBMIT: Send a query or manuscript (photocopies accepted only if very clear). Keep queries short; include a rundown of your writing credits. Include clips, as discussed.

REJECTIONS: Personalized replies are sent to all contributors, with encouragement "if we think there's any hope."

GOOD HOUSEKEEPING

The Hearst Corporation
959 Eighth Avenue
New York, NY 10019
(212) 262-5700

SOURCE: Joan Thursh, articles editor

IN SHORT: Difficult, very competitive market.

ABOUT THE MAGAZINE: Monthly. All feature articles are free-lance–written. *Good Housekeeping* is a women's service magazine, "for women whose prime concern is the home. While we do run some career-related articles, our readers buy the magazine for its service." This includes food and recipes, home decorating and management advice, needlework and crafts, fashion and beauty articles (all separate departments), as well as articles on varied subjects. *Readership:* mostly women; the median age of readers is 40; 67% are married, most with children; 53% are employed; 36% have attended/graduated college; the median household income of readers is $22,500. *Circulation:* 5 million. *Estimated readership:* 17 million. *Areas open to free-lancers:* All articles; regional sections; "The Better Way." *Rates:* Full-length articles: $1500 minimum. *Payment:* On acceptance. *Expenses:* Pays reasonable expenses. Kill fee: 25%. *Rights:* Generally buys all rights, by letter of agreement. *Number of submissions received weekly:* 200–300. *Reply time to queries:* "We try for two to three weeks." *Advance dates:* Lead time is three months. Issues are often planned five months in advance.

FREE-LANCE POSSIBILITIES: *Good Housekeeping is* open and willing to try new writers, but the competition and high standards make it a difficult market. Articles editor Joan Thursh says that some months nothing worthwhile comes out of the slush pile. She adds: "Though we look at all unsolicited manuscripts, we do not encourage them. We prefer queries."

Basically, there are five kinds of articles run (with examples in parentheses from the November '82 issue):

All service articles are written in-house (most by experts in The Good Housekeeping Institute).

Celebrity articles, such as "Marlo Thomas Keeping Fit After Forty" (Nov. '82), often have a service or news-related angle.

Thursh adds: "Mainly we interview celebrities who are very well known. A celebrity interview is not a good area for a free-lancer to try for us unless he/she has a fantastic 'in' with a very popular person."

Reportage pieces, such as "Fast Food Restaurants: How They Grew and Grew" (Nov. '82), are "usually done within the frame-work of a narrative. They should not be written as a straight report; they must contain vignettes."

How-to articles, such as "How to Help an Alcoholic Without Making Matters Worse" (Nov. '82), are not run very often, "but they should be relevant to women, nontechnical, and easy to understand in both language and content."

Personal-experience pieces should be "unique and family-ori-ented. Some are the kinds of stories that make people feel good; others are personal medical experiences, etc. We usually don't run 'down' stories."

Of all categories through which to break in, the best—and the more usual—is with a personal-experience piece. Thursh says: "It's the best kind of unsolicited idea for us. But in a sense it's also the most difficult way in because you have to have a story worth telling. It's hard to explain what will make one piece work for us, and another not. But they require a specialness, almost always with a woman as the protagonist. We're not necessarily looking for the story of the biggest tragedy overcome." Gracie Chapman's "His, Mine . . . Ours" (Nov. '82) is a personal story of second marriage and the successful blending of two families. Joan Thursh describes it as "a really nice family story."

Essays and pure think pieces that are technical or too scholarly won't work at *Good Housekeeping*. Unsolicited material goes first to two editorial assistants, who pass on "anything with merit" to either Thursh or one of the associate article editors. Potential ideas are then discussed within the department. Most work is done on assignment; on spec is asked for "once in a while—when a writer has not much work to show or is basically an amateur with a good story to tell."

Rewriting, which is frequently needed, is done by the writer: "We give detailed instructions for the rewrite." Galleys are shown "only in rare instances—if it's a first-person personal ex-perience piece or a technical medical article."

One story in makes the next easier. "We *could* call the writer —if we're impressed with their work, or if a writer is located in a particular area of the country where a story is breaking. But we prefer writers to generate their own ideas. Usually a writer who is not able to do this is not going to get far with us."

"The Better Way" is the *Good Housekeeping* section printed on colored pulp paper; it is included in every issue but December. Articles are only one page or a half page and are heavily service-oriented. The section, which includes about ten articles each month, is mostly staff-written; only one article a month, on an average, is likely to be assigned to an outside writer. Erika Reider Mark, "The Better Way" editor, comments: "We tend to use repeat writers because those who have written for 'The Better Way' know how to handle our subject matter and are familiar with our style. But we will consider any good ideas. We are very news-oriented and are interested in information that can be expressed as a chart or list. We would never do a piece, say, on general trends in education. That's too abstract. But we might do 'ten questions to ask your child's teacher.'

"We'd be interested in consumer-rights pieces, or legal rights, but writers should consult our subject index first so they don't suggest topics we've already covered. We try to avoid traditional women's page fillers, like 'how to get stains out of clothes.' We have regular people doing medical topics and financial stories, so we don't want queries for those. And we've done a lot of energy-saving pieces; there's very little more to say in this area.

"Typical of our kinds of pieces are these we've run recently: a report on victims' compensation laws, state by state; 14 ways to test tamper-proof packaging; summer camps with special programs." Most work is done on assignment. A list of sources is required with the manuscript. Editing varies; "some manuscripts need more than others. Galleys are not usually shown, but it's not unusual for one of our editors to contact a writer for more information or clarification on a story." "The Better Way" pays $350 for a half page; $500 for a full page. It buys first North American serial rights.

Good Housekeeping also publishes regional editions. Chances are very limited here, and free-lance contributions are not really encouraged. This section, which varies throughout the country, publishes localized service articles provided by The Good Housekeeping Institute and travel articles provided by the travel editor. Regionals editor Shirley Howard comments: "The New York Metro section is the only one open for free-lance writers. We'll consider local personalities, places, and events connected with New York, Connecticut, and environs." Assignments are possible, but on spec is more usual.

HOW TO SUBMIT: Send general article submissions to Joan Thursh, who advises: "Unless there is time pressure on a piece, you're better off to write a query." Photocopied manuscripts are accepted. On queries: "Most ideas are more salable if the writer puts some time and effort into the query. A first-time writer has to do this. It's unprofessional not to scratch the surface; a pro knows you have to do this." Include clips.

For "The Better Way": Submit to Erika Reider Mark. Queries are preferred. Include one or two clips "similar to our kinds of articles. They don't have to be consumer magazine clips, but they should show adaptability to 'Better Way' style."

For regional editions: Submit to Shirley Howard. Queries are preferred. Include clips.

REJECTIONS: A form rejection is used mostly. Personal, "regretful" notes are sent occasionally.

HARPER'S

Two Park Avenue
New York, NY 10016
(212) 481-5220

SOURCE: Helen Rogan, associate editor

IN SHORT: Prestigious market that welcomes ideas, new writers.

ABOUT THE MAGAZINE: Monthly. All articles are free-lance–written. General-interest magazine with a nonfiction mix of criticism, reportage, and political analysis. Says Helen Rogan: "We try to be very provocative, to present articles that say: 'Things are not what they seem.' " *Readership:* male/female ratio fairly evenly split; median age is 34.3. Readers are basically middle-class, college-educated; the ranks include many academics and professionals. Readers are spread throughout the country. *Circulation:* 140,000. *Estimated readership:* 473,000. *Areas open to free-lancers:* All. *Rates:* $750–$2500 (and occasionally higher). *Payment:* On publication. *Expenses:* Pays all incidentals. *Kill fee:* 25%. *Rights:* Buys first North American serial rights on agented material; all rights on nonagented material. By written contract. Negotiable. *Number of submissions received weekly:* 25–50 queries; 120–130 mss. *Reply time to queries:* Three to five weeks. (Inquire by mail, not phone.) *Advance dates:* Lead time is two months. Issues are planned very close to the issue.

FREE-LANCE POSSIBILITIES: *Harper's* is a surprisingly open market. There are four writers doing regular reviews and less than ten others writing for the magazine on a constant basis. The rest of the field is open to free-lancers, and you do not have to be a big-name writer. New writers break into the magazine about six times a year; one or two of these are likely to be previously unpublished writers.

Elaine Weiss, whose piece about the marketing of Stimorol gum ran under the title "King of the Chews" (October '82) called up with the idea and was told to go ahead. Says Helen Rogan: "Stimorol was, incidentally, an idea that occurred to at least three writers that week; we thought Weiss had the most coherent approach."

In the May '82 issue, Floyd C. Stuart's rural reportage piece was published as "Only Cows Were Killed"; he had sent in the manuscript over-the-transom. Avery Chenoweth, a young humorist living in Princeton, sent in an over-the-transom parody of the Donohue show; it was bought and published in June '82. Jim Traub sent in a proposal for a piece about West Indians in Brooklyn. The piece was commissioned and after minor editing ran in June '82.

Not only is it possible to break into *Harper's*, it's also possible to go on from there to write regular pieces. Says Helen Rogan: "We're always looking for people who are willing to go out and do legwork, rather than sitting at home making an argument. And if you do one good piece for us, we'll be likely to be on the phone to you asking: What are you going to do for us next? We're always looking for new names; we don't *want* to use the same names that you'll see in *The Atlantic* or *The New Yorker* or *Playboy*. We're hunting for new people who are good and reliable, people who can become regulars."

All over-the-transom material is screened by an editorial assistant, who then passes along everything but the immediate rejections to the small editorial staff. All promising submissions, generally there are five to ten weekly, go into a proposal file that all the editors peruse and are briefly discussed at the weekly editorial meeting. Perhaps one submission may be given a go-ahead. The writer is then contacted and the idea is discussed further, by phone or in person.

Once an idea is accepted, chances of an assignment (as opposed to on spec) are good. Less-experienced writers are likely to be paid the lower, starting rate, and sometimes writers will be asked to work on spec. "But we're always candid. We'll tell you we're asking you to work on spec because we're not sure the piece is going to work out.

"One of the mistakes contributors make is the too-jocular approach. Or they'll give us too much slant. We'd much rather see a vague direction, then discuss it and hope to be surprised. If the writer is not approaching the piece with an open mind, then it probably won't work for us." Often, article ideas may not be quite right, but a submission may spark interest in a new writer. "This could lead to an article down the road."

Helen Rogan adds, "Remember: We can't handle anything that's too timely. Or anything that's too much like a newspaper piece. We turn down a lot of people who are good newspaper-style writers. We don't just write about a subject; we always have a specific point of view. We never do straight interviews or profiles—in that they will be profiles of people you probably wouldn't have thought about, people who exemplify something, even if it's simply contradiction. And we often have to reject ideas because they're too local; we are mostly read out of New York. As far as writing style goes, we aim for 3000 words maximum in front-of-the-book pieces, and 8000 words for the middle. We don't have the space to write at a leisurely pace like *The Atlantic* or *The New Yorker* does."

Most often *Harper's* editors will do any editing while consulting at length with the writer on the phone or in person. "We'll always call the writer and consult with them before we make any changes," Helen Rogan says, "and we always show galleys. There are no surprises for the writer in print."

HOW TO SUBMIT: Send submissions to any editor listed on the masthead. Completed mss. are preferred "if the story is already written." No photocopies. Otherwise, send a query, with clips. Multiple submissions are accepted "as long as we know about it." Preferred length on queries: 1–1½ pages. Include a rundown of your writing credits. And a heartening last word from Rogan: "Don't worry about your submission; we never lose anything."

REJECTIONS: A standard rejection letter is used. "Sometimes we'll write notes saying, try us again. But we never say that unless we mean it."

HARPER'S BAZAAR

Hearst Corporation
1700 Broadway
New York, NY 10019
(212) 903-5000

SOURCE: Richard A. Kagan, features editor

IN SHORT: Very limited possibilities; publishes work from regular writers.

ABOUT THE MAGAZINE: Monthly; 50% free-lance–written. *Harper's Bazaar* is a fashion, beauty, and stylish living magazine. "Our aim," says Richard Kagan, "is to provide the relatively sophisticated woman with service in the areas of personal living, investment, travel. And to be brief and to the point, and not boring." *Readership:* 97% female; the reader's average age is 34; 54% are single; 68% are working, 54% of them in professional/managerial positions; 78% have attended college; the average household income is $48,000. *Circulation:* 700,000. *Areas open to free-lancers:* Everything except fashion copy. *Rates:* $250–$750. *Payment:* On publication. *Expenses:* Pays limited expenses. *Kill fee:* 25%–50%. *Rights:* Buys all rights, by letter of agreement. Negotiable. *Number of submissions received weekly:* Four. *Reply time to queries:* A few days to a month maximum. *Advance dates:* Issues are planned up to a year in advance.

FREE-LANCE POSSIBILITIES: Richard Kagan sums up the situation here frankly: "I really don't need any more writers. I have enough people I can call on for articles; the chances for an unknown writer coming in over-the-transom are very slim."

About 75% of the article ideas are generated in-house. The rest come from PR, advertising and merchandising contacts, as well as from writers coming in by reputation or connections. Most by-lines here belong either to name writers or to well-established free-lancers whose work appears frequently in major magazines. As prestigious as it is for the fashion designer to be showcased in *Harper's Bazaar,* so it is for the article writer. It rarely happens that a writer with limited experience breaks in. "Just so much depends on timing," Kagan says. "A while back I was thinking about a piece on trends in music, and a query came in from a writer I didn't know, but he had the right angle on the best new recordings of the season."

Because over-the-transom possibilities are connected directly to timing, it's difficult to pinpoint subject matter that might work. There's no interest in articles on politics or religion, or straight human-interest topics. The emphasis here is on fashion, beauty, health, personalities, trends, and style.

Kagan describes travel as "one of the hardest areas to break into, because every writer is able to travel these days and every writer wants to do travel stories."

Profiles: "They have to fit in with our needs at the time"; when profiles are done, the emphasis is generally heavy on photography. Money and personal investment stories are a possibility, but, Kagan qualifies, "only if I can get the right slant for our audience." Health, nutrition, medical: A submission here could be worthwhile mainly because these are often-covered areas. One area where Kagan *would* consider more queries: "new frontiers in psychological well-being."

As for the actual submission, avoid "cutesy letters. Not getting to the point. Being presumptuous—saying something like: 'I'm sure if you spent just half an hour reading my manuscript you'll find it worthwhile.'"

Writers are rarely asked to work on spec here. Kagan always asks to see clips; if they're not impressive, that is, if you don't have the "heavy writing experience" *Bazaar's* regulars do, the magazine will probably decline your idea. Once in, it becomes a lot easier. Even with really impressive clips, *Harper's Bazaar* is a market the writer must build up to.

Editing varies. Rewrites are done by the writer, "depending on the time frame, and if we feel they're competent enough to redo the piece." Galleys are "rarely shown."

HOW TO SUBMIT: Mss. are read, but not returned without SASE. Photocopied mss. are okay. Queries are "definitely preferred." Multiple submissions are okay. Keep queries short—about one page. Include clips.

REJECTIONS: A standard form rejection is used. Personalized notes are "rarely" sent.

HEALTH

149 Fifth Avenue
New York, NY 10010
(212) 598-0800

SOURCE: Joan L. Lippert, managing editor

IN SHORT: Best chances with "Breakthroughs."

ABOUT THE MAGAZINE: Monthly; 90% free-lance—written. *Health* is a medical news/health information magazine for the person who is health-and-fitness-oriented. The average reader is female, aged 24–34, and married. 40% of the readers have attended college; 58% work. *Circulation:* 850,000. *Estimated readership:* 2.3 million. *Areas open to free-lancers:* Features and "Breakthroughs." *Rates:* Articles (1000–2500 words): $250–$1000. "Breakthroughs" (250–600 words): $75. *Payment:* On acceptance. *Expenses:* Pays all incidentals. *Kill fee:* 20%. *Rights:* Buys all rights, by written contract. Negotiable. *Number of submissions received weekly:* 15–20. *Reply time to queries:* Four weeks. (Can take up to two months in very busy periods.) *Advance dates:* Lead time is two months. Issues are planned six months in advance.

FREE-LANCE POSSIBILITIES: In 1981, six "Breakthroughs" were done by writers new to *Health;* four of these were the writers' original ideas, the other two were assigned after the writers had approached the magazine with other ideas that weren't quite right—but the writers were. No newcomer's by-line appeared on a feature. Says Joan Lippert: "We're short-staffed and really can't take a lot of chances." But she adds that new writers' ideas will always be considered, and she is encouraging when talking about building up the regular writer ranks. There are currently about 30 regular free-lancers here; these people are doing between two and three stories a year. Lippert comments: "Three of these people started off by coming in over-the-transom with a 'Breakthrough.' "

"Breakthroughs," the front-of-the-book "hot-off-the-press stories straight from the frontiers of science, health, and medicine," are the more likely way in here simply because they are short pieces and several are run each issue. A piece on bone transplants, another on hormones and breast cancer, another on a woman in the Midwest who runs a cognitive therapy program in her area—these all came in over-the-transom. A catch that applies to both "Breakthroughs" and features is that *Health*'s readership buys the magazine for the *latest* health/medical/fitness news. It's the free-lancer's task to come up with the "inside scoop." The editors here aren't interested in seeing a rehash of an item that has appeared in another consumer magazine. They want news that is fresh, innovative, and informative. They want ideas that have an upbeat slant, and solutions to problems that are unusual and optimistic in tone. And they want to get the message across in terms the layman can understand. What won't work: negative reports; reports that involve animal studies, unless results will be crucial to human health; developments that won't be available to the general public within a two-year period; reports that do not explain complicated medical terms; story ideas based on press releases; essaylike prose; frightening or depressing topics.

Assignments are the norm here. Clips will be asked for before an assignment is made. Without clips (newspaper and small magazine clips are fine), you will have to show specialist background for the article you're suggesting.

A last word from Joan Lippert: "Too often writers simply name the subject they want to write about without showing or explaining *how* they would write about it. And we're looking for ingenuity; we have plenty of ordinary ideas ourselves!"

Galleys are generally not shown to writers, but may be shown on request. (See "Portfolios and Positive Thinking," pages 7–9.)

HOW TO SUBMIT: Send manuscript or query. The query should run as long as it takes to present the idea; include as much in the way of personal background as you can; you must prove to the editors that *you* are the writer for the particular story idea, even though this is a specialized field. Clips are not required at query stage. Photographs are usually needed on "Breakthroughs." So if you have them, or have access to suitable photos, say so. And on any submission, don't forget the SASE.

REJECTIONS: A standard reply card is used. Personalized notes are sent to "writers who are on the right track, people we want to encourage."

HOUSE & GARDEN

Condé Nast Publications
350 Madison Avenue
New York, NY 10017
(212) 880-8800

SOURCE: Jerome H. Denner, managing editor

IN SHORT: Virtually closed market.

ABOUT THE MAGAZINE: Monthly. At least 50% of the magazine is free-lance–written. With the January '83 issue, *House & Garden* marked its new era with a change of content (dramatically different from previous times), a new target audience (the affluent, literate, well educated, and sophisticated), and a reduction of circulation to 650,000 (with subscriptions being encouraged over newsstand sales). *House & Garden* had been a magazine of home decorating, gardening, architecture, and life-style; but now there are no more service or how-to articles, no merchandise you can buy, no entertaining features or recipes. Instead, readers are toured through the world's most stately/opulent houses and gardens. "Now the magazine concentrates on architecture, decorating, and the fine arts with features on antiques, collecting, painting and sculpture, tastemakers, etc.," says managing editor Jerome Denner.

FREE-LANCE POSSIBILITIES: *House & Garden* now publishes writers like Arthur Miller, Susan Sontag, and Norman Mailer, and its photography is by outstanding practitioners such as Snowdon and Horst. It is no longer a likely market for the general free-lancer. Says Jerome Denner: "We're almost a closed shop. We're assigning articles to writers whose work we are familiar with or to experts in a particular field. We do not accept unsolicited manuscripts and are discouraging queries."

Field experts and specialists *may* approach the magazine by writing directly to Shelley Wanger, articles editor, or Denise Otis, editor. Free-lance writers may do so also, but Denner stresses contributors should be thoroughly familiar with the sort of material *House & Garden* now uses.

HOUSE BEAUTIFUL

The Hearst Corporation
1700 Broadway
New York, NY 10019
(212) 903-5000

SOURCE: Carol Cooper Garey, senior editor/copy

IN SHORT: Very limited possibilities.

ABOUT THE MAGAZINE: Monthly. *House Beautiful* is a magazine centering on the home, covering interior design and architecture. It is aimed primarily at women, and is strongly service-oriented with emphasis on the "comforts and creativity of home." *Readership:* 78.5% female, 21.5% male. The median reader's age is 43. Half of the readers have attended college; 28% are college grads. The majority of readers are middle income; 68% are married; 43% are parents; 45% of the women readers are working full-time. *Circulation:* 872,000. *Estimated readership:* 4.5 million. *Areas open to free-lancers:* Free-lance contributions are occasionally used for travel, gardening, renovation, and "innovative" home articles. *Rates:* Declined to comment. *Payment:* On acceptance. *Expenses:* Pays reasonable expenses. *Kill fee:* 15%. *Rights:* Buys all rights, by letter of agreement and check endorsement. Negotiable. *Number of submissions received weekly:* Declined to comment. *Reply time to queries:* Two weeks to two months. *Advance dates:* Issues are planned four to six months in advance.

FREE-LANCE POSSIBILITIES: Very few articles are accepted here from new writers; there is a reliance on regulars and a reluctance to discuss over-the-transom possibilities. However, Carol Cooper Garey comments: "We don't want to be unduly discouraging." She adds: "We are primarily interested in timely, informative articles dealing strictly with the home environment, both rural and urban." Most articles run 1200–1500 words.

The most common reasons for rejections are: "Ideas recently covered; ideas not suitable for the magazine; ideas not well developed; topics too broad or narrow; ideas not timely."

Writers are encouraged to send clips with queries. If there is interest in the idea, the writer will still most probably be asked to submit on spec, but clips may be requested beforehand. It is possible to approach the magazine with biographical material and clips. See "Portfolios and Positive Thinking," pages 7–9.

HOW TO SUBMIT: Completed manuscripts are read, but queries are much preferred. Include "outline of story idea, detailing how to be developed; whether photos are available; and why this idea is timely and interesting." Include clips. No submissions are returned without SASE.

REJECTIONS: A standard form is used but "some personalized notes" are sent.

HUSTLER/CHIC

Larry Flynt Publications
2029 Century Park East
Los Angeles, CA 90067-3054
(213) 556-9200

SOURCE: Richard Warren Lewis, articles editor for both magazines.

IN SHORT: *Hustler:* limited market; *Chic:* good possibilities.

ABOUT THE MAGAZINES: Monthly. *Hustler:* 98% free-lance–written; *Chic:* 100%. Both *Hustler* and *Chic* are men's magazines. Most of the material published in them is X-rated. But they also publish provocative, reportorial articles and pay top rates. The emphasis is on investigative reports that are hard-hitting and controversial (example: "Suicide: A National Epidemic," *Hustler,* December '82); profile subjects are often leading people who warrant national news attention (examples: George Steinbrenner and John Belushi). *Hustler* is aimed at men 18–50; *Chic* is aimed at 21–45-year-olds. *Circulation: Hustler:* 1.4 million. *Chic:* 300,000. *Areas open to free-lancers: Hustler:* everything except "Advise & Consent" and reviews. *Chic:* everything except humor, music, and trivia column. *Rates:* $1200–$1500 for *Hustler.* $500 for *Chic. Payment:* On acceptance. *Expenses: Hustler* pays all incidentals, up to $200. *Chic* pays no expenses. *Kill fee:* 20%. *Rights:* Buys exclusive worldwide magazine rights, by written contract. Not negotiable. *Number of submissions received weekly:* 15. *Reply time to queries:* Six weeks. *Advance dates:* Issues are planned about six months in advance.

FREE-LANCE POSSIBILITIES: Chances at *Hustler* are limited because most assignments go to proven, known writers capable of the "hard-hitting, investigative" style required. In the past two years, only one new writer broke in over-the-transom, with "Nixon's Last Secret Tape," which ran in the October '82 issue.

A new area where there *may* be chances for free-lancers is the monthly 5000-word Q. & A. interview. While these interviews are being assigned to known writers, Richard Warren Lewis says: "If the subject idea is provocative enough and if the writer had the access, we would probably be willing to take the chance on him." The key word is "provocative" as far as subject possibilities go; the magazine does profile celebrities but has an inclination toward the newsworthy but lesser known.

At *Chic*, free-lance opportunities are much better. Probably 50% of all articles published are the result of over-the-transom submissions, and Lewis says: "This will be happening increasingly at *Chic*." New writers are appearing "all the time," he added. For instance, a report on an insanity trial in Massachusetts came in over-the-transom and was bought. Another writer who sent in an interesting query was assigned to do a piece on a series of murders in Key West, Florida, while his original proposal was still being discussed.

Assignments are the norm at both magazines. On spec will be ased for "only if the idea is marginal." Lewis sees all the unsolicited material; potential ideas are then discussed with the editorial director and publisher for a final decision. Editing can be on the heavy side. Copies of the edited manuscript are sent to writers on request.

Once in, chances of future assignments are definitely increased. Commented Lewis: "It's difficult to find good writers."

HOW TO SUBMIT: Completed manuscripts are read (photocopies okay). Multiple submissions are accepted. Queries should be typewritten, about 1½ pages in length, and clips should be included. The best query is one that is "well written and provocative." When reviewing clips sent with queries, the editors are looking for "the ability to write simply and provocatively."

REJECTIONS: A standard rejection slip is sent in most cases; occasionally a personal note will be sent to encourage more submissions.

INC.

38 Commercial Wharf
Boston, MA 02110
(617) 227-4700

SOURCE: George Gendron, executive editor

IN SHORT: Difficult market; business writers have best chances.

ABOUT THE MAGAZINE: Monthly. 25% free-lance–written. First published in 1979, *Inc.* bills itself as "The Magazine for Growing Companies." It is a "resource guide" for people in small and medium-sized businesses with emphasis on the entrepreneurial. Says George Gendron: "We're based on the assumption that smaller companies don't have access to the kind of resources large companies do. We cover individuals and individual companies, as well as general business topics, and serve as a forum for people in smaller companies. There is a sense of loneliness when you're running your own business. One of the things that does set us apart from the other business magazines is that we're not interested in the fact that a company may have grown quickly, and that it may have solved certain problems. We're interested in *how* that company has done it." *Readership:* 90% male; 70% of readers are aged 25–50; average age is around 40; 90% have at least a college education; average income is $60,000. *Circulation:* 500,000. *Estimated readership:* 2.5 million ("a substantial number of subscribers receive the magazine at work"). *Areas open to free-lancers:* "People & Innovations," "News & Trends," and all features. ("Speaking Out" is written by invitation only; all other areas are regular columns and are staff-written.) *Rates:* Features: $750–$2000. *Payment:* On acceptance. *Expenses:* Pays all incidentals. *Kill fee:* One-third. *Rights:* Buys all rights, by written contract. Possible but difficult to negotiate. *Number of submissions received weekly:* 100. *Reply time to queries:* Queries: four weeks; mss: could be up to eight weeks. *Advance dates:* Lead time is two months. Issues are planned six months in advance.

FREE-LANCE POSSIBILITIES: *Inc.* is three-quarters staff-written; this includes all the columns (a good half of the magazine). Of the five features run monthly, four are generally written by free-lancers. Only one of these is likely to have a newcomer's by-line, and the author is most likely to be a business writer "fairly well plugged into his local business community."

This is a tough market; it's particularly so for the general-interest writer. George Gendron explains: "Before we can make an informed decision on whether a story is appropriate, the free-lancer has to do a good deal of research to back up his idea; it's a complaint we hear often from free-lancers. But we have to know exactly what is there that's interesting about this company or individual that would make it a good story for *Inc.* And we need specifics. For general free-lancers, this can be very diffi-cult. The free-lancers who *do* break in are most likely to have written about business before or they have some business back-ground or expertise. We require a certain amount of business sophistication."

There are no specific guidelines on features. "It's probably easier to talk about what we *don't* want," George Gendron says. "We don't run industry overviews or wrap-ups—a look at the micro-computer industry, for instance. We concentrate on com-panies and people within them, on companies working well with their employees, on companies that have found interesting ways to obtain capital, on companies with interesting marketing or financial strategies."

The following features originally came in over-the-transom: "The Solid Gold Rollercoaster" (by Theresa Engstrom, April '82), a piece on a Boston collectibles company that has survived some volatile times in the market, and how they did it; "Man-aging Billy Martin" (by Jay Stuller, cover story June '82), a look at the Oakland As and the club's president, giving an insight into the operation of a baseball franchise.

The two front-of-the-book columns open to free-lancers, "Peo-ple & Innovations" and "News & Trends," are an easier way in. There are no specific guidelines for these areas either, although the magazine should be read to get a feeling for both these de-partments; basically they are short items summed up by both column titles.

The *Inc.* senior staff meets for a story conference once a week. It's here that any promising queries are discussed. Writers are not asked to work on spec; assignments depend much more on the idea and its presentation than on clips. Impressive clips by themselves won't get you an assignment. "We're more reluctant to assign a story to a writer with weak clips, but then again it all depends on the idea. We do take risks quite often." He admits they are calculated risks, and there has been a recent, more studied approach to free-lance queries and a decision to go only with writers who look capable, on a story idea that looks fairly certain to pan out.

Queries are rejected ("Nine out of ten of them after reading the first paragraph") for the following reasons: "When there's no sense the contributor is aware of what *Inc.* is all about; when the idea is incredibly underresearched; when the query presents a topic that has been covered to death—either by us or the other business magazines." A writer file *is* kept but is rarely used as a source. "The burden really is on the free-lancer to keep his name in front of the editors," Gendron insists. The magazine *is* looking for stringers with business writing experience. See "Portfolios and Positive Thinking," pages 7–9.

One story in *can* lead to future assignments. Editing varies: "It depends on the piece, but we probably edit more heavily than most." Rewriting is done by staff "if there's no time for the writer to do it, or if the manuscript is really disappointing." Writers are given manuscript photocopies to review before publication.

Note: Business people wishing to submit to *Inc.* should query first, following the "How to Submit" guidelines.

HOW TO SUBMIT: Mss. are accepted, "but we're very reluctant to read them. Sometimes, when we get very backlogged, we have to return them, unread. We'd much rather have a query." Photocopied mss. are okay. Multiple submissions? "We don't read them." Submit general queries to George Gendron; on specialist queries, call and ask the name of the appropriate department editor. Says Gendron: "The ideal query for us is one single-spaced manuscript page, giving us three components: first, the basic background information about the company in question: where is it, what does it do, how fast has it grown, who are its competitors, etc. Secondly, the specific angle of your story, and *specific* information to help us make an informed decision. Don't tell us something like: 'Their success is due to a brilliant strategy.' Tell us what that strategy is. And thirdly, tell us about yourself: who you are and what professional writing credits you have." Clips are not required at query stage.

REJECTIONS: Standard rejection forms are used by some editors. But George Gendron stresses: "Any editor who wants to hear from you again *will* send a personalized note saying so."

INTERVIEW

19 East 32nd Street
New York, NY 10016
(212) 685-1800

SOURCE: Robert Hayes, editor

IN SHORT: Closed market.

ABOUT THE MAGAZINE: Monthly. All interviews are written by known contributors. *Interview* is Andy Warhol's newspaper-sized magazine of celebrity Q. & A. interviews. Each interview (eight to ten are included per issue) is illustrated with b/w photography. Says Robert Hayes: "We try to be visually exciting; every photo is an original work done expressly for *Interview*. And we try to get material the other magazines don't get, can't get, or else don't do very well. We try to work in advance of other publications. We don't wait until a movie opens, for instance, to interview the leading actor. Our reader is the slightly more sophisticated person who wants to know things in advance, to anticipate rather than follow." *Readership:* slightly more male readers than female. The average reader is likely to be college-educated, single, and of upper-middle income. The typical reader is a big-city dweller. *Circulation:* 96,000. *Estimated readership:* 425,000. *Rates:* $200 per interview (higher rates are paid to regulars). *Payment:* On publication. *Expenses:* Pays necessary travel costs. *Kill fee:* None. *Rights:* Buys all rights, by letter of agreement. Rights revert to author six months after publication. Author receives 50% of any resales during this six-month period. *Number of submissions received weekly:* Ten. *Reply time to queries:* Two weeks (and only with SASE). *Advance dates:* Lead time is six weeks. Issues are planned from a few months to a few weeks in advance.

FREE-LANCE POSSIBILITIES: *Interview* is virtually a closed market. There are 30–50 known people the editors call upon to do interviews, and Robert Hayes comments: "We don't have enough space for *these* people." If a newcomer breaks in over-the-transom (a rare occurrence—it happens only once every couple of years), it's because the submission fulfills one of these requirements: "The writing is extraordinary and the piece is already completed. Or a writer can get to someone we can't." The latter is not easy; *Interview* has ready access to celebrities and contacts.

There *is* another way in: to interview a more obscure subject the editors might not be thinking of. However, this approach can be chancy; you're gambling on the editor's interest in the interview subject. *No* queries are accepted; only completed manuscripts will be considered, and Hayes even discourages these.

So how does one become a regular at *Interview?* Basically, through a recommendation or some personal contact. Most of the pieces that have been accepted over-the-transom have turned out to be one-shot deals.

For those free-lancers willing to try for publication here, these are Hayes's guidelines: "We're not looking for a particular slant. What we want is a good interview subject, and then not an encyclopedic listing of their achievements but rather an interesting conversation."

HOW TO SUBMIT: No queries are accepted. Send completed ms. only; photocopies okay. Replies are sent only if SASE is included.

REJECTIONS: Personal notes sent, or else submission is simply returned—but all depends on the weekly workload.

JET

Johnson Publishing
820 South Michigan Avenue
Chicago, IL 60605
(312) 322-9200

Weekly. Digest-sized general-interest magazine for black readers. Covers all subjects: black history, education, politics, current affairs, society, sports, celebrities, people in the news.
Accepts only very occasional free-lance pieces, and these will
be assigned by the editors to writers known at the magazine.
Completed manuscripts are not accepted, and queries are not
encouraged.

LADIES' HOME JOURNAL

Three Park Avenue
New York, NY 10016
(212) 725-1700

SOURCE: Sondra Forsyth Enos, articles editor

IN SHORT: Open, but very competitive market. Difficult to sell.

ABOUT THE MAGAZINE: Monthly. All articles are free-lance–wrtten. "We see ourselves as a thinking woman's magazine," says Sondra Forsyth Enos. "The *Journal* is the magazine a woman picks up when she's in the mood for meaty, gutsy, real-world topics that will stretch her mind, written in a reportage style. We also run service articles and interviews with celebrities; that's the fun, useful and entertaining stuff." The average reader is a 42-year-old woman, with some college education, who is married and has two or three children. She probably works (often part-time) and most likely doesn't think of her job as a career. However, she is involved in her community and, having come of age in the sixties and seventies, is interested in the world at large in a more profound way than middle-aged woman were even a generation ago. She is independent, young at heart, well informed, and thoughtful. *Circulation:* 5 million. *Estimated readership:* 18 million. *Areas open to free-lancers:* Everything except decorating, food, fashion, beauty, child care, animal care, money, celebrity profiles, and "Can This Marriage Be Saved?" *Rates:* $250–$3500. Top rates for name writers. The average starting fee for a 3000-word feature is $1000. *Payment:* On acceptance. *Expenses:* Pays reasonable expenses. *Kill fee:* 25%. *Rights:* Generally buys first North American rights, by written contract. *Number of submissions received weekly:* 100–250 queries; 100 manuscripts. *Reply time:* Queries: up to two weeks; manuscripts: up to six weeks. *Advance dates:* Lead time is three months. Issues are planned several months in advance.

FREE-LANCE POSSIBILITIES: At first glance the breaking-in statistics at *LHJ* are very disheartening. Of all the thousands of queries received each year, only between five and ten of them are ever pursued, and similarly, of the thousands of unsolicited mss. received yearly, only one or two ever make it into print. But Sondra Forsyth Enos insists: "It's not because we don't welcome ideas and submissions. We read everything that comes in and are delighted when we do find someone whose idea we can use. We like to try out different writers and we certainly have no bias; we don't reject people just because we've never heard of them. But we do have a large staff of people who read all kinds of publications, even obscure ones, making notes and clipping ideas, so it's very difficult for free-lancers to come up with ideas we haven't already thought of."

What does work? Hard-hitting, newsy pieces should tell the story but include service information as well. "Ordeal" stories, either first-person or as-told-to, should be moving accounts of triumph over tragedy. Contemporary close-ups focus on the varied life-styles of today's Americans (ordinary people, not well-knowns). "Emotional" pieces (e.g. how to stop putting yourself down), should include both quotes from specialists/experts and case histories. "I'd like to see more ideas for emotional articles because these are such a treat for the reader, a chance for her to talk with herself," Enos says. "But these are probably the most challenging to pull off, both because the topics are hard to think up and because the pieces have to be written in a mature, sophisticated way." Possibly the easiest way to break in is through the regular feature "It's Not Easy to Be a Woman Today." But with this category, as with all articles in *LHJ*, targeting your idea is of primary importance; you must *know* the magazine and keep the readership in mind.

Most writers work on assignment at *LHJ*, but here Enos advises: "We have to ask most fledgling writers to work on spec. But new writers *should* be glad to work on spec because it's really the only way to break into magazines. If we give you a go-ahead, on spec, we're giving you an honest chance and we're really hoping the article will work out."

Editing varies tremendously—from none at all to heavy rewrites—depending on the shape of the manuscript. But the first rewrite is always done by the author, and a galleylike printout of the piece is always sent to the author before publication.

Your chances of getting a rejection from *LHJ* will be increased if you're guilty of any of these: bad spelling and grammar; untidy, messy queries or manuscripts ("If I notice coffee and orange-juice spills, if you haven't changed your typewriter ribbon for 53 years, or if you spell my name wrong," Enos comments, "you won't convince me you'll be able to write a professional article for us.") Other faux pas: "Being pushy and trying to boss us around. Claiming that you're querying us with an idea that *will* be right for *Ladies' Home Journal*. Not targeting properly, querying us with ideas that are not right for our audience or for areas in the magazine that are staff-written. Sending queries written in business-letter style—that's a big mistake. Querying us on a subject that's too broad, without a slant or hook."

HOW TO SUBMIT: No phone queries ("even known writers must send us written queries"). Manuscripts will be read, but queries are much preferred. Photocopied manuscripts or queries are okay, but Enos likes to be informed that you're not sending her a multiple submission. "I like to be offered something that's exclusive, that you want to do for *LHJ* only."

Keep queries short—one page if possible. Forget personal details: "If you write a fabulous query letter I really don't care about your credentials," Enos insists.

Send a couple of clips if you have them. Newspaper and trade clips are okay: "Plain good writing is what I'm looking for."

REJECTIONS: A standard rejection form is used in most cases; personalized notes are sent to contributors who are on the right track, and are meant as a sign of encouragement. If you receive a rejection that's not a standard form, keep trying. And remember: one story and you're in!

LADYCOM

Downey Communications
1800 M Street, N.W.
Suite 650-S
Washington, DC 20036
(202) 872-0960

SOURCE: Sheila J. Gibbons, editor

IN SHORT: Very open to both beginning and experienced writers.

ABOUT THE MAGAZINE: Monthly, except July and December; 80% free-lance–written. The January issue is a special: *The Ladycom Reference Book for Military Wives*. *Ladycom* is a women's magazine for military wives, which is distributed free in commissaries in the U.S. (A smaller edition is also sent abroad.) Also available by subscription. *Ladycom* is a privately owned publication, not directed or controlled by any section of the military. Says Sheila Gibbons: "We're trying to make the magazine a very good mirror of military domestic life. We're trying to provide the military wife with a magazine that helps her interpret and cope with service life." Food, fashion, crafts, health, and child care are included with articles by both free-lancers and readers. The majority of readers are aged 25–34; half have attended college; two-thirds are married to enlisted men, one-third to officers; about half are working full- or part-time; most have small children and most will be military wives for many years. *Circulation:* 400,000 (U.S.); 75,000 (overseas). *Estimated readership:* one million. *Sample copy:* $1. *Areas open to free-lancers:* All. *Rates:* $50–$700 (higher payments for extensive research, and to known writers). *Payment:* Pays professional writers and regular contributors on acceptance. *Expenses:* Phone calls, mileage. *Kill fee:* One-third. *Rights:* Buys first North American serial rights, by letter of agreement. *Number of submissions received weekly:* 25. *Reply time to queries:* Two to three weeks. *Advance dates:* Lead time is six months. Issues are planned seven months in advance.

FREE-LANCE POSSIBILITIES: *Ladycom* runs 10–12 articles per issue, plus departments. Yearly, editor Sheila Gibbons writes about six articles; editorial assistant Karen Jones does the same. The rest of the magazine is written by free-lancers; there are about 15 regular writers, half of them military wives (who tend to move on fairly frequently). The rest of the material comes from general free-lancers and reader contributions. In an average issue, about five articles are by writers new to the magazine. All of this adds up to a wide-open field and good opportunities for the free-lancer.

The catch is: How does the general free-lancer come up with an idea and obtain article information relevant to a reader who is the wife of a serviceman? Sheila Gibbons is encouraging: "I always work pretty closely with the writer and will help in any way I can. I don't expect free-lancers necessarily to know military wives or to have the military contacts; I can help with those. What I need is a good article idea that will either affect or interest a woman who also happens to be a military wife."

In the October '82 issue, Kathy Conlan Phillips wrote "Christmas Shipping Simplified," from a query. The writer happens to be a navy wife, but this was a general consumer piece. Two controversial reports—one about child abuse among military families (September '82), by Stephanie Bobrowsky, and "Recruiters' Families," by Bruce Friedland (August '82)—were done by general-interest writers with no prior connections with the military.

Social issues are of particular interest here, as are personal and human-interest stories: "Human interest stories has the biggest value for us, particularly stories of hurdles overcome. There's a lot of tragedy in military life; there's also a lot of bonding among wives and families, and there's a tremendous amount of competition between the service member's job and his family life. Military families also experience a great deal of adventure. All this makes for good human-interest material. Anyone who comes to me with an interesting angle on a military family will get listened to."

Parenting is a good area: "We want to give reassuring, useful advice to parents. A lot of our readers are far away from their families and friends. We are always looking for parenting articles by people who are well credentialed, or by people who can get input from child care experts."

Crafts is a possible area. Here, how-tos for interesting, useful crafts are needed. Personality profiles are good, "but we're only interested in people with some connection with the military. Not military women particularly; we want military wives who are doing something really interesting."

Gibbons adds: "Our writing style is friendly, not cute, but down-to-earth. We're looking for writers who are respectful of other people's points of view and who are willing to get out there and get them. We need people to be resourceful, and a query tells us a lot about a writer's willingness to go out there and 'specialize' for us. You have to talk to *all* branches of the military, and there's no one phone number that works for them all. You have to be willing to do legwork."

Food, although open, is not a good area for the free-lancer—there are a number of regular contributors.

Gibbons also advises: "Often I reject submissions because they're not specific enough. An article on how military wives are coping with work is not focused enough or of sufficient interest. And often free-lancers don't know our magazine—an article on a civilian woman running a day-care center in California may be a good story, but it doesn't affect our readers." Gibbons will sometimes reject an idea but will suggest another as a possible assignment if she's impressed with the presentation of the query, and the clips enclosed.

She will ask to see clips before giving an assignment. You could be asked to work on spec if your clips are weak (major magazine clips are not required) or "if your query sparks interest but it's not passionate interest and I still need to be convinced."

Any extensive rewriting is done by the author. Minor editing/reorganizing is done by staff, but Gibbons comments: "I don't think we overdo it on the editing. We certainly don't feel obligated to make changes." Writers are not shown galleys or informed of editing alterations. See "Portfolios and Positive Thinking," pages 7–9.

HOW TO SUBMIT: Completed mss. are accepted (originals preferred over photocopies), but queries are preferred. Multiple submissions are accepted if the author informs the editor. The query should be no more than one page, single-spaced. Advises Sheila Gibbons: "Spell out your sources, how you're going to attempt to get the information. I want to see how much enterprise you have." Include clips—"that's an advantage."

Newspaper clips are good—"this is the kind of writing we do."

REJECTIONS: A standard rejection form is sent to all contributors, "except those I'd like to hear from again, with other ideas."

LADY'S CIRCLE

Lopez Publications
23 West 26th Street
New York, NY 10010
(212) 689-3933

SOURCE: Ardis Sandel, editor

IN SHORT: Good market for beginners.

ABOUT THE MAGAZINE: Monthly. At least 80% free-lance–written. *Lady's Circle* is a women's service/entertainment magazine, aimed at homemakers. Half of the readers are 18–39, the others are over 40. The readers are high-school–educated. Many readers work from home, but generally not outside the home. *Areas open to free-lancers:* Everything except "What's New in Medicine," "How to Get Things Free," and "Time & Money Savers." *Rates:* Features: $125 standard. *Payment:* On publication. *Expenses:* Not applicable. *Kill fee:* Not applicable. *Rights:* Buys all rights, verbally. Negotiable. *Number of submissions received weekly:* 100–150. *Reply time to queries:* Outright rejections: immediate response. Submissions under consideration: can take several months. *Advance dates:* Lead time is two months. Issues are planned six months in advance.

FREE-LANCE POSSIBILITIES: *Lady's Circle* is mostly free-lance–written and new writers appear in every issue. About 75% of the article ideas come in over-the-transom.

The drawbacks: Payment is on publication; reply time can be very lengthy (and calling to inquire won't speed up the process); and *all* work is done on spec, whether you're known at the magazine or are a newcomer.

But writers are not asked to work on spec unless the idea looks worthwhile, and decisions are not made on the writer's experience or on clips, but solely on the idea.

The "people" area, as well as the how-to, are fertile areas for the free-lancer. Ardis Sandel offers these guidelines: "We do one celebrity piece per issue, usually an actress, who also appears on the cover." (There are limited possibilities in the celebrity profile area, unless you have unique access.) "Other than those, we do stories about ordinary people who are helping others, or overcoming handicaps, or making a success in some venture." Published examples: a homemaker who makes folksy dolls with dried-apple faces; a woman who began an emergency "hot line" for the deaf, using a computer communications hookup; a couple who opened a facility for married pregnant women suddenly alone.

"We often get 'personal experience' pieces—like 'How I Stopped Coloring My Hair' or 'My Child Is Off to College.' These won't work; we need more substance. Mostly, our articles are upbeat." Examples: "23 Ways to Look Younger Longer," "A Psychologist Tells How to Break the Binge Habit," "A Doctor Tells How to Stop Playing with Your Life."

Editing can be extensive here, but any rewriting is done by the author, with close editorial guidance. Galleys are generally not shown.

HOW TO SUBMIT: Completed mss. are accepted (but not returned without SASE). Photocopied mss. are okay. No multiple submissions. Queries are preferred—no preferences on length. Writing résumé/credits or clips are not required.

REJECTIONS: A standard form is usually used. Personalized notes are sent to encourage more submissions.

LIFE

Time, Inc.
1271 Avenue of the Americas
New York, NY 10020
(212) 586-1212

SOURCE: A senior editor who has since left the magazine. A replacement had not been named when we went to press, but other editors did concur with the information given.

IN SHORT: Surprisingly, very open.

ABOUT THE MAGAZINE: Monthly. *"Life* is a magazine of feature photojournalism. We're looking for stories that are topical, but not necessarily front-page material." Articles cover both national and international issues. This is a coffee-table magazine of the highest quality; the magazine's heaviest concentration is on lavish photography. Readership is roughly half female, half male. Median reader age is 35; 72% of all readers have attended college and they're basically middle and upper middle in income. *Circulation:* 1.4 million. *Estimated readership:* Over 8½ million. *Areas open to free-lancers:* "Portrait," text pieces, picture stories. *Rates:* Payment starts at $1000 for short features, $2000 for longer pieces. *Payment:* On acceptance. *Expenses:* Pays all incidentals, up to an agreed-upon limit. *Kill fee:* Negotiable. *Rights:* Buys first North American serial rights, by confirming letter. *Number of submissions received weekly:* 25–30. *Reply time to queries:* Three weeks. *Advance dates:* Lead time is two to three months. Issues are planned five to six months in advance.

FREE-LANCE POSSIBILITIES: One of the best ways into *Life* is through a picture story, for which the magazine has always been renowned. In these, free-lancers are sent out to do the reporting only; a staff writer then writes the piece. But the reporter does get involved in the production of the piece. One editor said: "Possibilities for picture stories are limitless. And we probably need that kind of suggestion more than anything else." One such recent story was about a group of scientists who re-create natural phenomena—like lightning, the shifting of sands, and tornados—in the laboratory. Another story showed the lack of serious law enforcement in narcotics; the focus was on marijuana fields in

California. Writers are paid slightly less for picture stories, but expenses are added. (The photo editor assigns photographers, however.) Picture story suggestions are welcomed over-the-transom. "Just keep thinking pictures first," was the editor's tip.

In addition to the picture stories, there are two other monthly feature stories open to the free-lancer. This translates into 24 feature stories a year. And unknown writers manage to succeed three or four times out of the 24—not bad odds, particularly when you consider the prestige of this publication. The senior editor said: "We happen to have a particular interest in new writers, and many of the people who break in to the magazine are young—sometimes just a few years out of college. Getting into *Life* requires no great complicated rigamarole. Assignments are the norm and to get one you do *not* have to be widely published. What you do have to do is come up with an idea that's right and to impress the editors in the telling. Doug Hand, who wrote the piece on Dr. Helen Caldicott (June '82) from a query, had been published previously in the Vermont magazine, *Country Journal*. Larry Engelmann, who submitted, unsolicited, a manuscript which later became "The Ghost Blimp" (July '82) is a historian, based in San Jose, California. Bertram Gabriel III, who wrote the June '82 piece on an Oregon rancher caught smuggling cocaine and who was tortured in Peru, got the assignment with an unsolicited query. The Lindbergh baby story (March '82) resulted from a query from Tom Zito, a *Washington Post* reporter who had already written a smaller version for the paper.

Should you try with a "Portrait" or a text piece? Neither is harder than the other to accomplish, but as the editor pointed out: "The 'Portrait' is much shorter (it generally runs about 1500 words) and involves less reporting. But it does require very stylish writing. You have to be able to display an ear and a feel for dialogue, and what I call 'sights and sounds reporting,' to create the anecdotes. These pieces have to be very atmospheric." "Portrait" subjects are "by and large people whose names are easily recognized, or else the handle for the name is known. For instance, we ran a "Portrait" on the composer Vangelis; most people wouldn't know his name but they do know the music from *Chariots of Fire*, which Vangelis wrote. Generally free-lancers are more successful at thinking up text pieces because they tend to think too small, too localized, with 'Portraits.' 'Portrait' subjects are not everyday people; they're not quaint and they're not overexposed. They can be actors, politicians, people in the arts, businesspeople if they're colorful."

A text piece "has to be fairly broad-based in its appeal. It can't be too obscure or limited in its interest. It can be a good narrative. Or it can be focused around a single personality. We did one in 1981 on Francis Ford Coppola." What made the Coppola piece different from a "Portrait" was that the piece showed the director at work; it was not a straight profile. "We thought people would like to see him at work and listen to what he had to say."

Life editors do not ask free-lancers to work on spec. "Either we'll assign the piece or we won't." And often they'll take a chance on a writer, negotiating with a kill fee arrangement that will cover the magazine. Every now and then an *idea* will be bought, "but only if we're really unsure of the writer's ability."

HOW TO SUBMIT: Send a query or completed manuscript. Photocopied manuscripts are okay; simultaneous submission, however, "takes the edge off. It isn't a politic thing to do unless the story is a very urgent one." With "Portraits," probably the best approach is with a query. For a text piece it might be worth considering submitting a manuscript, particularly if the story is offbeat (like the blimp story), the reason being that the editors may be less enthusiastic to assign an offbeat piece to a writer unknown to them, particularly if it would involve travel and other expenses.

There's no set rule for queries, but "generally they should be on the shorter side. Some of the best ideas we've seen have been told in two or three paragraphs." The query letter is important here. "The query letter is the only way you know that person. Any mistakes or flaws are going to make an editor very wary. You're going to be wary, anyway, even with an immaculately prepared query letter! Editors look for some wit or flair; so many queries are so wooden that they only make me think: If I had so much trouble reading this letter, how would I react to a 6000-word piece by this writer? And I don't think it's asking too much for a free-lancer to be familiar with the magazine—and the name of the editor. We get queries addressed to the editor who was here two years ago!"

If you're unknown at the magazine, include one or two nonreturnable clips. But still include a rundown of your writing experience: "Often that's more helpful than the clips themselves." (See "Portfolios and Positive Thinking," pages 7–9).

REJECTIONS: A standard rejection form is used. "But if there's any spark at all, we'll try and write an encouraging note."

McCALL'S

230 Park Avenue
New York, NY 10169
(212) 551-9500

SOURCE: Don McKinney, managing editor

IN SHORT: Open, but very competitive market.

ABOUT THE MAGAZINE: Monthly. Articles are 85% free-lance–written; "Right Now" section is 50% free-lance–written. Says Don McKinney: "We are aiming to a great extent at young women from their early 20s to mid 30s. We try to deal, for the most part, with subjects that directly relate to the needs of these women, who are not a lot of different from a cross section of American women." *Readership:* half fall into the above-mentioned age category. Half of all readers work outside the home. *Circulation:* 6,200,000. *Estimated readership:* 15 million. *Areas open to free-lancers:* Articles, "Right Now," "Women on the Job," "Back Talk," and regional editions. (Beauty; fashion—including "Good Looks"; home management—including "Good Living"; and food are staff-written.) *Rates:* "Right Now": $150–$300. Main section: $1000–$3000 (and occasionally higher). Regional editions: $200–$500. *Payment:* On acceptance. *Expenses:* Pays all incidentals. *Kill fee:* 20%. *Rights:* "Right Now": Buys all rights. Other areas: Buys exclusive North American serial rights. By written contract. Negotiable. *Number of submissions received weekly:* 300–400. *Reply time to queries:* A few days to two to three weeks (manuscript submissions slightly longer). *Advance dates:* Lead time is seven weeks. Issues are planned three months in advance.

FREE-LANCE POSSIBILITIES: The only stumbling block at *McCall's* seems to be the competition; 300–400 over-the-transom submissions are received weekly, and only about 5% of these work out. The statistics aren't heartening, but Don McKinney offers some encouragement: "We have about 10 to 12 people writing regularly for the magazine, and a total of 20–25 people we might assign our ideas to. But only about 65% of our material is staff-originated, and we get happily surprised with material that comes in over-the-transom. We don't have any particular hang-ups about where a writer has been published before; the idea is what's important. We don't keep a list of unassigned ideas, and we almost never have more than four or five pieces in inventory at one time."

He also adds: "There isn't any magic way to break in," but acknowledges that the easier route is through "Right Now," for which editor Martha Hewson gives the following guidelines: "We're looking for anything that lives up to the section's name; it should be current and trendy, with national appeal. Anything that would relate to our women readers. We're always looking for ideas—from 200 to up to 700 words. Occasionally we buy ideas, but mostly we assign and don't ask people to work on spec. You can tell a lot from the query letter. We prefer to be queried first, and writers should list publication credits. It's not necessary to include clips; you can if you wish. But we *have* assigned to people who haven't been well published. We're looking for ideas, not credits."

In the general articles area, a first reading is done by trainee editors who will pass along anything with any kind of promise." From there, an appealing idea is assigned, "if the writer has a proven track record with magazines similar to ours." Without major magazine clips, the writer will be asked to work on speculation. On speculation may also be required, regardless of the writer's experience, "if the idea is somewhat amorphous—a personal essay, for instance, or a bit of short humor."

McKinney offers these general guidelines: "One of the good things about writing for a women's magazine, as far as the freelancer is concerned, is that we tend to go back to the same ideas; when you're dealing with the problems of human relationships you tend to touch on the same broad subject areas from time to time. We're addressing our readers' emotional concerns, health concerns, and their interests; more than half the magazine is geared in this direction. In the women's-interest narrative, we try to choose subjects our readers can identify with and possibly experience. For instance, we bought a piece from a writer over-the-transom who wrote about never having understood her mother till she became a mother herself. It has to either provide information or help the reader understand a problem she might have, and it has to have a direct bearing on the conduct of her life. So we wouldn't be interested in, say, the life of the wife of King Hussein.

"The human-interest narrative is always a good area. It can be the story of someone who's been through some kind of personal trial. Or it can be a story that illuminates a national problem. Like the piece we bought from a woman in Oregon; she had had a miscarriage and so had a number of her neighbors. She decided to investigate and was able to amass enough evidence that a pesticide used locally was at blame and to prevent further use until the facts were known."

The emotional/psychological story tends to be written by a writer known at the magazine. "These are hard to assign"; a newcomer would probably have to do this kind of piece on spec.

Celebrity profiles are *not* a good area. "We're doing fewer and fewer of these, and they'll almost certainly go to a writer we know. We're increasingly moving away from the straight profile into ones where we can weave some kind of service angle."

Editing varies. "We sometimes do a lot of editing, but it really depends. If we think the writer could just use some redirection we'll give it back to them. But if the manuscript is basically complete and well organized, but sometimes sloppily written, it's generally easier to fix it ourselves. But edited copy is always shown to the writer, and we try to satisfy them if there are any differences."

Don McKinney adds: "I'm always impressed when somebody has obviously taken the time to read the past couple of issues and knows the kind of articles we do, rather than just throwing all their ideas on the table and hoping one of them can stick."

It will take two or three published pieces in *McCall's* to become a regular who may be given future assignments. A writer coming over-the-transom with a good idea that can't be used at the time will probably not be kept on file. It's up to the writer to contact the editors again. And approaching the magazine only with bio. and clips and a desire to contribute is generally a waste of time. "Nothing much ever comes from that kind of contact," McKinney says.

HOW TO SUBMIT: Send article submissions to Don McKinney; "Right Now" to Martha Hewson. Says McKinney: "One of the mistakes is that some people don't make any effort to establish a relationship with an editor. It's always a good idea to develop a relationship with somebody on the staff, and that's really not very hard to do." So don't just send your submission to "The Editors."

Completed manuscripts are read (photocopies okay), but queries are preferred. No multiple submissions. Says Don McKinney: "The query should be long enough, to tell the editor what the idea is; how you, the writer, intend to develop it; and where the information is going to come from. The query should be a kind of teaser." Include clips. "Pick out two, at the most three, that are similar in style, if not content, to the article you're suggesting."

REJECTIONS: "The bulk of the unsolicited material will receive a standard rejection form, but we will send a personalized note if we see something promising either in the writer or in the expression of the idea."

MADEMOISELLE

Condé Nast Publications
350 Madison Avenue
New York, NY 10017
(212) 880-8800

SOURCE: Katherine Ball Ross, associate editor

IN SHORT: A difficult market for the beginner.

ABOUT THE MAGAZINE: Monthly. All articles are free-lance–written. Katherine Ball Ross describes *Mademoiselle* as "a general magazine, for college-educated, young working women." She elaborates: "To a large extent it's a service magazine, but we also feel we go beyond that. What we try and do is present beauty and fashion, and articles on a broad range of subjects." *Mademoiselle*'s readership is young; 91% are under age 30, and the median age is 22; 65% of all readers have attended college, 82% are working, and most are single. *Circulation:* one million. *Areas open to free-lancers:* All articles and "Feeling Good" (which is part of "Good Looks and Health"). Fashion and beauty and the regular columns (listed in the magazine's table of contents as "In Every Issue") are all written by staff or regular contributors. *Rates:* Full-length features (around 2500 words): $1250–$1600. Smaller articles (around 1250 words): $700. *Payment:* On acceptance. *Expenses:* Pays reasonable expenses. *Kill fee:* 25%. *Rights:* Buys first North American rights, by written contract. All rights revert to author three months after publication. *Number of submissions received weekly:* 150. *Reply time to queries:* Four to six weeks. *Advance dates:* Lead time is four to five months. Issues are planned at least six to seven months in advance.

FREE-LANCE POSSIBILITIES: *Mademoiselle* carries about ten full-length pieces per issue, and all are open to free-lancers. The scope is wide. A typical issue (October '82) included the following topics: "Pregnancy Roulette," "Were You Born to Work?" "How to Be an Optimist," "Beyond the Pill: Contraceptives of the Future," "The Guardian Angels Are Watching You" (a report on the volunteer youth corps that patrols the New York subways), and "What's Good About a Bad Affair." Although the magazine has its regular writers, new writers are very welcome.

Adds Katherine Ross: "We definitely try to use a writer more than once. When we give a writer an assignment, we hope it's the start of a working relationship."

But the catch is: You really have to be a fairly well-established writer to publish at *Mademoiselle*. Although about ten writers each year *do* break in over-the-transom, they're experienced. The editors want to see clips before they'll agree to an assignment. Ross says: "You don't have to have written for a major magazine to be a good writer; we would never discount clips from smaller publications." But the clips still have to be of high standard, and your idea, of course, has to be really "first rate." Even if the idea is appealing, if clips are weak the idea is likely to be forfeited, unless you ask to work on spec. "If a writer volunteers to work this way, we'll probably agree to it. But we won't encourage her, because we really feel working on spec isn't fair." (A way around this, if your clips are mediocre, is to send a completed manuscript.) Katherine Ross adds: "Inexperienced writers virtually never appear in *Mademoiselle*."

Most article ideas are either generated in-house or are suggested by regular writers. Queries coming in over-the-transom reach the articles editor only if they pass the first screening by an editorial assistant. Often the magazine will contact writers whose work they have seen in other magazines.

Still, it *is* possible to break in with a major feature. General-interest subjects are best; there is usually one celebrity interview in each issue, but this is assigned. Ross offers these guidelines: "Writers will often query us with something like, 'I'd like to do a piece on stepparents.' Or 'I'd like to write a piece on alcoholism in young women.' But what's important for us to know is: What *about* stepparents? Or alcoholism? What would be the specific focus of the article?"

The editors' chief complaints? "Writers who don't do their homework. Sending us ideas such as an article on the problems of menopause in marriage—ideas which tell us they haven't even looked at the magazine to see the kinds of articles we do, and the kind of reader we have."

Editing varies. A copy of the edited manuscript is sent to writers.

HOW TO SUBMIT: Send submissions to Katherine Ames Brown, articles editor. Completed manuscripts are considered (if a photocopy, it must be clear), but queries are much preferred. Present your idea, plus an explanation of how the article would be executed. Working titles are not required, but they help. A pet peeve: "Poorly structured, rambling query letters." Include clips. "If someone is really serious about getting an assignment from us, she has to send clips." What will be considered in your clips will be "the originality of your ideas and general good writing."

REJECTIONS: Unsolicited manuscripts receive a standard form rejection. On queries, "it depends—if it deserves special attention, it gets special attention."

METROPOLITAN HOME

Meredith Corporation
750 Third Avenue
New York, NY 10017
(212) 557-6600

SOURCE: Charla Lawhon, assistant managing editor

IN SHORT: Difficult to sell specific ideas; but submissions welcomed.

ABOUT THE MAGAZINE: Monthly; 40% free-lance–written. *Metropolitan Home* is an interior design and architectural magazine, with a heavy emphasis on home furnishings. Readers range in age from 25–50; median age is 31. Most readers are college-educated, they are in professional occupations, 45% are married. Average income of readers is in the low $30,000s. About half are male, half female. According to the editors, "They're people with an urban sensibility. They want to establish equity, they want to be smart about investments and real estate. They're interested in traveling and entertaining and they are intensely interested in renovation, rehabbing, and design." *Circulation:* 750,000. *Areas open to free-lancers:* Everything except "Hot Properties" (although stringer fees will sometimes be paid for information); "The New American Cuisine"; "Object Lessons"; and the "Metropolitan Home of the Month" and "Style" interior design spreads. *Rates:* $600–$1200. *Payment:* On acceptance. *Expenses:* Pays reasonable expenses. *Kill fee:* 20%. *Rights:* Buys all rights, by written contract. Not negotiable. *Number of submissions received weekly:* 15–20. *Reply time to queries:* About 6 weeks. *Advance dates:* Lead time is two months. Issues are planned about six months in advance.

FREE-LANCE POSSIBILITIES: Unlike most of the interior design/home magazines, you do not have to be an expert in the field to be published here; most of the free-lance by-lines appearing in *Metropolitan Home* belong to general-interest writers, not specialists. The magazine is always looking for good, reliable writers; the editors welcome ideas. Assignment chances are good, even for new writers; writing on spec is rare.

But only about 5% of the over-the-transom ideas are succeeding here. The idea may be wrong for the market. Says Charla

Lawhon: "We're an interior design magazine. We don't use articles about pets or party giving." Or, because most articles are staff-generated, the timing is often off on ideas coming in from the outside. Lawhon says: "The idea may not work, but we *may* see a talent in the writer." With the writer's permission, the editors may keep him on file and have often been known to reach into their files to hand out assignments.

The editors' advice is to forget the design spreads and the other areas not open to free-lancers, and forget "High Profile" if you are not a known writer. Try for a more general piece. Write a good proposal and include clips; these will be asked for. Query even if you do not have impressive clips. If your query is impressive, you could still have a chance (if you're in New York, you might be asked to come in and discuss your idea).

HOW TO SUBMIT: Completed manuscripts are read but only for the writing style. Chances of acceptance with a manuscript are very slim. Tips for queries: Present a good sense of the idea. Including a proposed lead paragraph is a plus, as is including a list of the people you would be interviewing for your information. Also include clips, a rundown of where you have been published, and your interests if they are relevant to the idea being proposed.

REJECTIONS: A standard rejection letter is sent if the idea is way off-target. If the idea is a reasonable one but the timing is off, or if it's obvious care has been taken with the presentation of the query, a personal letter will be sent, with reasons for rejection.

MODERN BRIDE

Ziff-Davis Publishing
One Park Avenue
New York, NY 10016
(212) 725-3888

SOURCE: Cele Lalli, editor
Mary Ann Cavlin, managing editor

IN SHORT: Very open market with wide scope.

ABOUT THE MAGAZINE: Bi-monthly. Most articles are free-lance—written. *Modern Bride* is a magazine for the bride-to-be and is heavily service-oriented. It is primarily bought on the newsstand. The average reader buys two to three issues. Fashion copy is aimed at the bride, but articles address both the bride and groom as a couple. The magazine is aimed at the first-time bride who is usually 22- or 23-years-old; the groom is typically 24–25. *Modern Bride* is divided into three main areas: wedding fashions, home furnishings and tableware, and honeymoon destinations. *Circulation:* 360,000. *Areas open to free-lancers:* General articles. (All etiquette and merchandising-related copy—fashion, gifts, home furnishings—is staff written.) *Rates:* 20–25 cents a word. *Payment:* On acceptance. *Expenses:* Rarely paid. *Kill fee:* 20%. *Rights:* Buys first periodical rights, by check endorsement. *Number of submissions received weekly:* 10–15. *Reply time to queries:* Two to four weeks. *Advance dates:* Lead time is four months. Issues are planned four to five months in advance.

FREE-LANCE POSSIBILITIES: *Modern Bride* is a good market for the beginning writer in particular. Ideas come from both regular writers' queries and over-the-transom submissions, and they do not have to be unique. Explains Cele Lalli: "It's amazing how many different angles you can put forward on a bridal subject. Because our reader turnover is high, there are certain topics we're always repeating. What we're looking for is good writing."

Features are open, but the best way into the magazine is through a short feature or short take. Completed manuscripts are preferred, but queries (with clips) are considered—the piece to be done on spec.

What kinds of articles is the magazine looking for? The editors look for subjects relevant to the bride-to-be: how to manage your home, how to keep the love light burning, how to juggle marriage and career, how to cope with long-distance marriages, how to deal with your in-laws, how to make new friends as a couple, how to keep your old friends now that you're part of a couple, how to be part of your neighborhood community. "How-tos" dealing with the most basic problems are also a good bet, as are articles on finances and budgeting. Articles on second marriages and family planning are possible (but not articles on child *raising*). Stay away from first-person narration if possible. And remember that article information should be aimed at both the bride and groom.

Although travel is open to free-lancers, it is limited to writers with proven travel background.

Editing is generally not heavy here. If a manuscript needs a complete rewrite, it is returned to the author to be resubmitted after revision. Galleys are not shown.

HOW TO SUBMIT: A written query or ms. should be directed to Mary Ann Cavlin. Be specific in your query; include one or two clips if possible.

REJECTIONS: Unsolicited mss. receive a form rejection. Queries receive a personalized reply.

MODERN MATURITY

AARP
215 Long Beach Boulevard
Long Beach, CA 90802
(213) 432-5781

SOURCE: Florence Gross, articles editor

IN SHORT: Good possibilities, but competitive market.

ABOUT THE MAGAZINE: Bi-monthly. About 40% free-lance–written, but this varies. *Modern Maturity* is the magazine of the American Association of Retired Persons; it is also sent to members of the National Retired Teachers Association. Available only by subscription, the magazine is aimed at the retired and at preretirees, aged 50 and over. It is a general-interest publication with a service orientation. *Circulation:* Over 8 million. *Estimated readership:* Over 13 million. *Sample copy:* Send 50 cents postage. *Areas open to free-lancers:* Everything except AARP business. *Rates:* $300–$2000. *Payment:* On acceptance. *Expenses:* Pays reasonable expenses. *Kill fee:* 25%. *Rights:* Buys all rights, by written contract and check endorsement. Rarely negotiable. *Number of submissions received weekly:* 250–300. *Reply time to queries:* Two to four weeks. *Advance dates:* Lead time is two months. Issues are planned four to six months in advance.

FREE-LANCE POSSIBILITIES: For experienced writers, major features are a possibility. Break-in opportunities on short pieces for departments are a possibility for beginning writers. But competition is strong. Of the 250–300 unsolicited submissions received weekly, less than ten will get a second reading.

It is important to study the magazine and keep the audience in mind. These are *active* older people, many of whom are involved in second careers. They read *Modern Maturity* for entertainment and service. The April-May '82 issue, for instance, carried this mix: "I Covered the Lindbergh Kidnapping," by journalist Adela Rogers St. John, now 88; "Where the Horse Is King—A Tour Through Kentucky's Beautiful Bluegrass Region"; "Thelma Wiliams, 70, Basketball Coach"; "The Worst of Halley's Comet—A Cosmic Chronology of the Troubles It Has Caused"; "In Search of Forty Winks—Sleep Patterns Change with Age: Here's What to Expect and How to Make the Adjustment Easier"; and "When Adult Children Return Home."

Another area for free-lancers is the profile. Profile subjects, who should be in the 50-and-over age group, can be well-knowns, or unknowns of note—like Arabella Williams, who's an active water-skier at 85 (December '81–January '82).

Service features are also welcomed, e.g. "What to Do About Brown Spots" (same issue); "New Kind of Snow Fun—Oldsters Are Finding That Cross-Country Skiing Is the Ideal Fourth-Season Sport" (same issue). Note here that *new* angles on retirement subjects are needed.

"Stories of Our Times" relives interesting historical moments. "Spotlight on People" profiles lesser-knowns. For both departments 750 words is ideal, and the latter is an easier sell if contributions are accompanied by black-and-white photos, or if photography is available.

Florence Gross sees all submissions; decisions are made with the editor. An impressive, appealing query will generally be followed up by a phone discussion, and an assignment will be made. Clips are not required to land an assignment. But if the writer isn't experienced, or if an idea is still undeveloped, on spec may be asked for.

Any necessary rewriting is done by the author. Editing varies, but it can be heavy. Galleys are not shown and writers are not informed on changes.

HOW TO SUBMIT: Manuscripts are accepted (photocopies okay), but short queries are much preferred. Florence Gross cites oversell as one of the common mistakes she sees in queries. Include a brief explanation of writing qualifications. Clips are not required, and sending a lot of clips doesn't help. SASE is required: "We won't reply as readily without one." *Note:* "Writers who pester are a bore. One call to be certain material has arrived is permissible, but constant checking is annoying."

REJECTIONS: A standard form is used. Personalized replies are often sent "when the writer deserves more special attention." Gross will also often suggest alternate markets to writers.

MONEY

Time, Inc.
1271 Avenue of the Americas
New York, NY 10020
(212) 586-1212

SOURCE: Joseph S. Coyle, senior editor

IN SHORT: Open, but difficult to sell. Experienced writers have best chances.

ABOUT THE MAGAZINE: Monthly; 10–15% free-lance–written. *Money* is a magazine of personal finance that covers investment, taxes, spending (large-purchase goods, services), money saving, careers, and travel. The magazine has a people-oriented editorial slant. *Readership:* 60% male, 40% female. Readers' median age is in the mid 40s. Readers are middle to upper middle in income. *Circulation:* 1,100,000. *Estimated readership:* 3.6 million. *Areas open to free-lancers:* All feature articles. *Rates:* $1500 minimum for articles. *Payment:* Half on acceptance, remaining half on editing. *Expenses:* Pays all incidentals. *Kill fee:* 25%. *Rights:* Buys all rights, by written contract. Not negotiable. Sixty-day postpublication time limit placed on subject matter of article. *Number of submissions received weekly:* "Professional submissions —no more than a couple." *Reply time to queries:* Two to four weeks. *Advance dates:* Lead time is one month. Issues are planned at least three months in advance.

FREE-LANCE POSSIBILITIES: *Money* relies heavily on its staff writers (this is a substantial group) and a few regular contributors. Of the 20-odd features run monthly, two to three are free-lance–written and only one—in a good month—has a newcomer's byline. But the editors are trying to find more free-lancers who have the talent and responsiveness to become regular contributors. There is not a lot of free-lance competition. "We're not getting a *lot* of ideas over-the-transom," Joseph Coyle comments. And if your idea is appealing, you do not have to show major magazine clips to get a go-ahead. Says Coyle: "We do try writers who are unknown to us. Most of the time the experiences aren't good. But we continue to do it because we want to throw the nets out as wide as possible for ideas. And secondly, you just never know. . . ."

Still this is not a beginner's market. New writers who break in tend to be fairly seasoned, with a dynamic idea. It's that kind of combination that has the best chance here. Coyle advises: "*Money* writing is very demanding—both in the prose and in the sophistication of the information and the approach. You've got to have a point and you've got to be able to sustain that point. You've got to have control in both the reporting and the writing, and that's something that really comes from experience."

The best area for the free-lancer is life-style, especially the catching of a trend. "A free-lancer came to us with an idea for a piece on parents who are buying apartments in college towns and allowing their college-student–children to live in them. It turned out to be a trend we hadn't noticed. Catching a trend can create a fresh story and really make us sit up and take notice. We went with another over-the-transom idea like this earlier on grown children coming home to reroost rather than moving out of home for ever. The life-style story will work for us if it's an emerging trend and one that hasn't been overwritten elsewhere. Some of our best material comes in that way. It's the kind of material that's available; it comes out of everyday life, the kinds of things you see among your family and friends. It can be such a rich source of ideas. And you can do the story without having to scour the country for information. Life-style is the area where free-lancers probably best connect with us."

The back-page stock picker "*Money* Profile" is open to free-lancers, but Coyle comments: "You have to be a fairly experienced business writer to do one of these." The short-take departments are not open at *Money*. "Money Letter," "Current Accounts," "Moneymakers," and "Top Deals" are all staff-written. Roundup features, a *Money* favorite, are almost always staff-done because of the logistics involved in locating and highlighting a half-dozen people, or couples, in diverse areas of the country. Travel is not a good bet, simply because it's not done, feature-length, very often. When travel is covered, "it has to be a pretty special piece" and it must be money-oriented. Past examples: barging through Europe for a cheaper, less conventional vacation and how the dollar situation is making the alpine ski package financially viable.

A good area for ideas is in investment: this covers art, oil and gas, land, etc., as well as stocks. Here, however, it should be remembered that *Money* is a personal consumer magazine.

What's not wanted is an angle or approach that would be better directed to the business magazines.

If an idea is appealing and the writer is experienced, chances are he will get an assignment, and that the piece will be used fairly fast. "We order stories for specific issues. And we don't have a large inventory." Writers are seldom asked to work on spec; it happens if the editors aren't too sure about the writer's ability to handle the piece suggested. It's a fine line here. Good clips can often be the determining factor. Without them, you must be able to present a good query and back it up with knowledge and information. The main reasons for rejection here are: "The idea doesn't appeal enough. Or the writer doesn't appeal enough; we get a sense he won't be able to handle the story."

Rewriting is done by the author. Advises Coyle: "Revisions are almost universal." Staff does further editing and fact checking. Generally, the writer is asked to come into *Money*'s offices, if this is feasible, and work with the editors on closing the story.

HOW TO SUBMIT: Mss. are read ("photocopies do make us a little suspicious"), but queries are definitely preferred. Brief queries are best. "If we like the idea, then we'll ask for more detail." Include "a couple of examples of very good writing, preferably the manuscript of the article rather than the clip." Magazine pieces are preferred over newspapers. A word about responses: "We try to get replies out fast. But everything does have to be passed on to the managing editor; so it can take a few weeks. Writers can drop me a note to inquire about a submission."

REJECTIONS: No standard form is used. All responses are personalized. Says Coyle: "I'll make an effort with the reply if I want to encourage the writer, of if I feel he or she has gone to a lot of trouble with the query."

THE MOTHER EARTH NEWS

P.O. Box 70
Hendersonville, NC 28791
(704) 693-0211

SOURCE: Roselyn Edwards, submissions editor

IN SHORT: A very good market for writers willing to work on spec.

ABOUT THE MAGAZINE: Bi-monthly. A little less than 50% free-lance—written. A "no frills" magazine, covering alternate life-styles, natural health, alternate energy sources, and natural living. Roselyn Edwards describes the content as "back-to-basics and how-to." The magazine is aimed at "today's turned-on people of all ages. The creative ones. The doers. The folks who make it all happen. Heavy emphasis is placed on alternative energy and life-styles, ecology, working with nature, and doing more with less." *Readership* is 59% male, 41% female; median age is 38. Most readers are high-school—educated and 26% have attended college; 81% are married. *Circulation:* 1,050,000. *Estimated readership:* 4 million. *Sample copy:* $3. *Areas open to free-lancers:* All areas are open but the following are generally staff-written: "Economic Outlook," "Last Laugh," "*Mother's* Herb Garden," "Plowboy Interview," and "Seasons of the Garden." *Rates:* Approximately $100 per published page. But the following departments pay in subscriptions: "Successful Swaps," "Bootstrap Businesses," "Getting There." *Payment:* On acceptance. *Expenses:* Included in manuscript/photo package fee. "Exceptions only by advance negotiation." *Kill fee:* "We have never killed an article that was a definite assignment." *Rights:* Buys all rights for *The Mother Earth News'* use (author free to resell article). *Number of submissions received weekly:* 50. *Reply time:* Queries are responded to within a week. Response for mss. may take three months, but editors respond immediately if unacceptable. *Advance dates:* Lead time is at least two months. Issues are planned at least six months in advance.

FREE-LANCE POSSIBILITIES: With the right idea, and if you're willing to work on spec, this magazine is an excellent market. Only about one-third of the ideas are staff-generated; the rest come in over-the-transom. And says Roselyn Edwards: "I believe we're unique in the proportion of material we buy from first-time authors."

For writers with specialties, *Mother Earth News* offers these areas: gardening, old-time and traditional crafts, home decorating, food (recipes and preserving), environment and conversation, holistic health, livestock raising, and workshop projects. A typical issue (July/August '82) carried the following specialized stories: "The Art of Worming for Trout," "Stop Soil Erosion with 'Softflow Screens,' " "A Home in the Wilderness: Survival Cooking," "Build a Bike from Junk," "Building a Cedar Strip Canoe," and "How to Control Garden Pests Without Killing Almost Everything Else."

For the general-interest writer there are article possibilities in small businesses, unusual self-employment enterprises, low-cost ($3000 maximum) shelters, alternative energy projects, energy-efficient homes, smalltown and urban self-sufficiency, and what the magazine calls "down-home adventure and travel." For instance, in the July/August '82 issue, the magazine carried the following stories: "A Barge on the Bayou" (a personal story of a couple who decided to try houseboat living after their home was destroyed in a flood, run as a "Report from Them That's Doin' " —one of the best areas in which to break in over-the-transom); "Run a Rural Ice Delivery Service" (another personal account, discussing a profitable home business); "Alaska: Land of Opportunity?"; and "Backpacking with 'Buggie' "—an article about backpacking with a baby.

Also open to free-lancers are several of the columns and departments, specifically: "Profiles" (250–500 words): articles about interesting people and their accomplishments (examples: a couple in Ohio who are making a living, in their farmhouse, creating and restoring historical stringed instruments; a school-teacher turned performer who now tours schools, teaching with song and slide shows). "Newsworthies": articles about people who have achieved success in a field related to the magazine's philosophy (examples: Congressman Morris Udall and his struggle against Interior Secretary James Watt; actor John Burstein, who as "Slim Goodbody" appears on TV to teach children about good health and eating habits). "Successful Swaps": hints on bartering and skill-and-labor exchanges; "Bootstrap Businesses": short (500-word) reports on successful home businesses that were inspired by an article in *The Mother Earth News*;

"Getting There": travel tips; "Mom's Marketplace": new product information; "Access": short pieces detailing contacts-available information geared to the magazine's life-style.

The magazine *assigns* only staff-generated ideas. Anyone coming in with an idea is required to work on spec, even if the writer has impressive clips to show. But queries from writers willing to work on speculation are welcomed.

The magazine prefers to buy copy/photo packages. Lack of good photos can mean the difference between acceptance and rejection, so photo possibilities should always be kept in mind and submitted with the query or manuscript.

If only timing is off on a submission, the editors may keep the writer's name and idea on file until a more appropriate time. Editing varies; it can be on the heavy side. Rewriting is done on staff. Galleys are not shown.

Roselyn Edwards concludes: "We don't keep track of the frequency with which newcomers break in to the magazine. But quite probably it happens every issue. Chances—with the right idea—are excellent."

HOW TO SUBMIT: Submit to appropriate department editor (e.g. "Successful Swaps" Editor) for the following columns and departments: "Profiles," "Newsworthies," "Successful Swaps," "Bootstrap Businesses," "Getting There," and "Access." Submit "Mom's Marketplace" items to New Products Editor. All other submissions should be sent to Roselyn Edwards.

Send completed mss. (with photos) or query. Photocopied mss. are okay. If multiple submission, "tell us who else is considering the piece." Include in query "enough information to make it possible to evaluate the idea." The editors also like to see a bibliography of the material you have used for information. Clips are not required.

PHOTO REQUIREMENTS: Send color slides in protective-plastic transparency-holder pages. Color should be sent with articles in the following areas: crafts, wild foods, gardening, and decorating. Color prints (with negatives included) are accepted, but reluctantly. Black-and-white 8x10 glossy prints preferred; also include negatives. Include captions and your name on every photo.

REJECTIONS: A standard form is sent, but this is detailed, allowing editors to check the reason for rejection.

MS.

119 West 40th Street
New York, NY 10018
(212) 719-9800

SOURCE: Rhoda Katerinsky, editorial research

IN SHORT: Competitive market; *new* ideas needed.

ABOUT THE MAGAZINE: Monthly; 75% free-lance–written. *Ms.*, the original feminist magazine, started in 1972. Its core of women readers is the 18–34 age group; roughly half are married and half single; more than half have attended college; most are working —about one-third in professional or managerial positions. Interestingly, about one-quarter of the readers are men. *Circulation:* Around 500,000 monthly. *Estimated readership:* 1.5 million. *Areas open to free-lancers:* All. *Rates:* From $25 for a "Gazette" item to $1000 for major reporting story. *Payment:* On acceptance (but allow eight to ten weeks for processing). *Expenses:* Pays all reasonable expenses. *Kill fee:* "Standard." *Rights:* Buys first North American serial rights, by written contract (reverting to author three months after publication). *Number of queries received weekly:* 80–100. *Reply time to queries:* Four to six weeks. *Advance dates:* Lead time is three months. Issues are planned about four months in advance.

FREE-LANCE POSSIBILITIES: The catch in selling to this magazine is to come up with an idea that hasn't been done to death; if it's basic, chances are *Ms.* has covered it already, and if the subject is to be used again, a new "hook" will be needed. It's the idea that's the challenge here.

You don't have to be widely published to be noticed. "Credentials are not what's most important," insists Rhoda Katerinsky, who deals first with all over-the-transom material. "I take each manuscript or query, I read it carefully, and I care only about that particular manuscript or query."

If an idea is accepted, you may be asked to work on spec if you're unknown to *Ms.* editors—"until we can see what you can do." There's rather a shoestring budget here; editorial staff is at a minimum and editing is generally light. Thus, all stories must be exceptionally well written.

Most of the article ideas are generated in-house (only about one slush-pile idea in 50 works out), making it difficult, though not impossible, to break in with a feature. It's easier to try for a "Gazette" piece; what's needed are short "quickies": an update, a what's new, a what's timely. It *must* be informative; this is a news section. (Often "Gazette" pieces are taken, too, from longer articles that haven't materialized into main features; you're competing against those and staff-written material.)

Major profiles go to name/known writers; but there are possibilities with people less in the spotlight. "When we do profiles we talk not just about the woman, though, but also about her work and the times," Katerinsky says. "It's difficult to make a choice when it comes to profiles. There are lots of women out there doing wonderful things. But for us to write about her she has to be doing more than just breaking a stereotype."

Well-documented health and informed arts articles are always good possibilities. Book reviews are done by writers known to the editors. But if you have book-review experience and would like to do *Ms.* reviews, it's worth sending samples.

Personal pieces "have to be so extremely good that they go beyond the cliché. Something may be hurting you but can you write about it in such a way that it will also affect the reader? Personal anecdotes help make a story more textured.

"Humor is another sought-after commodity. It's hard to describe what's funny till you see it, but our readers love to laugh —and so do we." The small sidebars used throughout the magazine are staff-written.

Don'ts: "Whenever there is a political event, we get dozens of badly written manuscripts from earnest, concerned people presenting their opinions. This is a reaction to the six o'clock news; this is not what constitutes a good article. Pastiches and mood pieces do not an article make." Another problem is manuscript length. Often articles are much too long—3000 words is the maximum possible here.

And it's worth taking note of these points: "Our readership is intelligent. They're everyone from teenagers to 80-year-olds. They are not a highbrow intellectual audience, but they're intellectual enough. There's no reason to talk down to them. These are politically aware people; they're definitely today's people. And they're unlikely to also be readers of, say, *Seventeen* or *Woman's Day.*"

HOW TO SUBMIT: Send all submissions, marked either "manuscript" or "query," to "The Editors." Photocopies are okay. Keep queries to one page if possible, and put your name and address on the same page as the query. Clips are "helpful." And courtesy *is* noticed here: "Please remember: An editor's eyes are her livelihood. Don't give us purple ink on green paper. And change those typewriter ribbons!"

REJECTIONS: A form rejection is used but Katerinsky says: "Rest assured everything is read carefully."

NATIONAL ENQUIRER

Lantana, FL 33464
(305) 586-1111

SOURCE: Paul F. Levy, senior editor

IN SHORT: Excellent, well-paying free-lance market. Looking for material.

ABOUT THE PUBLICATION: Weekly; 60% free-lance—written. *National Enquirer* is a mass-market tabloid, sold in supermarkets and at some newsstands. It is a general-interest publication with strong concentration on celebrities, human interest, medical issues, self-help and the offbeat. The editors like news-breaking, controversial stories. The readership is 60% female, 40% male; middle income. *Circulation:* 5¼ million. *Estimated readership:* 21 million. *Areas open to free-lancers:* All. *Rates:* $175–$600, on acceptance. Additional fees paid on publication: $150–$300 extra for page lead; $1000 bonus for main page-one stories. *Expenses:* Pays all incidentals. *Kill fee:* $125 a day. *Rights:* Buys all rights, by check endorsement. *Number of submissions received weekly:* 750. *Reply time to queries:* Three to six weeks. *Advance dates:* Lead time is one to six weeks. Issues are planned three weeks in advance.

FREE-LANCE POSSIBILITIES: The situation here is heartening. Not only is the *Enquirer* a well-paying market, its editors are *very* open to free-lance contributions. Comments Paul Levy: "In the past three years we've used more than 2500 stories from free-lancers around the world. Seventy percent of our pieces come from free-lance queries."

Competition is intense. Some 750 queries are received weekly; only about 10% of these work out. Most are "too long, lacking detail, lacking attribution, of no interest to the paper's editorial policy."

It's important to study the *Enquirer* before submitting, and to note these policies: "All interviews must be tape-recorded; medical-journal articles must be included for a medical story. Every story must have multiple sources; all stories are checked by our research department."

Articles are also totally rewritten in-house. Levy explains this process: "The writer gives us a detailed file—of interview and research notes and the article's rough draft. A staff writer then uses the file to write the finished copy; the file normally runs five to seven pages for every page of the written, finished version." Galleys are not shown.

However, writers are never asked to work on spec. If clips are satisfactory, an assignment is made. If clips are weak, the writer is given a go-ahead, but is paid instead on publication and will then be given another assignment as compensation.

Once in, a writer may be given future assignments generated by the *Enquirer*'s staff. It's also possible to approach the *Enquirer* with bio and clips. See "Portfolios and Positive Thinking," pages 7–9.

HOW TO SUBMIT: Send submissions to "The Editor" or to a specific department editor. Phone queries are discouraged: "Call only if the story has immediate news value." No photocopied manuscripts are read. Queries are preferred to manuscripts. "The query should be three to four sentences maximum, giving main point, source of idea, and backup (doctors, etc.) who will support it." Include clips.

REJECTIONS: A form reply is sent, which is sometimes personalized; phone calls are also made.

NATIONAL GEOGRAPHIC

National Geographic Society
17th and M Streets N.W.
Washington, DC 20036
(202) 857-7000

SOURCE: A submissions editor

IN SHORT: One of the hardest markets to sell.

ABOUT THE MAGAZINE: Monthly; 50% free-lance–written. *National Geographic,* the publication of the National Geographic Society, is devoted to travel, exploration, and discovery throughout the world, and is renowned for its text/photo coverage of exotic people and places. It is available only by subscription (actually, membership in the Society). *Readership:* slightly more male readers than female; the median age of men is 42, of women 44; close to half have attended/graduated college; readers' income is middle to high. *Circulation:* 8.5 million in U.S., with another 2 million worldwide. *Sample copy:* $1.90 (recent issues). *Areas open to free-lancers:* All. *Rates:* Pays top rates. *Payment:* On acceptance. *Expenses:* Pays all incidentals. *Kill fee:* Generally 50%. *Rights:* Buys one-time world magazine rights, by written contract. Negotiable. *Number of submissions received:* About 500 a month. *Reply time to queries:* Depends on urgency of query. Timely submissions receive immediate replies. Replies to less timely submissions could take up to two months. *Advance dates:* Lead time is four months.

FREE-LANCE POSSIBILITIES: *National Geographic's* articles blaze trails and its editors are willing to take a chance on a new writer with an appropriate idea. They won't ask free-lancers to work on speculation; they'll give assignments, for which they'll pay top rates. Said the editor interviewed: "Our attitude is: if we're not willing to invest in a story, then let's not go with it."

Statistically, free-lance opportunities appear heartening: half of the article ideas come from the outside; regular free-lancers number only 15–20; half the magazine is written by free-lancers, and in an average issue one or two of the writers are likely to be newcomers.

But there are a few catches at *National Geographic:* Standards are very high. The chances of an unpublished or little-published writer doing a piece are extremely slim; most people who break in here are *experienced* magazine or newspaper feature writers. Also, a large inventory of articles is maintained. At most times there are likely to be about 80 text/photo pieces waiting for space; as a result it can take two to three years in some cases for a story to appear.

And many good story ideas must be rejected for what the editor termed "one enormous caveat": lack of first-rate photography. Assigning a photographer to illustrate an over-the-transom story idea generally means a substantial financial commitment on the magazine's part, particularly if an overseas locale is involved; this will only be done for ideas genuinely and enthusiastically wanted. "Going out and doing the story only, without pictures, is extremely risky," the editor commented. So, if your idea is not one that is so unique or appealing you know the editors won't be able to resist it, the best way to approach *National Geographic* is to offer them a text/photo package. That's the way writer Robyn Davidson and photographer Rick Smolan broke in with "Alone Across the Outback" (May '78). A first-rate writer/photographer team has the best chances here. Said the editor: "I would urge the free-lancer to get together with a photographer who has an excellent portfolio, then approach us."

When thinking of story ideas, it's important to note that while a particular place may sound remote, exciting, and exotic, chances are it has already been, or is in the process of being, covered by a *Geographic* staffer. Said the editor: "There really are very few unexplored, exotic places left. You have to try and come up with a real focus. Usually, the smaller the focus the better."

National Geographic stories are also written by writers who are experts on their chosen subject. "Often we'll reject a submission because we'll feel the writer doesn't know the subject well enough. A lot of people want to take on too much. If you approach us with: 'I've been doing a lot of reading about Sierra Leone and I'd like to do a story on it,' if you don't *know* the place, it's unlikely we'll take the chance on you. Natural history and adventure are really successful categories for us, but for both of them you need to know your stuff." For instance, Eleanor Storrs broke in to the magazine in the June '82 issue with "The Astonishing Armadillo." Storrs has been conducting biochemical research on the animal for the past 18 years.

One story in, and it's likely you'll still have to come up with your own future story ideas; there's a large, able staff here.

HOW TO SUBMIT: Queries are required ("Don't ever send the manuscript"). Phone queries are accepted. "If there's a ghost of a chance, however, I'll ask you to send me a written proposal." Multiple submissions are okay. Queries should be "short, but sufficient." Include details of your professional background. "Don't include clips. If we're interested in your idea, then we'll ask to see writing samples." Possible ideas go before a group of 10–12 editors, who meet once a month on the average; hence the length of the reply time. Unless you have sent an urgent query, don't call. "There's really no point."

REJECTIONS: Personalized replies go to those contributors seen as professionals. "It means courtesy only." Worth noting: "If an idea is not acceptable today, it probably won't be next year either."

NEW WOMAN

P.O. Drawer 189
Palm Beach, FL 33480
(305) 833-4583

Monthly. Covers fashion and beauty, health, finances, careers, life-styles, relationships, self-growth. Highlights achieving women. Uses mostly reprints. Declined to participate. Editor/publisher: Margaret Harold Whitehead.

NEW YORK

755 Second Avenue
New York, NY 10017
(212) 880-0700

SOURCE: Laurie Jones, managing editor

IN SHORT: Very competitive, focused market. Not easy to break in.

ABOUT THE MAGAZINE: New York City's weekly magazine, *New York* covers the metropolitan area. Emphasis is on city life-style, issues, and personalities—geared mainly (but not exclusively) to the apartment dweller living in Manhattan. Roughly half the readers are male, half female. *Circulation:* 410,000. *Estimated readership:* 1.27 million. *Areas open to free-lancers:* All articles. (Columns and reviews are all staff-written.) *Rates:* $850–$1500 (higher rates paid for features; lower for service articles). *Payment:* On acceptance. *Expenses:* Pays all incidentals. *Kill fee:* $150. *Rights:* Buys all rights, by written contract. Negotiable. *Number of submissions received weekly:* 100. *Reply time to queries:* Two to three weeks. *Advance dates:* Lead time is one week. Issues are planned only a few weeks in advance.

FREE-LANCE POSSIBILITIES AND HOW TO SUBMIT: *New York* has a fairly large staff and a long, impressive list of contributing editors. It's stiff competition for the free-lancer, particularly if you're unknown. Only about one in 100 over-the-transom submissions is pulled for further consideration.

Still, the editors *are* open to newcomers. Most important is the right idea. The magazine is interested in personality profiles such as "Maxwell Caulfield—The Next Overnight Sensation" (March 22, '82); "The Young and the Riklis" (January 25, '82)—a piece on actress Pia Zadora and her husband Meshulam Riklis; "The Princess of Playboy" (June 21, '82)—a profile of Christie Hefner; "Amanda of Broadway: It's All in the Genes" (May 10, '82)—a profile of Amanda Plummer; "The New Queen of the Art Scene" (April 19, '82)—a profile of Mary Boone, art dealer. The key here is New York personalities, or, in the case of show-business people, entertainers who are or will be appearing in New York. But forget the Westbury Music Fair brand of visiting celebrity. And forget big stars or personalities unless you're able to get a truly exclusive interview. Think ahead of up-and-coming personalities; just make sure they're headed to the top. Profiles of interesting New Yorkers who are less well known are also a possibility.

Some examples of the magazine's investigative, exposé pieces include "The Met's Own Foreign Affair" (March 29, '82)—the story behind the Metropolitan Museum's cancellation of an archaeological exhibit from Israel; "Trouble Boys" (August 30, '82)—a two-part article questioning the guilt of four teenagers accused of murdering a neighborhood youth; "A Message for Tony" (August 16, '82)—the mystery behind the slaying of a Citicorp executive. Here, look for unusual angles or particular connections you might be able to use to get somebody to talk only to *you*.

Health/medical/behavioral topics that have been done in the magazine include "Conquering Pain—New Treatments, New Hope" (March 22, '82); "Stress Can Be Good for You" (August 2, '82); "The Subway Syndrome" (August 9, '82).

Some examples of published life-style articles include "Attitude" (July 26, '82)—a story about the life-style of the eighties, following the protest of the sixties and the narcissism of the seventies; "Downward Mobility—You Thought You'd Live Better Than Your Parents Did. Wrong" (August 16, '82).

How-to service pieces that have been published include "How to Hire a Pro—Lawyer, CPA, Investment Adviser, Decorator" (January 25, '82); "How to Find the Right Pediatrician for Your Child" (May 10, '82); "Protecting Yourself Against Crime" (February 8, '82); "Adult Education—How to Find the Best Courses" (August 30, '82).

New York also publishes tales of the city. Some recent pieces include "The End of the Rainbow—A Texas Dream Dies in a Columbus Avenue Boutique" (July 19, '82); "The Collector—How a Quiet Doctor Squirreled Away Millions in Stolen Art Treasures" (May 31, '82); and "Breaking Up—A Tale of the Hamptons" (June 14, '82).

The best approach is to submit your idea to Laurie Jones. (Jones reads all submissions and makes decisions with editor Ed Kosner.) What she prefers is a short, succinct query; if there's interest she will contact you requesting an expansion of the idea. Include a couple of clips with your original query. If the idea's right and your clips are impressive, you'll get an assignment. But clips must be of a high standard. Without impressive clips, you have two choices. (Jones will ask for a piece on spec only "if I'm reasonably enthusiastic about the idea and the writer's ability to pull it off"), or send in a completed manuscript in the first place. "Although I prefer to read queries over manuscripts, the writer who has had no connection with the magazine and whose work is unknown to us probably has a better chance approaching us with a manuscript," she concedes. Photocopied mss. are okay, but no multiple submissions.

What gets a fast rejection? "Query letters that haven't been proofread; spelling errors and messy queries are off-putting. Poorly written query letters that don't give enough detail. Ideas that are very similar to ones we've just done; if we run a piece on a particular subject, that's that; we're not likely to want to do a similar piece for a very long time. Ideas about people and events that have little to do with New York. Sending us a piece you've had published elsewhere, asking if you can rewrite it for us. Phone queries. Asking us: 'How much will you pay?' before we talk about anything else. Calling up and asking us our address. Obvious mistakes in queries that show us you aren't familiar with the magazine or haven't read it for a long time."

A standard rejection slip is never used at *New York*. Each reply is individually typed. You will be told the reason for rejection, and words of encouragement will be meant.

Very careful fact checking is done here on articles. Writers are shown galleys before publication.

A new writer's article makes it into *New York* about once every couple of months. Half of these articles turn out to be one-shots. The writers of the other half will go on to write more for the magazine; some will even be asked to write a staff-generated piece. But while one piece in the magazine is a nice credit, it does not ensure an open door in the future. If you publish once in *New York*, you'll still have to keep the standards high to get in again.

NEW YORK SUNDAY NEWS MAGAZINE

220 East 42nd Street
New York, NY 10017
(212) 949-1234

SOURCE: Pucci Meyer, editor

IN SHORT: Limited possibilities; chances are best for experienced writers. New York slant required.

ABOUT THE MAGAZINE: Weekly; 25–50% free-lance–written. *New York Sunday News Magazine* is the Sunday magazine of the *Daily News,* "of local (New York metropolitan area) interest, covering all subjects—from politics to life-style, from crime to fashion, food and home." *Circulation:* About 2 million. *Areas open to free-lancers:* All. *Rates:* $600 for articles of 2500 words. *Payment:* Just prior to publication. *Expenses:* Pays limited expenses. *Kill fee:* $150. *Rights:* Buys first publication rights, verbally (in writing if requested). *Number of submissions received weekly:* 50. *Reply time to queries:* One to two weeks. *Advance dates:* Lead time is six weeks. Issues are planned two months in advance.

FREE-LANCE POSSIBILITIES: "We are always open to good writing and good ideas," comment the editors here. But while about 25% of the articles do come from outside writers, it's not often that new writers break in. Nonstaff articles tend to be written by experienced writers with very good clips; clips are always requested before assignments are given. Without impressive clips, the story idea is likely to be dropped; it's "unusual" for a writer to work on spec.

The editors emphasize the importance of "reading the magazine and being familiar with its format and approach." A New York angle is needed, and a straightforward writing style is required.

The magazine often runs on-the-scene pieces of various areas within, say, the New York City Police or Fire Departments; real-life drama stories that highlight New Yorkers who aren't celebrities; and trend stories. The one area where the editors would like to discourage queries is celebrity interviews (inventory here is generally very strong).

Any required rewriting is done by the author. The extent of editing varies. Galleys are shown if time allows.

HOW TO SUBMIT: Both completed manuscripts (good photocopies okay) and queries are accepted. Simultaneous submissions are discouraged. Preferred query length is one-half to one page; include an "angle and news peg." Also include clips.

REJECTIONS: Standard rejections forms are usually sent.

THE NEW YORK TIMES SUNDAY MAGAZINE

229 West 43rd Street
New York, NY 10036
(212) 556-1234

SOURCE: The editors here preferred not to be named.

IN SHORT: Very difficult, competitive market.

ABOUT THE MAGAZINE: Included weekly with the Sunday edition of *The New York Times*, the magazine is aimed at an intellectual audience, *nationally.* Issues covered and people profiled are all of national/international stature and of political/cultural/social significance. Main articles typically run 3500–5000 words. *Areas open to free-lancers:* All articles. (Design, fashion, food, and wine are generally all staff-written.) *Rates:* $1500 and higher. *Payment:* On acceptance. *Expenses:* Pays reasonable expenses. *Kill fee:* $250. *Rights:* Buys first North American serial rights, by written contract. *Number of submissions received weekly:* 300–400 manuscripts, 150 queries. *Reply time to queries:* Four to six weeks. *Advance dates:* Lead time is four to six weeks. Issues are planned one to two months in advance.

FREE-LANCE POSSIBILITIES: The magazine gets some 300–400 manuscripts on an average week, and 150 queries. If you dare work that out on a yearly basis, the total comes to a startling 15,000-plus manuscripts and over 7000 queries.

Over the past three years, only five or six unsolicited submissions have seen print. Still, the editors *do* have some encouraging words: "We're always looking for new writers; we have no regular stable. We always read the unsolicited submissions with the hope of finding something we can use." Joyce Colony submitted an unsolicited personal essay in defense of domesticity which was published in the *Magazine* as "Diary of a Glad Housewife" (December 6, '81). Andrea Lee, who had been educated at Harvard, went to Russia, taught there, and returned to tell her story—"An English Lesson for Moscow Jews" was published in the September 7, '80 issue. Lorian Hemingway, one of Ernest Hemingway's granddaughters, sent in a proposal, unsolicited, on marlin fishing. It was commissioned and published in the September 21, '80 issue as "The Young Woman and the Sea." Essentially, either you have to be a known writer, or you have to come up with something that is so unusual only *you* can write it. As the editors point out: "The unsolicited submissions that *have* worked out have mostly been personal accounts, written really well, with depth and insight." Forget profiles. "We're talking about writing 5000 words on a subject. The author is going to have to have the experience and the background for us to assign something like that."

Some reasons for rejection: "A lot of the time the ideas being suggested are too local; we have a national orientation. Often, too, the ideas are either too trivial or else too embarrassingly personal. But the caliber of the writing is the biggest thing that works against almost all of the submissions. You have to have the right article idea and you have to be able to write *extremely* well to be considered."

If an editor spots a submission with possibilities, it's carefully considered by several other editors. It all adds up to a grueling test.

HOW TO SUBMIT: Send all submissions addressed simply to "The Articles Editor." Manuscripts are accepted (photocopies okay), but queries are preferred—short ones ("a précis of about a page"). Include your writing background, your qualifications for the story, and one clip. If the story would require interviews, indicate the *kinds* of people you would approach.

REJECTIONS: Standard forms are generally used. However, "the better the writer, the more promising the proposal, and the more seriously it was considered—the more likely you are to get a personalized reply."

THE NEW YORKER

25 West 43rd Street
New York, NY 10036
(212) 840-3800

SOURCE: The editor interviewed here preferred not to be named.

IN SHORT: A market for very few writers.

ABOUT THE MAGAZINE: Weekly; 10–25% free-lance–written. *The New Yorker* is a weekly magazine famous for its reporting pieces, reviews, essays, fiction, poetry, drawings, and cartoons. From its inception in 1925, the magazine has consistently published articles and fiction that meet the highest literary standards, and has introduced many of this century's leading writers. Circulation is over 500,000. *Areas open to free-lancers:* Profiles and other articles; fiction; and poetry. ("Talk of the Town" and reviews are staff/contributor written.) *Rates:* $4000 minimum for full-length articles. *Payment:* On acceptance. *Expenses:* Pays "anything agreed upon in advance." *Kill fee:* Not applicable. *Rights:* Buys first world rights, by check endorsement. *Number of submissions received weekly:* Hundreds. *Reply time to queries:* Can take several weeks. ("Call after a few weeks.")

FREE-LANCE POSSIBILITIES: Said the editor interviewed here: "We want writers to feel that *The New Yorker* is open to them if they have a piece that is a *New Yorker* piece and if they're capable of writing it. We don't want to feel that we're sealed off. We don't care about names and credentials. We care only about the talent and ability of the writer."

But the facts are these: *The New Yorker* is probably the best—and hardest—place for a writer to make his mark. In an average year, only eight to ten articles would result from over-the-transom approaches, proving chances here to be very limited, for two reasons. Staff writers number about 75 and, amazingly, finding space for these writers' work in the magazine is a problem. The other limiting factor is the obvious one. The editor conceded: "The article idea has to be an irresistible one." And the quality of the writing has to be outstanding.

There is actually no distinction made between staffers and

free-lancers; the assignment process—which is a unique one—applies to both kinds of writers. Nothing is commissioned. Technically, all work is done on speculation, with editorial right to accept or decline. But here the editor made this clarification: "Each assignment—what we term 'an approved project'—is a very serious one. We never consider anything lightly. And when we give a writer our encouragement, the piece is almost certain to work out. We do everything possible to make a manuscript work."

Each "assigned" subject is reserved for the writer—indefinitely. Such reservations have been known to last 20 years, and lapse only when the writer informs the editors he will not be going ahead with the manuscript. Until the writer makes this decision, the subject will not be "assigned" to any other writer.

Although the editor interviewed stressed that *all* submissions —"every letter, every manuscript"—are read and considered, he added: "What's rarest is for somebody to send in a manuscript and have it published. Writers should send us a query first—because 99 out of 100 ideas would be wrong for us. The *best* possible procedure is to send us an outline." Outlines should be detailed, anything from a few sentences to several pages. "The outline is all-important; in a certain way, the longer the better. We're then able to get an idea of what the writer's approach to the subject is and what kind of mind the writer has. . . ."

Writing samples will probably be requested if the writer's work is unknown to the editors. "If we're familiar with the writer's work through reading it elsewhere, that takes care of that. But if it's a writer we're not familiar with, we would always like to see samples. Sometimes we will take chances on writers; we've published people who've written only for a newspaper or college paper. We'll take a chance if the writer is talented and looks as if he could develop into a *New Yorker* writer. The point is: There are writers who are talented and who write well but because of their particular tone or style can't write for *The New Yorker*. Both subject and the writer have to be right for *The New Yorker*."

It can take a year or two for a piece to appear.

Commented the editor: "We're not actively seeking nonstaff pieces, but we think it's very important to keep the door open."

HOW TO SUBMIT: Send all submissions to "The Editors." Writers are not encouraged to submit to individual editors. Photocopied manuscripts are accepted. Clips are not required at query stage.

REJECTIONS: A standard rejection form is used.

NEWSWEEK

444 Madison Avenue
New York, NY 10022
(212) 350-2000

The only area open to free-lancers in this staff-written weekly news magazine is the "My Turn" column. This is a regular personal opinion column, running one page (1000–1100 words). The following information pertains only to "My Turn": *Rates:* $1000. *Payment:* On publication. *Rights:* No rights bought. *Number of submissions received weekly:* 500. *Reply time:* Up to a month.

There are no specific guidelines for "My Turn"; all subjects are considered. No reprints are accepted. And manuscripts are not accepted from people either in, or campaigning for, political office. No queries are accepted; contributors should send the completed manuscript, with return postage, to "My Turn Department."

NORTHWEST ORIENT

The Webb Company
1999 Shepard Road
St. Paul, MN 55116
(612) 690-7295

SOURCE: Jean Marie Hamilton, editor

IN SHORT: Limited feature possibilities. Better chances with columns.

ABOUT THE MAGAZINE: Monthly; 90% free-lance–written. *Northwest Orient* is the in-flight magazine of Northwest Orient Airlines. Says editor Jean Marie Hamilton: "We're most interested in travel and business/management topics. Science, finance, sports, and health are also important. And arts and culture rate high because our readers are affluent." *Readership:* 68% males, 32% females; 41% are aged 35–49; 60% have graduated college; 66% are in professional/managerial positions. *Circulation:* 150,000. *Estimated readership:* 421,000. *Sample copy:* $2. *Areas open to free-lancers:* All. *Rates:* Columns (800–1500 words); $200–$300. Features (2000–3000 words): $300–$1000. *Payment:* On acceptance. *Expenses:* Pays documented expenses, agreed in advance. *Kill fee:* 25%. *Rights:* Buys all rights (lasting 60 days after publication), by written contract. Not negotiable. *Number of submissions received weekly:* 30. *Reply time to queries:* One to two weeks if being rejected; a month or more if accepted/under consideration. *Advance dates:* Lead time is two months. Issues are planned in six-month groupings, about six months in advance.

FREE-LANCE POSSIBILITIES: Some 60–75% of the magazine's column ideas come in over-the-transom from writers with major magazine exposure and from less-credentialed writers. A column idea is the best way into *Northwest Orient*. Subject areas: science, personality profiles, sports, health, cities, personal finance, travel, the arts, books, coping. A "Pop Quiz" is also run occasionally; specialist psychology writers are encouraged to submit ideas for this.

Hamilton offers these guidelines for personality profiles: "Profile subjects should be truly outstanding or unique in their field. They should be people who are making significant contributions to society, who affect the way we live, or who add to our entertainment value." *Northwest Orient* has profiled Buckminster Fuller, Judith Guest, Dick Cavett, Ellen Goodman.

As for submitting a travel idea, Hamilton says: "In the travel field, we try not to do the obvious travel stories. We need a real angle." (Travel pieces have included: the gentlemen's clubs of London, the Seattle-Asian business boom, the deepest China that so far has eluded the tourist throngs.) "The number-one rule is: If the airline doesn't fly there, we won't be interested. This point should be an obvious one by now, but amazingly many writers still haven't caught on." (Editorial guidelines, available with a business-size SASE, list Northwest Orient Airlines destination cities.)

Only one or two main features a year are the result of over-the-transom submissions, and the authors tend to be experienced. Three examples are: "Finding Your Place in the Sun," an article on solar developments, in the March '81 issue; "In Scotland with James Michener," in the October '80 issue; "The Oil Money Market," September '80.

No essays, please, and no more humor. Jean Marie Hamilton adds: "Some writers think that having been on vacation is the basis for a wonderful article. Writing is *work*, not a vacation."

Hamilton will make an assignment (1) if clips are satisfactory and (2) if the article can be slotted into her issue schedule. "I hate to have a big story backlog, no matter how good they are," she explains. A writer will only be asked to work on spec "if I may, perhaps, be thinking of featuring a story on some topic and a writer with little experience or credentials submits that very idea. I'll then go with the writer on speculation. If the manuscript is poor, the story idea is dropped."

Manuscripts are returned to the author for any necessary rewriting. Editing varies. Galleys are shown "if the article is a complicated one, or if the author requests it."

HOW TO SUBMIT: Manuscripts are accepted, but queries are preferred. Multiple submissions are accepted on queries, but not manuscripts. Short queries are preferred. Personal details are not needed "unless it directly applies to the story topic." Include a rundown of your writing experience, and three or four clips. SASE required.

REJECTIONS: A standard rejection form is sent to most contributors. A personalized reply will be sent "if it's a good idea but we just don't have the space for it. If it's an idea that just didn't quite make it. When we hold something awhile for consideration, and then decline it, we feel an explanation is in order."

OMNI

909 Third Avenue
New York, NY 10022
(212) 593-3301

SOURCE: Paul Hilts, managing editor

IN SHORT: Specialized market, but good possibilities with the right idea.

ABOUT THE MAGAZINE: Monthly; 80% free-lance–written. Published by Bob Guccione/*Penthouse*, *Omni* is a magazine of the future. Comments Paul Hilts: "We write about what's going to happen in the future, based on the science and technology of now. We're a science magazine, but we're not like, say, *Scientific American*. We're read by people with an interest in what's happening in the world, but they're not necessarily scientists. We're always looking for the futuristic angle, how today's developments are going to change the world. So we do almost no coverage of natural sciences or earth sciences, the things that are happening now—unless they relate to the future." *Readership:* 63% male, 37% female; median age: 20.4; readers are mostly college-educated; average income is $28,500. "Readers are everyone from college students—who love the fiction—to the older folks who are professionals, engineers, etc.—who just want to keep up with what's happening in the world." *Circulation:* 800,000. *Estimated readership:* 4.5 million. *Areas open to freelancers:* Everything except "Games." *Rates:* "Continuum" (200 words): $75–$100. Front-of-the-book columns (800 words): $500–$800. Features (2500–5000 words): $1500–$2000. *Payment:* On acceptance. *Expenses:* Pays all reasonable expenses. *Kill fee:* 25%. *Rights:* Buys first worldwide periodical rights (English language), and first rights in other languages for one year after English language publication. Also buys open-ended nonexclusive worldwide rights, and nonexclusive licensee rights. By written contract. Negotiable. *Number of submissions received weekly:* 100. *Reply time to queries:* One to two weeks. *Advance dates:* Lead time: 2½ months. Issues planned five to six months in advance.

FREE-LANCE POSSIBILITIES: You do not have to be an experienced magazine writer to be published here; clips are much less important than the article idea. And Paul Hilts adds: "Once you've been published in *Omni*, your chances of getting in again are increased tremendously."

However, getting that first piece in is difficult in that a new, innovative story idea is required. Most contributors (there are 10–15 regulars) are science/technology specialist writers. "In order to get ideas for a magazine like ours, you have to be around the information sources. You have to read a lot in the field to get one good idea, and then you have to sit down and think about it in depth." But ideas come from both people in the field and from general-interest writers, and all have an equal chance.

A good half of the ideas that lead to features come in over-the-transom. In the June '82 issue, free-lancer Barbara Rowes wrote "Housewives in Space," a piece about NASA placing want ads in newspapers and supermarkets, looking for "ordinary people" to participate in a functioning-in-space testing. In March '82, Dr. Roy Walford, Jr., an immunologist, wrote "Cool Immortality," outlining his technique for cooling the body and thus allowing humans to live longer. It was his first magazine piece.

However, there are generally only four features run per issue. So chances are better in areas like "Continuum" ("This is a good area to get known. We want odd little bits; the writing doesn't have to be particularly flashy"); "Last Word" (the back-page humor column; send ms. here rather than a query); or in the 16–20 columns run monthly ("Column ideas mostly come from outside the magazine").

"Interview" is a possibility, too, but Hilts advises: "You really have to know what you're talking about beforehand." Most "Interview" subjects are scientists, but they don't have to be; subjects *have* included personalities like publisher Malcolm Forbes, and General Sir John Hackett, who wrote a book about World War III.

About 100 submissions are received weekly, but Paul Hilts estimates only 30% of these come from "serious writers writing serious proposals." Of these, 10–20% end up in the magazine (four to five pieces appear monthly by newcomers). Hilts also says: "Probably 5–10% of stories end up the way the author originally intended them." Writer/editor discussions are what tend to make the difference here, rather than the amount of editing involved. "If an editor thinks your idea has promise, three or four editors will discuss it. Then an editor will call the writer to discuss it in more depth and to give direction. We don't always ask to see clips; we're interested in how well you express yourself, either on the phone or in your proposal. Editing is to be expected if you've never written for us before. But we edit a lot less heavily now than we used to because we like to give the writer a lot more in the way of specific guidelines."

Most work is done on assignment. But sometimes writers *are* asked to work on spec "if they've never published before, or if their idea of the story differs significantly from ours."

Hilts cites as "the single biggest problem" with over-the-transom submissions "the lack of a fully developed idea." He adds: "Just being excited about a story idea is not enough to get you into *Omni*. You have to convince us."

More on editing: "We try to keep all cuts and fills to under ten lines. If we need more than that, we'll go to the author for help." If a rewrite is needed, "we'll give it back to the author. But the manuscript should be pretty close the first time round; the editor does keep in constant contact with the writer. If it takes, say, two complete rewrites, somebody is not communicating." Galleys are shown on request, "for information but not for changes." He adds, however: "Usually we try to tell the writer about any changes we make."

HOW TO SUBMIT: Submit query or ms. to a specific editor listed on the masthead, or to "*Omni* Editorial." (Submissions to the latter are logged; if you call to inquire, a tracer can be put on the submission.) Original mss. are preferred over photo or word-processor copies; multiple submissions are discouraged. Phone queries are accepted, "but the editor will probably still ask for a written query." Queries should be detailed. "It's better if your query is on the longer side; the more writing the editor sees, the better he'll feel about the writer. Tell us your suggested approach; including an outline is ideal. If you haven't written for us before, an outline will really improve your chances. The more specifics you can give us the better; a good, innovative idea backed up by quotes and, if possible, figures, is on its way to getting into *Omni*." Clips are not necessary at query stage.

REJECTIONS: A standard rejection form is used for most submissions; encouraging replies will be personalized. "If we really like a person's writing and it looks like they know what they're doing, we'll generally try to be encouraging."

OZARK

East/West Network
5900 Wilshire Boulevard
Suite 800
Los Angeles, CA 90036
(213) 937-5810

SOURCE: Laura Doss, editor

IN SHORT: Good possibilities for ideas with midwestern slant.

ABOUT THE MAGAZINE: Monthly; 95% free-lance–written. *Ozark* is the in-flight magazine of Ozark Airlines; it is a "general-interest magazine with a strong midwestern base." *Readership: males 60%, females 40%; aged 30–60. Circulation: 40,000. Estimated readership: 200,000. Sample copy: $2.* Write to Dottie Hogan. *Areas open to free-lancers:* All articles and departments except "The Ozark Traveler" and "Outdoors." *Rates:* Columns: $250–$300. Features: $450–$600. *Payment:* On acceptance. *Expenses:* Up to 10–12% of article fee. *Kill fee:* 25%–30%. *Rights:* Buys first North American rights, by written contract. *Number of submissions received weekly:* 15–20. *Reply time to queries:* Two to four weeks. *Advance dates:* Lead time is three months. Issues are planned three to six months in advance.

FREE-LANCE POSSIBILITIES: *Ozark* generally publishes work from experienced writers. But editor Laura Doss comments: "That doesn't mean to say we wouldn't publish a beginner. If I've never worked with a writer before, and if they don't have good clips, I would probably ask them to work on spec. But I don't do that unless I really want the story. And because we run more columns than features, there *are* areas where a beginning writer could try us."

There is a real advantage here, however, if you're a writer located in Ozark Airlines territory. "I'm looking for writers living in the Midwest," Doss explains. "I'm trying to use other writers less; I'd much rather have someone on the scene." (See "Portfolios and Positive Thinking," pages 7–9.

So, for those with midwestern knowledge and a midwestern slant, here are some guidelines: The magazine runs columns covering "Life-style," "Outdoors," "Media," "Business," "Technology," "The Right Stuff," "Sports," and "Hometown." The titles aptly describe the copy. In the June '82 issue, for instance, "Life-style" discussed the return to traditional weddings. "Outdoors" talked about the challenge enjoyed by southwest Missouri fishermen each spring—trying to shoot gar with bow and arrow. "Media" talked about the future of TV news. "Business" can cover any topic relevant to the midwestern traveling executive: anything from foreign stock investments to tax breaks to personalities in business. "The Right Stuff" has published a range of subjects: from a piece on a wonderful car, to art in the Midwest. "Sports" can profile personalities or cover any aspect of midwestern professional or amateur sports.

General-interest features should have an Ozark slant. Of profiles, Laura Doss says: "I'm always looking for midwestern personalities, people with some name recognition in the region." Profile subjects have included: Chicago author Richard Dunlop, who wrote *Donovan: America's Master Spy*, "Garfield" creator Jim Davis, and syndicated columnist Bob Greene. Travel is not a good area for querying on a specific story because, like the other in-flight magazines, travel stories are determined well in advance by the airline. But Doss stresses: "If someone sends me, say, a Nashville piece, I'm probably not going to need it; Nashville has probably already been assigned. But that doesn't mean I wouldn't want to see the piece. Because if it's good, the next time I need a Nashville piece I'll have the writer on file."

Editing: "I try not to edit heavily. I *like* not to edit at all." Galleys are not shown, but writers are informed of any major changes.

HOW TO SUBMIT: Manuscripts are accepted (photocopies okay), but queries are preferred. No preferences on query length. Clips are requested from writers unknown at *Ozark*. Multiple submissions are discouraged, but they will be considered "as long as I know I would be getting first North American rights."

REJECTIONS: All contributors receive a personalized reply letter.

PAN AM CLIPPER

East/West Network
34 East 51st Street
New York, NY 10022
(212) 888-5900

In-flight magazine. Editor: Gayle Welling.

Declined to participate. "We prefer to make our own assignments and accept very little unsolicited material."

PARADE

Parade Publications
750 Third Avenue
New York, NY 10017
(212) 573-7000

SOURCE: Bill Ryan, associate editor

IN SHORT: Open, but competitive market. Uses name writers regularly.

ABOUT THE MAGAZINE: Weekly. Mostly free-lance–written. *Parade* has the largest circulation of any weekly magazine in the world—22½ million—and a readership conservatively estimated at 50 million. It is a general-interest magazine distributed in 134 newspaper Sunday editions throughout the country. *Areas open to free-lancers:* All articles. ("Celebrity Parade," "Intelligence Report," and "Significa" are bought as syndicated packages.) *Rates:* $1000 and up. *Payment:* On acceptance. *Expenses:* Pays all incidentals. *Kill fee:* Negotiable. *Rights:* Buys first North American rights, by written contract. *Number of submissions received weekly:* 200. *Reply time to queries:* Immediately. *Advance dates:* Lead time is six weeks. Issues are planned four to six months in advance.

FREE-LANCE POSSIBILITIES: *Parade* has recently been looking to name writers for cover stories. Ideas are usually staff-generated. There are also about 20 people already writing fairly regularly for the magazine, and each issue contains only three articles. But this is a weekly, and a policy of openness to new writers (and healthy rates) makes this an inspiring market for the free-lancer. About 15% of the articles are done by writers coming over-the-transom.

The way in is with a story idea that will appeal to Sunday readers across the board. Associate editor Bill Ryan cites as an example a piece that came over-the-transom about the mining town of Weirton, West Virginia, and the attempt by the mine workers to save the town from going under by buying it. "The writer originally spotted this as a small newspaper item and suggested the story to us." Another writer suggested a piece on "gray models"—the trend toward using older people in advertising. The story was the writer's first published piece.

If an idea coming over-the-transom appeals to Bill Ryan, he will discuss it with the executive editor, the two will make a decision, and the writer is then contacted. Ryan would like to see a couple of clips with the original query, but it is the quality of the idea and discussions with the writer that will decide whether an assignment is given versus work on spec. "Every once in a while we even ask our regular writers to work on spec. It just depends on the story," Ryan explains.

Of the 200-odd submissions received weekly, only about ten are given a second reading, and only one or two of these work out. Says Bill Ryan: "A lot of people write queries that are too long, too involved and unfocused. You should keep it short and to the point and tell us what you think the story is going to show." The magazine does not run essays, humor, opinion, or personal experience pieces. General topics should have national interest and significance. Profiles must have a particular focus. "We don't do profiles on obscure people. And we don't do straight profiles. We'll never do, say, a profile on Dolly Parton. We like articles with a focus or aim; so a profile should have a news peg (but remember the six-week lead time), a specific angle, or some kind of focus that will make it different from any other old interview. We can usually get to most people. So don't approach us with a piece on Burt Reynolds unless you know something about Burt Reynolds nobody else does. What's needed is a unique angle." Articles generally run 1300–1500 words.

It's mostly generalists writing here, and if you want to write, say, an education piece, you don't *have* to be a specialist. But don't suggest a very technical piece unless you have the right background.

Editing can be heavy here (any rewriting is done by the author), and Bill Ryan adds: "Sometimes we have to do a lot of heavy editing on people who are well-known writers." Regular writers are shown galleys automatically; they will be shown to new writers on request.

One final note: If you get into *Parade,* you'll still have to keep coming up with your own ideas.

HOW TO SUBMIT: Mss. are read (photocopies okay), but queries preferred. No multiple submissions; "ideas should be original and exclusive to us." Send one or two clips; "please, not everything you've ever written." Newspaper clips are okay. "We rely heavily on people with a newspaper background."

REJECTIONS: A standard rejection form is used. "I'll send a personalized rejection to people I think are professional and serious and perhaps could use a little advice," Ryan says.

PARENTS

685 Third Avenue
New York, NY 10017
(212) 878-8700

SOURCE: Phyllis La Farge, managing editor

IN SHORT: Specialized market, but open and receptive to ideas.

ABOUT THE MAGAZINE: Monthly; 50% free-lance—written. *Parents* is a service magazine for young parents, aged 18–34 (average age: around 28). Most readers are married; most have some college education. Readers' interests are focused, to a large extent, on family life and child rearing. All articles are geared to help and instruct, rather than simply entertain. There is a heavy emphasis on the how-to. The magazine also runs pieces written by doctors/experts in the child-rearing field. *Circulation:* 1.65 million. *Areas open to free-lancers:* Feature articles, the "How-To" department, shorter service articles. *Rates:* Articles: minimum $500–$900. Short how-tos for service department: $350. *Payment:* On acceptance. *Expenses:* All reasonable expenses. *Kill fee:* Negotiable. One-third maximum. *Rights:* Buys first North American serial, or all rights, by written contract. *Number of submissions received weekly:* 50. *Reply time to queries:* Two to three weeks. *Advance dates:* Lead time is four months. Issues are planned at least six months in advance.

FREE-LANCE POSSIBILITIES: About half of the features here are written by free-lancers, most of them regular, known writers. A newcomer breaks in with a feature only four or five times a year. But Phyllis La Farge says: "We're always looking for writers who are good, and reliable, and who have good ideas. We're getting more choosy, but we're very much open to ideas from free-lancers."

There's one problem: This is a very specialized market, and a writer trying to break in has to offer either something very new, or else a new slant that will bring a fresh, unique flavor to a topic. And while the focus is a special one, it can't be too narrow. For instance, the editors would be interested in an article on children's earaches (because that's relevant to so many readers and their families). But forget a topic like childhood arthritis;

while it's a worthwhile subject, it won't be right for *most* of *Parents'* readership.

It can be a lot easier to land an assignment here than at many other magazines. A good idea, presented well, can mean an assignment even for a new writer. Assigned work is the general rule here. Phyllis La Farge explains: "I tend to reserve on-spec work for personal experience pieces where I can't really tell just how a piece will work out."

The personal experience piece is welcomed; so is humor. And there's a constant need for article ideas in the areas of child development, health, medicine, psychology, better time management, and ways to make life easier. Also needed are article ideas covering a range of age groups. It *is* possible to break in with a feature, but La Farge's advice is to try first with a shorter, how-to article. In this area there's a need for ideas on crafts (especially if they involve kids), activities and service pieces that cover subjects like safety, household management, and child care. The following ideas came in over-the-transom and were published as features: how to encourage children to appreciate the natural world; a personal piece, written by a father, on settling arguments with his two children; children and eating—the different kinds of eaters.

Phyllis La Farge adds: "To know what kind of magazine ours is, you've got to really sit down and read it. And not just one issue, but four or five. Writing for a service magazine *does* follow a formula. You have to present the idea, one that will be useful and informative to readers, and then back it up with authoritative information and quotes from experts. A lot of submissions have to be rejected because writers send us essays instead of articles."

Editing varies here, although major rewrites are not usual. Writers are not shown galleys.

HOW TO SUBMIT: Send submissions to Elizabeth Crow, editor-in-chief. Completed mss. are read (photocopies okay), but if you haven't written the piece, query first. Present not just the idea but also an indication of the way you would tackle the story; if you have published elsewhere, list your credits. Clips are not necessary, but they won't hurt. Take time and put effort into the query. "You can tell an awful lot from queries" is the attitude here.

REJECTIONS: A standard rejection form is used on general submissions. Submissions to a specific editor receive a form-letter rejection, with personalized notes sent to encourage more submissions in some cases.

PENTHOUSE

909 Third Avenue
New York, NY 10022
(212) 593-3301

SOURCE: Peter Bloch, senior editor

IN SHORT: Very competitive market; very limited possibilities.

ABOUT THE MAGAZINE: Monthly; 95% free-lance–written. One of
the classier of the men's "skin" magazines, *Penthouse* represents
an interesting juxtaposition in content: female picture spreads
with general-interest articles that are in-depth, usually investigative, and mostly hard-hitting and controversial. Subjects range
from nuclear war to child abuse. Also included monthly is an in-
depth interview; the magazine has profiled everyone from movie
stars to senators. As Peter Bloch explains, the editorial aim is "to
entertain and inform, to give readers a magazine that's fun to
read but which also contains information not available elsewhere. We don't have any particular editorial formula. But we
try to break news when it's possible with our lead time; we do a
lot of investigative reporting." Readers range in age, but a high
percentage are in the 18–34 group. They're everyone from
media people and politicians in New York and Washington, to
college students, to urban white-collar professionals, to blue-
collar workers. There are no definite figures on women readers,
but from reader mail Bloch guesses "there are a lot of women
out there reading *Penthouse*. We don't aim all our editorial material only at men; we know that women are concerned with
many of the issues and concerns that are also relevant to men."
Circulation: 4,100,000 in the U.S.; 5 million worldwide. *Areas
open to free-lancers:* All articles (reviews, columns, and quiz are
written by staff/contributing editors). *Rates:* Features: Payment
starts around $2000. *Payment:* On acceptance. *Expenses:* Pays
all reasonable expenses. *Kill fee:* 25%. *Rights:* Buys all (world)
rights, by written contract. Negotiable. *Number of submissions
received weekly:* 100. *Reply time to queries:* Within two weeks
(outright rejections get immediate replies). *Advance dates:* Lead
time is a minimum of three months, generally four to five
months. Issues are planned six months in advance.

FREE-LANCE POSSIBILITIES: *Penthouse* is not an easy market for
one big reason: space limitations. "Ninety-five percent of sub-

missions coming through agents have to be rejected because we just don't have space for them. And I'm rejecting over-the-transom submissions constantly—ones that actually look interesting —just because we don't have the space," Peter Bloch says. Four to five main features are run monthly. These are generally all written by free-lance writers already known at the magazine.

An unknown writer coming over-the-transom has to ask if his idea is strong enough to compete. A good idea backed up by good clips is not enough to get you in here. The idea *really* has to strike the right chord. Says Bloch: "I have very often turned down people with clips from publications like *The New York Times Magazine* or *Playboy*. It's the idea that has to be right."

But *Penthouse* shouldn't be considered a closed market. All submissions are considered, and Peter Bloch says: "If I see a good proposal for an idea that's really right for us, I'll assign the story." Studying a few back issues will give you the clearest idea of the kind of material used. Ideas must be provocative or news making.

Some examples: "The Selling of America," by Ernest Volkman (April '82), discussed the influence Arab and other foreign investors have bought for themselves in the U.S. "The American Cancer Society May Be Hazardous to Your Health," by Allan Sonnenschein (May '82), was an investigation of the Society. In "The Devil's Work" (March '82), Tom Kennedy and his daughter Kate told how he rescued her from the Reverend Sun Myung Moon's cult and of her deprogramming. "The Farce of Courtroom Psychiatry," by John Godwin (August '82), looked at the current, controversial legal hole: innocent by reason of insanity. Peter Bloch comments: "We get a lot of proposals based on something the writer has read elsewhere; they then try to con us into believing they have additional information that would be sensational. We're looking to break news."

There are no set guidelines for the *Penthouse* interview. "The only way to find out who we're interested in is to query us on the subject," Bloch advises. "But subjects have to have name recognition and something to say. Sometimes, though, we will interview people who are not especially famous but whose opinions are interesting." Like Michael Levin, a professor at City College in New York, who discussed torture as punishment (October '82). Other recent subjects have included: novelist Stephen King (April '82); Curtis Sliwa, leader of the New York subway "Guardian Angels" vigilante group (August '82); "Raging Bull" boxer Jake Lamotta (May '82); Robert Leuci, the New York City police officer who uncovered police corruption by working with city officials (January '82); Senator Howard Metzenbaum, "the toughest guy in the U.S. Senate" (November '82); and comedian Dan Aykroyd (January '83).

Writers will be asked to work on spec here "only occasionally —probably only if the idea looks marginal. If a piece would involve several weeks of research, for example, I would never ask anyone to work on spec."

If rewrites are required, they are done by the author "if it's something I think the writer can do and if there's no particular deadline involved." But excessive rewriting doesn't happen here. Galleys are usually shown. Even though the odds of getting published here are long, one article, well received, *will* get you in for the future.

HOW TO SUBMIT: Manuscripts are preferred (photocopied manuscripts okay). Multiple submissions are accepted—reluctantly—but the writer must inform the magazine. Submit feature queries/manuscripts to Peter Bloch. Query Bob Hofler, senior editor, on entertainment; senior editor Jonathan Black on service pieces, fashion, and life-style articles; interview editor Laurie Lister on interviews.

If possible, include three or four representative clips with your query, or else indicate where you have been published and the subject matter. Queries "should usually be no more than one page, single-spaced."

REJECTIONS: Standard rejection slips are sent to most contributors; personalized notes go only to those writers the magazine really wants to encourage. Considering the space problem here, these notes don't go out too often. But now and again Bloch will call a talented writer whose over-the-transom story idea has been rejected to discuss the possibility of tackling another idea.

PEOPLE

Time, Inc.
Rockefeller Center
New York, NY 10020
(212) 586-1212

People is a weekly pictorial magazine that profiles celebrities and people making news. The magazine is mostly staff-written. Occasional free-lance pieces are used, but these are all assigned to writers known to the editors.

PLAYBILL (and SHOWBILL)

American Theatre Press
100 Avenue of the Americas
New York, NY 10013
(212) 966-5000

SOURCE: Louis Botto, senior editor

IN SHORT: Not easy to sell, but open. Theater writers have the best chance.

ABOUT THE MAGAZINE: Monthly. *Playbill* is distributed free to Broadway theatergoers. Each theater has an insert concerning cast and cast/play notes; general theater articles remain constant and include interviews and current show/theater notes, reports, and nostalgia pieces. The magazine is also available by subscription and on newsstands. *Showbill*, like *Playbill*, is a digest-sized magazine, but distribution is in off-Broadway theaters. All *Playbill* information included here applies to *Showbill*—except that off-Broadway, rather than Broadway, is the focus. (*Playbill* is also published in Boston, Florida, and Philadelphia but by licensees, who have access to and use of editorial material purchased for all editions; this material generally first appears in the New York edition.) Circulation is over one million. *Areas open to freelancers:* Everything except "Fashion," "Celebrity Choice," and "At This Theatre." *Rates: Playbill* pays 5–20 cents per published word (lower rates paid to new writers). *Showbill* pays slightly lower rates with a top payment of $250. *Payment:* On acceptance. *Expenses:* None. *Kill fee:* 50%. *Rights:* Buys first North American rights, verbally. *Number of submissions received weekly:* 15. *Reply time to queries:* Immediately to two months. (Call to inquire after a month.) *Advance dates:* Lead time is three weeks.

FREE-LANCE POSSIBILITIES: Roughly 200 free-lance pieces are bought here yearly (from over 900 submissions). This figure includes the work of a number of regular free-lancers, most of them theater specialists. But there *are* possibilities for both the budding theater writer and the generalist.

Best chances are in "A View from the Audience." About 150 submissions are received yearly for this feature; six to eight are bought. The feature runs 750 words (payment is a standard

$100). It's always written essay-style about a play or a musical that has greatly influenced the author, something from which the writer has learned an impressive lesson. Adds Louis Botto: "It should be about a *Broadway* show; we want our readers to be able to identify with the piece, so it should be a show a lot of people would have seen." This is a particularly good area for first-time writers; completed manuscripts are required.

Fillers (about half-page column length) are always wanted. An actor recently sold a piece he'd written on an amusing conversation he had overheard in a play intermission. The "Did You Know?" column is open for trivia and facts about the theater. Roundup articles (e.g. actors who play tennis) are good "if you can get to the subjects. It's not easy," Louis Botto cautions.

An article that requires research could be a good possibility "if it's well done and amusing." In the days when Botto was a free-lancer, he sold one piece to *Playbill* on the really preposterous comments from critics over the years about musical songs that later became big hits; and another on famous theatrical feuds.

Then there are the offbeat personal stories that could amuse theatergoers. One contributor sold a piece (to *Showbill*) about the delights of actually living above a theater, hearing stage words and music as she goes about her daily life, and of sneaking down the stairs to listen in to the latest production. *Playbill* also bought a piece by a woman who had been working behind-the-scenes during the run of Jean Kerr's play *Lunch Hour.* It included an anecdote about a ticketbuyer who hastily hung up after the box office receptionist answered the phone with *"Lunch Hour,"* then called back an hour later to hear the same, and testily inquired, "So when do you people do any work anyway?"

Actor/director/lyricist interviews are *not* a good way into the magazine. Regular writers get these assignments, which depend on whether a new show will have a decent run. Generally, interview subjects are from established shows. "Ninety-nine percent of the time interviews are done by experienced theater writers —people we know," Botto explains. "The only way a writer unknown to us could do an interview (profile) would be to have an 'in' with someone we want but haven't been able to get." (And a query here would not get an assignment; it would have to be done on spec.)

What won't work at *Playbill?* "We have no interest in articles that have no relation to what's *currently* on Broadway. Approaching us with 'I had an opportunity to interview Shelley Winters; would you be interested?' when Shelley Winters is not, or is not going to soon be, on Broadway, won't work. We're not interested in theaters or theater groups that are not in Manhattan. We don't do articles on flops or flop shows; all our articles are upbeat. We don't do articles that are critical of the theater in general or articles about one specific theater. We don't want reviews of plays or books. We don't really use parody or satire; we rarely use verse. And we're not interested in articles on movies, health, travel; it has to be New York theater." And a word of caution: The New York theater is a fairly tight-knit community. Press agents, the connections to the stars, always check with *Playbill* before arranging interviews.

Writers are required to work on spec for the first *Playbill* piece. From then on, assignments are given. Mss. are returned to authors for any necessary revisions, if there's time. Galleys are not shown however.

HOW TO SUBMIT: Send all submissions to Joan Alleman, editor-in-chief. Send manuscripts, not queries, for "A View from the Audience"; on other articles, send query or manuscript (but no photocopied or multiple submissions). Keep queries short; include your writing background and one or two clips, preferably theater-related samples. Because of the first-story-on-spec policy, however, you will not be required to produce extra clips.

REJECTIONS: Personalized replies are sent, specifying reasons for rejection.

PLAYBOY

919 North Michigan Avenue
Chicago, IL 60611
(312) 751-8000

SOURCE: James Morgan, articles editor

IN SHORT: One of the toughest markets, even for a published writer.

ABOUT THE MAGAZINE: Monthly; 60–70% free-lance–written. *Playboy* is a men's magazine, combining female photo spreads with high-quality articles and fiction. The magazine is known for its often-controversial "Interview" subjects and in-depth, investigative/exposé articles. *Readership:* 75% male, 25% female; median age: 31; 59% have attended/graduated college; at least half are married; 55% are professional/managerial, 25% blue-collar; "readers are active participants in 'the good life.' They're interested in travel, sports, music, clothes." *Circulation:* 5 million. *Estimated readership:* 19.4 million. *Areas open to free-lancers:* Everything except book and movie reviews, "*Playboy* Potpourri," "*Playboy* on the Scene," "Grapevine," and "Sex News." *Rates:* Full-length features (about 5000 words): $3000–$5000. *Payment:* On acceptance. *Expenses:* Pays reasonable expenses. *Kill fee:* 20%. *Rights:* Buys all rights on interviews and special columns/sections. On other text, buys all rights until publication. By check endorsement. Not negotiable. (Copyright assigned on request; magazine retains periodical reprint rights, with set time limit.) *Number of submissions received weekly:* 150 queries; 50–100 manuscripts. *Reply time to queries:* Two weeks. *Advance dates:* Lead time is six months. Issues are planned six months in advance.

FREE-LANCE POSSIBILITIES: It's very difficult to break in to *Playboy* if you're an unpublished or little-published writer. There are a number of regular writers here, and newcomers almost always are writers who have written books or had articles published in the major magazines. A writer without a proven track record will break in "very, very infrequently. Probably not even once a year."

Approximately 90% of the article ideas are generated in-house and assigned to regulars. On over-the-transom submissions, clips are requested before assignments are given. If the writer has not been widely published, "but has an innovative, interesting idea," he may be asked to work on spec. This doesn't happen often. Some 250 unsolicited submissions are received weekly; less than 1 percent are successful. James Morgan describes some reasons for rejection: "The writers don't hit us with ideas *we* find relevant at that moment (timing is everything in this business); and they aren't compelling in their proposal of an idea *they* find relevant."

One of the biggest misconceptions is that *Playboy* wants pornographic/erotic articles. In fact, exposé, investigative, and reportage pieces of the highest quality are what's needed. *Playboy*'s writers have included David Halberstam, Arthur Schlesinger, Jr., Philip Caputo, Robert Sam Anson; and the following kinds of articles: "Behind the Lines in the Network News War" (September, '82); "One Last Chance for the Democrats" (November '82); "Campaign of Cunning: The Inside Story of Alexander Haig's Rise to Power" (August '82); "Circle of Deceit: The Hypocrisy of College Athletics" (November '82); "Holy Terror," a look at fundamentalist sects (June '82).

The *Playboy* "Interview" is assigned from the New York office. Chances on this feature are extremely slim; it is almost always assigned to a very experienced writer/interviewer. Exceptions occur when a newcomer approaches the magazine with special access to a personality the editors have been trying to track down; this happened when two Polish sisters were able to get hold of Lech Walesa and sold the interview to *Playboy*. The "Interview" talks with personalities of the caliber of Luciano Pavarotti, Marlon Brando, Muhammad Ali, Patricia Hearst, Jimmy Carter, and Sony founder Akio Morita. Queries are required for "Interview"; reply time is generally one to two weeks.

Rewriting is done by the writer "if we feel revision would be worthwhile." Galleys are shown.

HOW TO SUBMIT: General articles: Completed manuscripts are accepted (photocopies okay), but queries are preferred. Short queries are requested; a more detailed proposal will be asked for if there's interest in the idea. Include: "Briefly, what the author has published and any credentials regarding the subject." Clips are accepted, but not required at query stage. "Interview":

Send query, not manuscript, to Barry Golson, executive editor, in the New York office—747 Third Avenue, New York, NY 10017.

REJECTIONS: Standard forms are used. Personalized replies are sent as a courtesy to widely published authors, when a writer suggests a piece that has been done or is in the works, or when the editors would like to encourage more submissions.

PLAYGIRL

3420 Ocean Park Boulevard
Suite 3000
Santa Monica, CA 90405
(213) 450-0900

SOURCE: Judy Brown, articles editor

IN SHORT: Good possibilities for *published* writers with ideas for in-depth features.

ABOUT THE MAGAZINE: Monthly; 50% free-lance–written. *Playgirl* is a magazine aimed at young women, aged 20–29. It combines nude male centerfolds and erotic vignettes with health and beauty, fashion, and articles on general-interest topics, relationships, self-growth, and celebrities. *Circulation:* 800,000. *Estimated readership:* between 1 and 4 million. *Areas open to free-lancers:* Articles, interviews with major celebrities, "Erotica." (Columns are written by staff/regular contributors). *Rates:* Columns: $300 and up. Features: $750 and up. *Payment:* Within 30 days of final editing. *Expenses:* Pays certain reasonable (documented) expenses. *Kill fee:* 15–20%. *Rights:* Buys all rights, by written contract. Not usually negotiable. *Number of submissions received weekly:* 50–100. *Reply time to queries:* "No promises, but anywhere from one week to one month." *Advance dates:* Lead time is three months. Issues are planned five to six months in advance.

FREE-LANCE POSSIBILITIES: *Playgirl* only wants writers with published experience. Says articles editor Judy Brown: "We won't consider submissions from previously unpublished writers. Except for 'Erotica,' we will consider manuscript submissions only if they're accompanied by strong clips. We rarely buy unsolicited manuscripts; we prefer queries."

Only about 50% of ideas are generated in-house; most articles *are* written by writers with leading magazine/newspaper experience, but Brown adds: "I'm desperately searching for good, solid feature writers who can do in-depth relationship pieces, and I'm looking for ideas for trend and general-interest stories, feature-length health articles, investigative reporting for women."

One of the most common mistakes writers make in approaching *Playgirl* is, according to Brown: "Underestimating the quality writing we require or the in-depth subject matter. We're interested in hard-hitting feature pieces and well-rounded relationship and coping articles."

While the pictorials, the "Erotica" vignette section, and much of the advertising are of the "skin" magazine kind, the rest of the magazine is women's general-interest. The November '82 issue, for instance, carried this mix: Interviews with Margot Kidder and Matt Dillon; a quiz asking: "Do You Know the You that Others See?"; "Stalking America's Most Eligible Men," a report on the compiling of *The American Bachelors Register*; an article titled "Up and Down Relationships," by Howard M. Halpern, Ph.D.; an in-depth investigative report, "White Slaves," focusing on young women being lured into international prostitution rings; an article on erotic video cassettes and cable TV programs women are watching; as well as fashion; movie, book and music reviews; fitness/health/grooming/diet news; and a gossip/people column.

Says Judy Brown: "We don't want service: exercise, food, or diet. And not women and careers articles per se. I wouldn't encourage humor, unless it was in the framework of another category of article. And we do very little first-person, except for travel. But yes to how-to-cope pieces. We'll consider celebrity profiles, but these are generally done by writers we know; to consider a new writer, you would have to approach us either with an existing interview or an extremely good major celebrity contact. What we'd like to see are more ideas for general-interest pieces. We've done articles on the Moral Majority, women in the stock market, investing in diamonds. Relationships, coping—these are also good."

Writers with very strong clips and writers with proven expertise in a particular area generally work on assignment. Less-credentialed writers will most probably be asked to work on spec. Says Brown: "A lot depends on whether I think the writer can handle the story." Editing varies, but it can be heavy—depending on the manuscript.

HOW TO SUBMIT: Completed manuscripts are accepted, but only with clips. Photocopied manuscripts are okay but queries are much preferred. No length preferences on queries. Including clips is "a must."

REJECTIONS: A standard rejection form is usually sent. Personalized notes are sent to encourage more submissions.

POPULAR MECHANICS

The Hearst Corporation
224 West 57th Street
New York, NY 10019
(212) 262-5700

SOURCE: Bill Hartford, managing editor

IN SHORT: Very open, but highly specialized market.

ABOUT THE MAGAZINE: Monthly; 50% free-lance–written. *Popular Mechanics* covers the latest developments in the fields of science, mechanics, invention, industry, and hobbies—all with a mechanical slant. Heavy emphasis is on how-to. Says Bill Hartford: "We're trying to service the person who wants to be self-reliant and who wants to keep the mechanical things in his life working. We also direct stories to people who are fascinated by machines." *Readership:* mostly males (its advertising department terms this a "men's magazine"); median age: 36; median income: $25,000; just under half of the readership has attended/graduated college; 18% are craftsmen/foremen and 19% are in professional/technical fields. *Circulation:* 1.6 million. *Estimated readership:* 6 million. *Areas open to free-lancers:* All. *Rates:* Hints, how-to shorts: $15 (more with photos). Features: $300 and up. *Payment:* On acceptance. *Expenses:* Pays reasonable expenses to writers previously published in the magazine. *Kill fee:* Negotiable. *Rights:* Buys all rights, by written contract. Not negotiable. *Number of submissions received weekly:* 500. *Reply time to queries:* "If it's a terrific idea, same day. If it's borderline, we may need a couple of weeks to consider it." Outright rejections receive immediate replies. *Advance dates:* Lead time is three months. Issues are planned six months in advance.

FREE-LANCE POSSIBILITIES: *Popular Mechanics* relies heavily on free-lance contributions and is very open to over-the-transom material. "A new writer has as much chance as anyone," Bill Hartford says. "And with our kind of book we're unique in that we'll accept a design idea and information from say, a skilled craftsman, and we'll write it up."

But this is a highly specialized magazine. Fewer than 5% of the 500-odd submissions received weekly work out, and most people who do get published here are actually working in technical fields. Says Hartford: "If a potential writer *knows Popular Mechanics*, he's much closer to hitting the nail on the head."

Any area is a possibility for a short or a feature (eight to ten features yearly come in over-the-transom); even the regular columns are open to outside contributors. But keep in mind these points (from the magazine's excellent guidelines sheet): "The subject must be one of general interest and must have a wide application. We stress newsworthy, novel, and human-interest angles, and deal with facts that appeal to everybody. We prefer ideas that are *useful* as distinguished from those that are *merely interesting*." (This precludes machines or inventions applicable to a very limited field or industry, local-interest stories/personalities, historical or extremely technical subjects, informative material without a news angle. Other don'ts: "Subjects whose principal appeal is in their size. Pictures/accounts of accidents, freaks of nature.")

Patented/manufactured items must be on the market, that is, available for purchase; but there is a format (the "Technology Update" section) for presenting ideas not yet in the hardware stage.

With adventure stories (science, exploration, etc.)—a good area—the technological angle must be stressed. The how-to "Home and Shop Department" must include during-and-after construction photos and drawings (see requirements under "Photos/Illustrations").

Generally, departmental editors handle queries and assignments within their specific area. Assignments are the general rule. Editors may ask to see clips; a writer would be asked to work on spec "only if he's convinced he has a story and we're not sure."

Editing varies. Rewriting is rarely done by the author: "Usually we're on deadline, and *Popular Mechanics* editors are better tuned to preparing stories in the *PM* style." Galleys are shown "if they're requested, or if it's a story that's highly technical."

PHOTOS/ILLUSTRATIONS: If possible, your submission should include appropriate photos, sketches, or technical art. "News, novelty, human interest and action are the essential requirements." *Photos:* Clear, with plenty of contrast. "The photo should in itself tell the story, and should excite interest pictorially and serve to dramatize the article"; 8x10 glossy prints preferred;

color—only 35mm or larger slides. Captions should be typed on a sheet of paper and attached (not pasted) to the back of the photo; the caption must be easily removable.

SKETCHES: Rough, but accurate pencil sketches are required. Make sure they are adequate for a staff artist to copy (pencil preferred).

HOW TO SUBMIT: Submit general queries to John Linkletter, editor; send specific area queries to the department editor listed on the masthead. Completed manuscripts are read (originals preferred over photocopies). Queries should contain "enough information and facts to substantiate a story idea sufficiently." Including a rundown of writing credits "is always helpful." Clips are not necessary at query stage; these may be requested if interest is shown in the idea.

REJECTIONS: A standard rejection form is usually used. A personal reply will be sent "at the discretion of each editor."

POPULAR SCIENCE

Times Mirror Magazines
380 Madison Avenue
New York, NY 10017
(212) 687-3000

SOURCE: Everett H. Ortner, editor

IN SHORT: Good possibilities for writers with technical interests.

ABOUT THE MAGAZINE: Monthly; 40% free-lance–written. Editor Ortner describes *Popular Science* as "a facts magazine for the person who is curious about the physical world around him." Articles are aimed not at the scientist but at "the fairly knowledgeable layman," with emphasis on the mechanical sciences (electronics, computers, hifi, automobiles, etc.) and the earth sciences, including energy in all its forms. Each month there are reports on emerging technologies in science and engineering, and consumer information (including product testing). There is a strong emphasis on the how-to. The majority of readers are male; mean age is 32. A high percentage are college grads. They're lovers of gadgets and devices; many work in technological fields. *Circulation:* 1,800,000. *Estimated readership:* over 5 million. *Areas open to free-lancers:* Everything except columns and features under "Regular Features" on contents page. Most of the automobile coverage and a good part of the electronics material are also done by staffers. *Rates:* Articles: $250 per published page, minimum. "What's New" (photo and caption): $35. *Payment:* On acceptance. *Expenses:* All. *Kill fee:* Negotiable. *Rights:* Buys first North American rights, by written contract; after publication the magazine retains all nonexclusive rights. *Number of submissions received weekly:* 100–200. *Reply time to queries:* One to three weeks. *Advance dates:* Lead time is three months. Issues are planned four to six months in advance.

FREE-LANCE POSSIBILITIES: There are opportunities here, even for the unpublished writer. Contributors tend to fall into two groups: people working in technical fields or writers with a strong interest in and knowledge of technical fields. "You don't necessarily have to have a degree in an area to write for us, but you do have to have the right orientation," Ortner explains. "There's a technical vocabulary you have to know."

Because the magazine runs more than 20 articles each month, there's no question that the right idea—one that's *new*—from either a specialist (with inside information) or a writer (who's willing to dig for the information, interviewing specialists) will find an enthusiastic response.

But only about one idea in 20 or 30 works out. "Three-quarters of the queries have no relevance to us. And we get a lot of queries from people who aren't qualified to write the story. Also, we get far more submissions than we can possibly use, regardless of quality. And we have access to much more information than the average free-lancer has in these areas." Because of the volume of unsolicited material, the editors are unable to keep mss. or story ideas on file; the onus is on the writer to keep trying to break in.

Articles are done on assignment "if the query is convincing and we really want the story." Good possibilities: innovative and clever projects and products; energy projects (like wind power, solar energy); home improvement projects; and new developments either in communities or in science/technical companies ("insider" information).

The writer will also be expected to dig for appropriate art or illustration to accompany his story. B/w photos (with caption) are bought regularly for the "What's New" section.

The extent of editing and rewriting varies from story to story. Writers of the major articles are shown photocopies of the edited manuscript before publication.

HOW TO SUBMIT: Submit to editor-in-chief C. P. Gilmore, editor Everett H. Ortner, or appropriate department editor. Mss. are read (no photocopies), but queries are preferred. There's no preferred length on queries, "but give us an idea of your competence as a writer and sell your idea." Published writing experience or technical qualifications are important. Clips are not necessary, "but it doesn't hurt to include them."

REJECTIONS: A standard rejection form is used, but personalized notes are sent "to those who have sold us before, or those we wish to encourage."

PREVENTION

Rodale Press
33 East Minor Street
Emmaus, PA 18049
(215) 967-5171

SOURCE: John Feltman, managing editor

IN SHORT: Very difficult to sell; chances very limited.

ABOUT THE MAGAZINE: Monthly. Mostly written by staff/contributing editors. Tagged under its masthead as "The Magazine for Better Health," *Prevention* was the first of the magazines aimed at health-conscious Americans. It remains digest-sized and is printed on plain matte stock. *Prevention*'s circulation is around 2.5 million and readership is estimated at a low figure of 5 million. Readership demographics are sketchy, but the "typical" reader is female, in her 50s. *Areas open to free-lancers:* All. *Rates:* Features (1500 words): $450. *Payment:* On acceptance. *Expenses:* Phone calls, car mileage. *Kill fee:* Negotiable. *Rights:* Buys all rights, by written contract. *Number of queries received weekly:* 30–50. *Reply time to queries:* Immediately. *Advance dates:* Lead time is three months. Issues are planned three to four months in advance.

FREE-LANCE POSSIBILITIES: Possibilities are very slim here, mainly because most pieces are staff- or contributor-written. Only about one query in 50 works out. John Feltman is discouraging about the free-lancer's chances but suggests the following areas as being most open: profiles on holistic doctors, pieces on new trends in health, articles on holistic health clinics. "If the idea fits into our format there may be a chance. But generally the free-lancers who do publish in *Prevention* are in a place that's geographically difficult for our regular writers to get to." Assignments are given "if the person demonstrates a writing ability."

HOW TO SUBMIT: Send a short query; include your proposed lead, and also include clips.

PSA MAGAZINE

East/West Network
5900 Wilshire Boulevard
Suite 800
Los Angeles, CA 90036
(213) 937-5810

SOURCE: Al Austin, editor

IN SHORT: Possibilities for regional articles only.

ABOUT THE MAGAZINE: Monthly; 40% free-lance–written. *PSA* is the in-flight magazine of Pacific Southwest Airlines and is described by editor Al Austin as "general-interest with a regional slant." The magazine primarily covers California, plus Arizona, Nevada, and Washington. *Circulation:* 70,000. *Estimated readership:* 400,000. *Sample copy:* Send $2 to Dottie Hogan. *Areas open to free-lancers:* Features. (All departments are written by regular contributors.) *Rates:* $250–$750. *Payment:* On acceptance. *Expenses:* Pays all reasonable expenses. *Kill fee:* 33–50%. *Rights:* Buys first North American rights, by written contract. *Number of submissions received weekly:* 35. *Reply time to queries:* Five weeks. *Advance dates:* Lead time is two months. Issues are planned 3½ months in advance.

FREE-LANCE POSSIBILITIES: Roughly one-third of the article ideas here come in over-the-transom. While the magazine mostly publishes experienced writers, a newcomer appears perhaps every couple of issues and the regular writers include several people who originally approached the magazine with an unsolicited idea.

Subject matter is general-interest, but the regional emphasis is strong. For instance, the November '82 issue carried seven features, but all related to the Pacific Southwest area. They included: "Las Vegas—My Kinda Town," by Shecky Greene; a profile of Scott Newhall, "The Last Frontier Journalist"; "The Buzzword is Flattop," the fifties haircut returns to southern California; and an interview with West Coast advertising whizzes William F. Arens and Courtland L. Bovee.

Clips are usually requested if there is interest in an over-the-transom idea; "if the writer's professionalism is in doubt," he may be asked to work on spec. But generally an assignment will be made if clips are impressive and the idea is appealing, *and* if it can be slotted into an upcoming issue. A large inventory is not held here, so ideas *must* be wanted. The following articles originally came in over-the-transom: a piece on California wildcatters, an article on a study-of-garbage project at the University of Arizona, another on a novice working as a chef-for-a-night in a four-star restaurant.

Editor Al Austin doesn't want to see any more queries on women working in jobs traditionally held by men, or on entertainment profiles. Travel is not a good area. "We don't do too many straight travel stories; those we do are usually assigned to people we know." He lists what won't work: "Writers querying on an idea they've picked up from the previous week's *Real People,* stale ideas, stories outside of *PSA*'s region, poorly constructed queries—that are illogical or which neglect to get across why the story is important." Austin sees all submissions and makes final decisions with East/West editorial director John Johns. Any necessary rewriting is done by the author. Editing varies. Galleys aren't usually shown.

HOW TO SUBMIT: Manuscripts are accepted (photocopies okay), but Austin comments: "It's best to query." Detailed queries are preferred. Personal information included should be "brief and pertinent." Clips are not required at query stage.

REJECTIONS: A standard form is usually used. A personalized reply is sent "if the story might be suitable, reworked. Or if there's interest in the writer."

PSYCHOLOGY TODAY

12000 Seventeenth Street N.W.
Washington, D.C. 20036
(202) 833-7600

SOURCE: Christopher T. Cory, managing editor

IN SHORT: Specialized market; fresh material required.

ABOUT THE MAGAZINE: Monthly; 75% free-lance–written. *Psychology Today* is a magazine that combines news reports and feature articles (based on research and findings) relating to general topics about which psychology and social science can contribute fresh insights. Says Christopher Cory: "It's for well-educated, literate, general readers who are interested in the 'whys' of their own behavior and that of people, organizations, and societies." *Circulation:* 850,000. *Estimated readership:* 4 million. *Areas open to free-lancers:* All. *Rates:* "Crosstalk": $100. Features: $500–$2000. *Payment:* On acceptance. *Expenses:* Pays all incidentals. *Kill fee:* 25–35%. *Rights:* Buys all rights, by written contract. Rarely negotiable. *Number of submissions received weekly:* 50–60. *Reply time to queries:* Two to four weeks. *Advance dates:* Lead time is three months. Issues are planned three to five months in advance.

FREE-LANCE POSSIBILITIES: Roughly half of the submissions received at *Psychology Today*, and many of the pieces published in the magazine, come from scientists who have conducted the research on which the articles are based. Explains Christopher Cory: "Our pieces involve science reporting and do not carry themselves on good writing and bright ideas alone."

However, a writer who's a nonscientist but who can come up with a bright idea *can* make it here. "It helps to have some familiarity and expertise in the field, but we'd welcome a general-interest writer who's thoughtful and who's willing to dig into the science involved to back up an idea. They should dig hard though. Our material can be sophisticated and demanding; it's hard to handle well. But we're always open to ideas that are genuinely fresh and insightful and based on something more than just armchair speculation."

To editors here, "the ideal query letter" (or ms; mss. are, in fact, preferred) is one that presents a "new and surprising idea based on solid scientific research about something that's inherently interesting or currently on people's minds."

When both academics and free-lancers go wrong (and many do; only about one query in 30 works out), it's usually for one of the following reasons, as Cory explains it: "There are two kinds of research: that which establishes baselines and that which is news. Both are valuable to science, but we cover only the second kind. Our major pieces are often based on major research, and while a researcher's findings may be interesting and exciting to him or her, to work for us they have to be new and surprising, or to contribute freshly to a hot current topic. Many of the queries we get from writers tend to rely just on an academic's new information without asking whether the findings would be surprising to a reader.

"Often, too, the writing is not of a high enough caliber. Or people will tell us flatly just what the story is about, rather than what it will conclude. And often potential contributors are not aware of what we've published in the past or what's been published elsewhere."

"Crosstalk" is mostly written by staff and a small stable of regular free-lancers, but it *is* open for pieces that fulfill the already-mentioned article requirements, on a smaller scale. Assignments are the norm here. Editing tends to be heavy. Final-edited manuscripts are shown on major pieces.

HOW TO SUBMIT: Completed mss. are preferred over queries; photocoped mss. okay. Query requirements: Longer queries are preferred; "give us as much detail as possible." State where you've been published, if you've had any specialized training, what kinds of areas you write about. Include three or four clips (newspapers, trades okay); "we're looking for the ability to write and think straight." For proposals to "Crosstalk," attach a copy of the academic data on which the piece is based.

REJECTIONS: Sends both form letters and personalized notes. The latter is more likely "if the writer makes more than just the routine impression."

READER'S DIGEST

Pleasantville, NY 10570
(914) 769-7000

SOURCE: Philip B. Osborne and Ric Cox, senior editors

IN SHORT: A very difficult market.

ABOUT THE MAGAZINE: Monthly. Approximately half original material, half reprinted from other publications. *Reader's Digest* is a general-interest magazine, appealing to a readership (U.S.) that is fairly equally split male/female. Half are aged 18–44. Basically readers are middle income. *Circulation*: 18 million (U.S.), 60 million (worldwide). *Areas open to free-lancers*: All. *Rates*: Reprints: $900 per printed page (half of fee is paid to writer, the other half to original publication). Original material: $2850 for a first-time writer and for an area like "Drama in Real Life." "Unforgettable Character": $3500. *Payment*: On acceptance. *Expenses*: Pays reasonable expenses. *Kill fee*: $500. *Rights*: Buys all world periodical rights, by written contract. *Reply time to queries*: Two to three weeks. *Advance dates*: Lead time is three months. Issues are planned three to four months in advance.

FREE-LANCE POSSIBILITIES: *Reader's Digest* is a high-paying top-prestige market. It's also a very difficult sell. . . .

Fillers: It's stiff competition even in this area; 400,000 filler submissions are received yearly for departments like "Life in These United States," "All in a Day's Work," and "Laughter, the Best Medicine." But material is needed constantly, and it could be a way in. Both Phil Osborne and Ric Cox agree: "If you're serious about writing for *Reader's Digest*, you should be submitting to these areas." Departments are explained, and submissions requirements are given in the front of each issue.

Articles: Of the average 30 articles run monthly, half are reprints, half originals. Of the original material, one or two are likely to have come in over-the-transom; the rest are written by staff and known free-lancers.

The editors welcome published articles from writers for reprint consideration. If you think you have published a *Reader's Digest*–style article, send in the published piece—it's that simple. Original submissions, however, require a good deal of forethought. Unsolicited manuscripts are not accepted, according to magazine policy. But by directing your submission to one of the editors listed on the masthead, chances are you'll find an editor willing to review, at least. If the piece isn't written, send a query; queries are accepted.

If the query is picked up, the editor involved must do a three-step check: first, to the magazine's index and to *Reader's Guide* (to make sure a similar piece hasn't been done over the past five years), then to the magazine's inventory (to make sure a similar story hasn't already been bought), and then to the assignment files to make sure a similar piece hasn't already been assigned. If the magazine then wants to pursue the idea, an editor will contact the writer requesting an expanded proposal: three to four pages, double-spaced, presenting the idea in the style the piece would be written. Here Osborne and Cox offer this tip: "Two or three excellent, beautifully written anecdotes can sell your proposal quicker than anything else." They add: "Probably the best kind of *Reader's Digest* story is the extended anecdote, a personal narrative or a case study of someone who has gone through a tragic ordeal. If you can, tell a story through people. . . . our most successful pieces are 'Drama in Real Life,' the story of a drama that touches a human emotion or a common concern, a common urgency or a common problem. One that will engage and involve the reader.

"A lot of writers who approach us don't have a focus, a point of view. We need that. We see ourselves as a crusader, a champion of the common American—someone who's basically traditional. We're looking for solutions. We're in the business of helping people *solve* their problems. We'll tackle all kinds of issues. We're against the government wasting taxpayer money, for instance. *Reader's Digest* believes that you *can* change things, that people can make a difference. So we want stories on subjects, and about people, embodying those principles."

Once a proposal is accepted, the story becomes a project—an editor works closely with the writer throughout.

Reader's Digest gives assignments to writers who present strong, well-thought-out proposals. Sometimes writers without strong credentials will be asked to work on spec. All humor must be done on spec.

A drawback here *can* be the length of time between manuscript submission and publication. While the magazine is buying more selectively than in previous times and is keeping the assignment process a tight one, it is also maintaining a 150–200 story inventory. Five different editors take charge of the magazine on a rotating basis; each editor is free to choose the material he likes from the inventory.

Reader's Digest is a challenge. The beginning writer's best chance is with a personal experience story; the more experienced writer faces a good deal of competition. But it may be well worth the effort, keeping this point in mind: "We get a lot of the same ideas all the time."

HOW TO SUBMIT: Send query or manuscript to a specific editor. No simultaneous submissions. Clips are not required; however, including a clip or two is a good idea, if you're unknown to the editor, but "it's the proposal that has to sell itself."

Tips from both Osborne and Cox: "You have to be a salesman. Try to sell your idea; don't just ask, 'Are you interested in this?' Give us facts that will get us as excited about the story as you are. If you're not enthusiastic about the idea, then we probably won't be either." Enclose a SASE.

REJECTIONS: All contributors receive personal replies.

REDBOOK

230 Park Avenue
New York, NY 10169
(Watch out for possible address change)
(212) 850-9300

SOURCE: Susan Edmiston, articles editor

IN SHORT: Open, but very competitive market.

ABOUT THE MAGAZINE: Monthly. Most articles are free-lance—
written. *Redbook* is an entertainment and service magazine for
women aged 24-40. Fashion, beauty, exercises, food and nutrition (plus recipes), crafts, home decorating, and money management are covered. Articles concern relationships, sex, parenting,
reporting on issues of current interest, humor; articles run 1000–
3500 words. Most readers have some college education, most
work outside the home, most are married and have children.
They are busy women, leading full lives. *Circulation:* 3.8
million. *Estimated readership*: 13 million. *Areas open to free-
lancers*: All articles (Fashion, beauty and food usually are
staff-written). *Rates*: Articles: $750 and up; "Young Mother's
Story": $750. *Payment*: On acceptance. *Expenses*: Pays reason-
able expenses. *Rights*: Buys exclusive first and continuing North
American serial rights, by written contract. *Number of submissions received weekly*: "Hundreds." *Reply time to queries*:
2–4 weeks. *Advance dates*: Lead time is 5 months. Issues are
planned 4–5 months in advance.

FREE-LANCE POSSIBILITIES: A professional writer with good writing samples has a chance at *Redbook*. But beginning writers
break in over-the-transom only occasionally. As is the case at all
the women's magazines, there is a lot of competition.

Most general subjects are possibilities—personal experiences
(these should offer solutions, though, rather than just tell the
story), relationships, children, running a home, health, sex, issues and reporting of current interest. Celebrity interviews are
not a good area—the main interview is generally written by a
known writer in the field and "Talking With . . . ," while open
to free-lancers, is almost always done by one of the magazine's
regulars.

If your idea is appealing and if you submit a well-developed proposal, the idea will be discussed within the articles department—several editors will be involved. It's a good idea to send a few relevant clips with the query. Excellence of reporting and writing is of the utmost importance. Rare assignments may be given on spec to less-experienced writers whose ideas are particularly on target and whose queries demonstrate the ability to conceptualize a story well and to write well.

Writers work closely with an editor throughout.

HOW TO SUBMIT: Completed manuscripts are read (photocopies are okay), but proposals are preferred. Multiple submissions are considered "as long as we know." The query should include the idea, the approach, the purpose of the article, plus any relevant professional information. Keep it short—one page, if possible. A pet peeve regarding query letters: "When an idea is never fully or clearly explained."

REJECTIONS: A personal typed letter is sent to most contributors (this is merely a polite rejection). More detailed notes are sent to those writers the editors would like to hear from again.

REPUBLIC SCENE

East/West Network
5900 Wilshire Boulevard
Los Angeles, CA 90036
(213) 937-5810

SOURCE: The editor interviewed has since left the magazine; a replacement had not been named when we went to press.

IN SHORT: A market better suited to the experienced writer.

ABOUT THE MAGAZINE: Monthly; 100% free-lance–written. *Republic Scene* is the in-flight magazine of Republic Airlines. It is a general-interest magazine with business concentration. The average age of readers is 43; 63% are college grads; 68% are in professional/managerial positions. *Circulation:* 140,000. *Estimated readership:* 800,000. *Sample copy:* $2 to Dottie Hogan. *Areas open to free-lancers:* All. *Rates:* $400–$650. *Payment:* On acceptance. *Expenses:* Up to 10% of article fee. *Kill fee:* 25%. *Rights:* Buys first North American rights, by written contract. *Number of submissions received weekly:* At least 25. *Reply time to queries:* Two to four weeks. *Advance dates:* Lead time is three months. Issues are planned three to four months in advance.

FREE-LANCE POSSIBILITIES: Over-the-transom ideas account for about 25% of the articles run here; of these, about 5% carry the by-lines of writers new to the magazine.

Because both regulars and newcomers tend to be either magazine-experienced or newspaper writers in major cities, the beginning writer will most probably be asked to work on spec. This doesn't happen often, and the idea has to be really good. But beginning or experienced, all writers need to approach this magazine with a "sharp" idea and an impressive query. Even a seasoned writer may not be given an assignment if his idea does not suit the magazine's upcoming (regional, seasonal) needs.

Ideas are considered for both columns and features, in both specialist and general-interest areas. An article on giant inflatable billboards, for instance—which the editor interviewed described as a "colorful piece"—came in over-the-transom. Business, life-style, personalities, sports, science are all possibilities. The June '82 issue carried: "Wide-Open Welcome—from fertile farmlands to rugged badlands to friendly towns, North

Dakota offers hospitality in a big way"; " 'You Can Change What You Are' "—positive thinking works; "Splendor on the Grass" —polo, the sport of kings and cowboys; "Perfect Timing"— watches as gifts; "The Hidden West"—two adventurers discover the isolated beauty of an America that few people have seen; "A Report: Office Design." Plus a supplement on computers, and two columns: "Technology: the one-armed bandit goes electronic"; and "Sports"—catcher Gary Carter.

Not a good area, however, is travel. These stories—the locations and story scheduling—are decided, way in advance, by the airline. The editor said she would prefer not to see any more queries in the travel area.

She added: "We don't have much success with unknown freelancers who are not familiar with the magazine. Our needs are specific, our audience clearly delineated. Writers should have a national outlook, a timely news peg or slant that makes the idea topical, a familiarity with business and/or life-style trends, the ability to research and get facts that support the story. The stories should have strong angles or points of view, and not be simply an almanac of information about a given subject.

"Many writers send battered, much-used, nonindividualized queries of ideas they've obviously tried selling to every publication there is. And it's absolutely amazing how many 'writers' don't bother to present their ideas in an appealing manner, how many of them fail to proofread, check spelling, punctuation, and grammar, type properly, etc. When we have the choice of working with so many competent writers, why would any editor choose a writer who does not grasp even the basics of writing?"

The editor sometimes makes decisions alone; sometimes she will also discuss over-the-transom ideas with the executive editor.

Rewriting is done by the author, "if they seem capable." Editing varies. Galleys are almost never shown.

HOW TO SUBMIT: Send submissions to (Ms.) Max Gordon, assistant editor. Manuscripts accepted (originals are preferred over photocopies, "to ensure it's not a multiple submission"). Queries are preferred, however, fulfilling these requirements: "Clearly typed, well spelled, smart idea, well-angled—a selling pitch!" Clips should be included (preferably magazine clips). It may also be worthwhile to outline interview/information sources:

"This sometimes helps to make a case, especially if the writer can show that he or she has *access* to specialists."

REJECTIONS: A standard form rejection letter is used mostly. Personalized replies sent to "writers who seem promising."

ROLLING STONE

745 Fifth Avenue
New York, NY 10151
(212) 758-3800

SOURCE: David Rosenthal, managing editor
Alan Weitz, senior editor

IN SHORT: Very limited possibilities; most free-lance work solicited from known writers.

ABOUT THE MAGAZINE: Bi-weekly. About 30% free-lance–written. *Rolling Stone* is a newsprint publication begun in the 1960s as a rock'n'roll, youth culture magazine. It has now expanded into film and other forms of entertainment and politics. Says David Rosenthal: "We see ourselves as a general-interest magazine, with a particular interest in popular culture. We cover both the political and cultural scene; there's nothing we *won't* write about." Publishes controversial articles often noted in other publications. *Readership:* 68% male, 32% female; median age: 24; 48% have attended/graduated college; 71% are single; 76% are employed, 55% full-time. *Circulation:* 800,000. *Areas open to free-lancers:* Everything except "National Affairs" and record and movie reviews. *Rates:* Main features: $1000–$3000. *Payment:* On publication. *Expenses:* Pays all incidentals (according to a budget worked out with the writer in advance). *Kill fee:* 25%. *Rights:* Negotiable. By written contract. *Number of submissions received weekly:* At least 100. *Reply time to queries:* Within a month, usually sooner. *Advance dates:* Lead time is four to six weeks. Issues are planned two to four months in advance.

FREE-LANCE POSSIBILITIES: The over-the-transom approach is not highly recommended here. When new writers break in (and it doesn't happen often), they do so through an agent or a personal connection. Or they come in with unique access on a story. Says David Rosenthal: "Writers *can* take their chances, but breaking in over-the-transom is very rare. I can think of only one or two manuscripts we've bought that way."

He describes profiles as "almost impossible—one of the hardest ways to get in." These are always done by known writers. An exception was a writer who approached the magazine with an interview with Ringo Starr. Explains Alan Weitz: "I had met this writer very briefly, about a year previously. We had been trying —unsuccessfully—to get Ringo Starr. When the writer came in with the interview we assigned it, and it made the cover. But access was the deciding factor."

Rosenthal describes one of the most common mistakes free-lancers make: "Giving us ideas for profiles of people, when we're more than aware of their existence." Weitz adds: "We try to be timely. But sometimes there's another reason for a profile. A few years back we did a piece on Bob Hope. That wasn't timely, but in its oddness it worked for us."

Music: "Generally not a good area for the free-lancer. We have a number of regular writers working in this area," Rosenthal explains.

"Random Notes": Says Alan Weitz, "This section is basically done in-house. We'll probably pay for information from a couple of stringers each issue. In 90% of cases we would rewrite any item coming in; there's a particular tone we like to keep throughout this section. There are requirements; we're looking for personality tidbits, unusual or news-breaking stories about famous people. Basically, it has to be gossipy."

Essays: "We print personal journalism pieces only occasionally. It's not an area we'd recommend for writers trying to break in." Investigative pieces are also difficult. Says Rosenthal: "These have to be of *national* interest." He adds: "Writers would be well served if they were able to submit a story idea for an area where they have a particular interest or knowledge. Or unique access. We often have to reject ideas, too, because the story would involve a great deal of travel or other expenses. Sometimes it's almost *better* to send in the completed manuscript."

Articles are not always assigned at *Rolling Stone*; writers are sometimes asked to work on spec. Says David Rosenthal: "Assignments depend on factors like the writer's track record, how much work is involved, how exclusive the story is, how impressed we are with the idea."

Editing varies, but close contact is maintained with the writer. Galleys are shown.

Note: Poetry *is* accepted over-the-transom. All poetry published is unsolicited.

HOW TO SUBMIT: Send music submissions to "Music Editor," general-interest to "Editorial Staff." Send query or manuscript (photocopies okay). Multiple submissions accepted, "but we do not prefer it." Preferred query length: "the shorter the better." Include clips.

REJECTIONS: A personalized reply is always sent.

THE RUNNER

Ziff-Davis Publishing
One Park Avenue
New York, NY 10016
(212) 725-4244

SOURCE: Marc A. Bloom, editor

IN SHORT: Only writers on the run need apply.

ABOUT THE MAGAZINE: Monthly. Main features mostly written by staff/contributing editors. Marc Bloom describes the aim of this publication: "To help people enjoy their running and benefit from it, and to help runners better understand and appreciate the sport." He describes the readership as "runners and joggers who take their sport fairly seriously." Readers are 80% male, 20% female; the typical reader is 34–35; 90% are college educated; and income is high: $35,000–$40,000. *Circulation:* 225,000. *Areas open to free-lancers:* Everything except the "Footwork" column, "Pacesetters" (although finder's fees are sometimes paid), and "Race Highlights." *Rates:* "Warmups": $50. Columns: $200 and up. Features: $500 and up. (Average article fee: $750–$800.) *Payment:* On acceptance. *Expenses:* Pays all incidentals. *Kill fee:* 20%–30%. *Rights:* Buys all rights, by written contract. Negotiable. *Number of submissions received weekly:* 40–50. *Reply time to queries:* Two to three weeks. *Advance dates:* Lead time is two months. Issues are planned four to five months in advance.

FREE-LANCE POSSIBILITIES: To write for *The Runner*, two talents are required: You need to know the sport and you need to come up with a fresh, new idea. The latter isn't all that easy; there's a sizable staff and a wealth of contributing editors and stringers. So forget about major features. "These will be done by us, or we'll know about them; otherwise we're not doing our job properly," Marc Bloom says. And forget about that piece on "a running experience and how I've grown through it." That story is too clichéd now; anything obvious is not going to succeed. But it *is* possible to break in to the magazine in the following areas:
    "Off the Track": Frequently a humorous piece is used here; this is a column that has to be studied for style and content. "People" is a column run about every other month; it highlights

an interesting running personality; "it doesn't have to be a talented runner but it does have to be someone who's doing something unusual." "Flashbacks" highlights an event in running that happened at least ten years ago; "it could be an account of some kind of historic event in the sport or a personal experience recollection." "Training": "Mostly we get champion runners to do this, but a free-lancer could do it. We like to give very specific advice in this column; it can be an essay, it can be first-person, but it must present a new notion about basic running training." "Pros and Cons" is an opinion column (not run on a regular basis); "here we want to talk about an issue in running. Some of the topics we've discussed have been the increased commercialism in running, the influence of TV on running, the management of certain events." "Reviews" is a book-review column, run every second or third issue. "We would have to see clips to consider a writer here, not necessarily published book reviews but something that would show us the writer is someone who could give an intelligent appraisal."

"Warmups" is probably the best area through which to break in. Although most often writers work on assignment rather than on spec, the editors are going to be quicker giving an assignment for a short "Warmups" piece than anything else. "Breaking in with a major feature happens fairly infrequently. With 'Warmups' there's much less risk involved for us," Bloom explains. He adds that a wide range of topics will be considered for "Warm-ups"—whatever writers can come up with is worth the try.

If you're unknown at the magazine, it might be worth suggesting a feature on spec (ideas from unknown writers for major features can be rejected because of the risk of committing to an assignment). But query first if the piece isn't written; articles are balanced each issue and your idea may not fit into the content planned. These are some of the over-the-transom submissions that succeeded: a run through the war zones of Afghanistan, by Shawn Lyons (May '80, unsolicited ms.); a run from one end of Ireland to the other, tracing family roots along the way, by Bill Plunkett (1983, query); an interview with champion runner Roberto de Castella after he won a race in Japan, by Hanns Maier, Jr. (May '82, query). Here Marc Bloom adds: "If you want to do an interview, a Q. & A. might be the best approach. That also represents less risk to us."

The Runner is not interested in rehashes of ideas that have been done by their competitors. Editing generally is light-handed: "We don't have the time or the resources to do rewriting. If it needs to be done, we'll give it back to the writer."

HOW TO SUBMIT: Mss. are read (no photocopies), but queries are preferred—the exception being humor, essay or opinion pieces. Keep queries to a page: "Come right in and tell me the angle. The angles should be well defined; your query should tell me *why* this would be a good piece for us." Submit a neat query. "Anything that's sloppy makes me feel the person wouldn't be able to do the story; I've rejected queries because they're sloppy. And it would help to spell my name right." Include your writing credentials. Clips are necessary "only if they will add to the query. They can help in the case of a writer I wouldn't know."

REJECTIONS: Standard rejection letters are used most of the time; personalized notes are sent to those contributors the editors would like to hear from again.

RUNNER'S WORLD

1400 Stierlin Road
Mountain View, CA 94043
(415) 965-8777

SOURCE: Mark Levine, managing editor

IN SHORT: Possibilities for both running writers and generalists.

ABOUT THE MAGAZINE: Published 13 times a year (two issues in January); 75% free-lance–written. *Runner's World* is a magazine for running enthusiasts. Says Mark Levine: "Our readers are mostly what we like to call 'hard-core runners.' We publish articles on training, health and nutrition, and any other subjects that might be related to running or running training. For instance, about once a year we'll run pieces on swimming and bicycling —because a lot of runners use these sports to train." *Readership:* 60% male, 40% female; average age: 30–40. Readers are highly educated (most have advanced degrees), and income level is high. *Circulation:* 400,000. *Estimated readership:* 1.3 million. *Areas open to free-lancers:* All feature articles, and those columns which invite reader submissions. *Rates:* $350–$1500. *Payment:* On publication. *Expenses:* Pays reasonable expenses. *Kill fee:* If purchased piece is not used within a three-month period, magazine asks to extend their option to publish. If writer agrees, and the piece is then not used within a 12-month period, a kill fee of 10% is paid. *Rights:* Buys first world rights; retains rights for reprints and one additional editorial use. By written contract. Rarely negotiable. *Number of submissions received weekly:* 50. *Reply time to queries:* Two to six weeks; may be longer if being considered. (All submissions are logged; to inquire, write, attention editorial secretary.) *Advance dates:* Lead time is three months. Issues are planned nine months in advance.

FREE-LANCE POSSIBILITIES: There's room for the free-lancer at *Runner's World*—both the running writer who knows the sport well enough to write a specialized article and the generalist interested in a related article. (Best bets: health and nutrition— new stories on health diets/foods.) New writers are published in almost every issue. Writers mainly work on assignment. The policy is to start off an untested writer at a lower fee range rather than requesting work on spec. And Mark Levine adds: "We *do* take chances quite often. We've used top writers and we like doing that. But that can also destroy a budget fairly fast. So if a writer is willing to start off at a lower range and work up from there, we'll go with him."

But what Levine stresses is that you must be familiar with the magazine. "You should *know* the kinds of articles we publish, and just as importantly, the kinds of things we *don't* publish. The biggest problem with unsolicited submissions is that people don't understand the magazine. For instance, we must get 30 'Running with My Dog' pieces a month. Or we'll get 'Running in England.' Or China, or France. These sometimes have potential if they're exotic, but usually they're not different enough. We don't do stories on runners and ordinary people who run; we rarely do personality profiles for that matter. Our stories are much more general; we write about the sport, and how to train, and what's going on in the sport."

Levine sees all over-the-transom submissions. Any with promise go into his "Pending" file and are discussed with the executive editor and publisher at the next editorial meeting. Levine will contact the writer, asking to see clips, and will assign from there. The only times he might ask someone to work on spec is if the editors are unsure of the story, if the writer has weak clips (magazine clips preferred), or if the person is not a professional writer. But whether on assignment or on spec, if the first story works, chances of future assignments are promising. The writer should also keep pitching ideas in-between, however.

Two writers who recently broke in over-the-transom: Charles Farmer, who wrote the April '83 piece on training for running through backpacking (an example of the relevance of a related sport); and Bob Kriegel, who discussed runner's burnout and boredom in running in the May '83 issue (an example of the generalized scope of *Runner's World* pieces).

Editing varies here. Rewriting is done by the author, "as long as there's time." Galleys are not shown.

HOW TO SUBMIT: Completed mss. are "scanned" (no photocopies). Queries are much preferred. Multiple submissions are returned unread. Queries should be brief; "a few paragraphs is best." Personal background information is not necessary, and don't include clips at query stage. A brief listing of writing credits is "helpful." (No replies without SASE.)

REJECTIONS: A standard form letter is sent to most contributors. Levine will send a personalized note "if I know the writer." If he wishes to encourage a new writer, he will ask the editorial secretary to include a note with the standard form.

THE SATURDAY EVENING POST

1100 Waterway Boulevard
Indianapolis, IN 46202
(317) 636-8881

SOURCE: Ted Kreiter, executive editor

IN SHORT: Mostly publishes experienced writers, but open to all writers.

ABOUT THE MAGAZINE: Nine issues yearly. About 50% free-lance–written. *The Saturday Evening Post* is a general-interest magazine, aimed at a middle American family readership. Articles cover current issues of national importance, health/medical topics, celebrity interviews, travel, food, history/reminiscence, and sports. Articles often have a religious (Christian) slant. The magazine also includes cartoons and humorous anecdotes. The emphasis is on wholesome, entertaining reading. *Readership:* 55% women, 45% men; average reader age: 42–44; average household income: $25,000. While most readers do live in urban and suburban areas, the readers are more rural-based than at many magazines. Slightly less than half of the readership has attended college. *Circulation:* Rate base: 750,000. *Estimated readership:* 4 million. *Areas open to free-lancers:* Everything except "Post People" and "Medical Mailbox." *Rates:* $250–$1500. *Payment:* On publication. *Expenses:* Pays reasonable expenses. *Kill fee:* Negotiable; generally around 50%. *Rights:* Buys all rights, by letter of agreement. Negotiable. *Number of submissions received weekly:* 20–25. *Reply time to queries:* "Within a few weeks." (Calls accepted only after four weeks.) *Advance dates:* Lead time is three months. Issues are planned about four months in advance.

FREE-LANCE POSSIBILITIES: New writers break into the *Post* three to five times a year. While most writers published are experienced, major magazine clips are not a requirement; less experienced writers are published "fairly frequently."

General-interest is the best area for the free-lancer. Says executive editor Ted Kreiter: "We haven't been doing very much in the arts lately, but just about anything is fair game." Two general articles, maximum, are run per issue. The March '83 issue covered "Amish Farming: The Gentle Way of Life" and looked at unemployment, discussing "New Jobs: Who Will Create Them?" "We do have to stay away from truly newsworthy stories because of our lead time," Kreiter stresses. In the general-interest vein, the magazine often profiles people across the country with strong altruistic/community involvements, concentrating usually on their Christian and family life-styles. These are possibilities for the free-lancer.

Sports is another good area; it's a category the magazine covers regularly, often with profiles. "North Carolina's Determined Dean," a profile of UNC basketball coach Dean Smith, by Barry Jacobs, in the March '83 issue, came in as a proposal over-the-transom.

Travel is another regular area. It is about 75% free-lance–written. There's a preference toward domestic, rather than overseas locations. Travel pieces are generally short—around 1500 words—and preferred are general pieces rather than articles that focus in on a particular aspect of a destination. "Travel *can* be an area for the general free-lancer," Kreiter says, "as long as the piece is well documented. And we prefer to see photos as well." Queries on food/recipes are welcomed, but a specialist background is required. "We're looking more for health-type foods rather than traditional cooking."

The two areas where submissions are discouraged are health/medical articles and celebrity profiles. There is a strong emphasis on medical articles (two or three are run per issue), but free-lance work is rarely used in this area. "We generate our own ideas," Kreiter says. "And we prefer to have the articles written by doctors or people working in a research capacity."

Generally one or two celebrity profiles are run per issue, but Kreiter says: "We have several regular contributors who do these, and we have more profiles than we can use. If a free-lancer had a *super* interview, we *would* take a look at it. . . ." Celebrities profiled have included Bob Hope, Barbara Mandrell, Richard Chamberlain. "We like 'family' people, people who are into a healthy life-style."

All unsolicited submissions are screened by two editorial assistants. They pass on "possibles" to Kreiter. Clips are requested before an assignment is made; Kreiter prefers to see clips at the query stage. Without strong clips a writer would be asked to work on spec; this happens "quite often." Kreiter acknowledges that for the little-published writer, a manuscript submission might well be the best approach.

The most common reasons for rejection: "Hackneyed ideas, inappropriate ideas. The majority of the free-lancers approaching us haven't really looked at the magazine."

Once in, chances of future assignments are "definitely" increased.

Manuscripts needing rewriting are given back to the author. Editing varies. "We *do* edit heavily sometimes, but we really prefer not to." Galleys are not shown.

HOW TO SUBMIT: Phone queries are not accepted. Completed manuscripts are accepted (photocopies okay), but queries are preferred. Multiple submissions are accepted. Preferred query length: 1 to 1½ pages. Include list of previous publications; also include clips.

REJECTIONS: A standard form is usually sent. Personal, "encouraging" notes are sent occasionally.

SAVVY

111 Eighth Avenue
New York, NY 10011
(212) 255-0990

SOURCE: Wendy Reid Crisp, editor

IN SHORT: Open, possibilities; but all writers new to the magazine must work on spec.

ABOUT THE MAGAZINE: Monthly. Describing itself as "The Magazine for Executive Women," *Savvy* is aiming not at the woman on her way up but at the woman who has arrived—or, at least, has the top rung of the ladder in sight. Says Wendy Reid Crisp: "We're for the woman in business who has reached a certain level of maturity and who has been through a few fires already. We don't cover any women's service areas like beauty or fashion; we address the reader's business life and the personal life that surrounds her career." *Readership:* 28–40 age group; 80% are college grads; one-third have advanced degrees. They're roughly half married, half single; one-third are parents. It's primarily an urban audience. *Circulation:* 260,000 subscribers, with another 40,000 newsstand sales. Estimated readership: close to one million. *Areas open to free-lancers:* Everything except "Frontlines." *Rates:* Features: $500–$2500. Average article fee: $600–$800. (Rates are standard, even for top-name writers.) *Payment:* Payment is made on the 15th of the month before publication. *Expenses:* Pays all reasonable expenses. *Kill fee:* Up to $150. *Rights:* Buys exclusive North American rights, by written contract. Half payment is made to author on any additional sales. Rights negotiable. *Number of submissions received weekly:* 500. *Reply time to queries:* Outright rejections: within a week. Queries under consideration: up to a month. *Advance dates:* Lead time is four months. Issues are planned up to six months in advance.

FREE-LANCE POSSIBILITIES: *Savvy* is highly focused in its editorial content. "We are very clear on where we're going; we think *Savvy* 24 hours a day," editor Wendy Crisp says. "Free-lancers generally have a tough time trying to come up with ideas we haven't already thought of."
 The editors welcome well-credentialed writers (see "Portfo-

lios and Positive Thinking," pages 7–9). But known writers won't be published here just because they have a name, and prima donnas are not tolerated ("We discourage them even if they're good writers, because we don't want to put up with the emotional wear and tear"). If you have written for competitive career-woman magazines (like *Working Woman, Woman, Complete Woman*) it might not be worthwhile approaching *Savvy.* Certainly sending clips from these kinds of magazines is not a good idea. Wendy Crisp says: "I consider these other magazines to be our competitors and of less editorial quality, and I'm not interested in free-lancers who have written for them."

Although the magazine has published first-timers, this is a hands-on operation without staff writers. So revisions are done by the author. "We'll help people with promise and a good attitude," Crisp says, "but writers should be aware that they may have to go through six or seven heavy rewrites." *All* writers should be aware of this. One or two rewrites are usual; doing *several* rewrites (and complete rewrites, not just revisions) is common—even among experienced writers.

Savvy receives about 500 unsolicited submissions weekly. Crisp sees all those with any promise. Only one or two work out weekly; the rest are rejected either because the ideas, or the writers, are not good enough. To submit a successful idea, it's necessary to study *Savvy* back issues, both to get a feel for the specialized content and to avoid suggesting an idea that has already been done. This is especially necessary for general topics.

Profiles are possibilities, but suggesting a profile of a woman who's managing to succeed in a career—even an unusual one— and raising three children as well is not what will sell here. Ninety-nine percent of the profiles suggested by free-lancers are rejected. They have to go beyond the woman and her job into some other angle that will inform and educate; profiles should really be illustrations of women who've succeeded using the kinds of business strategies that are discussed in the magazine's general articles.

Health is an area with possibilities. But specialist health/medical writers have the best chances here. "I wouldn't suggest a general writer tackle one of our health pieces," Crisp says. She adds: "Don't use us to switch fields. If you're a health writer, suggest a health piece, not a business profile."

The back-page essay, "1000 Words," is a possibility for the general writer. A completed manuscript, not a query, is required however. "1000 Words" is not an easy sell, but it could be a fast one. And subject matter can range to fit the writer's whim: essays, opinion pieces, humor and satire have appeared here.

The "Tools of the Trade" section, which encompasses several articles monthly, presents specific business and economic ideas and strategies. It is *not* a good area for the general writer. "This is the best part of the book for a businessperson who wants to write and thinks she might have something to say," Crisp explains. "She doesn't have to be a professional writer; just give us the ideas and we'll fix them up. For this section the rule is: If you don't have a business background, don't try and write about it. I don't want a writer to go out and interview a stockbroker to get information for a story; we can get a stockbroker to write the piece herself." Honorariums are paid for articles in this sections.

No assignments are given first time around. Clips have to be satisfactory to get a go-ahead, on spec. The magazine *does* pay for ideas, so if your clips are not up to par but you are determined to do the piece on spec, you'll have to be prepared to plead your case.

Editing tends to be light at *Savvy* mainly because of the multiple-rewrite policy. But all rewrites *are* done by the author, with editor guidance throughout, and galleys are always sent to the author before publication.

HOW TO SUBMIT: Manuscripts will be read, but queries preferred. All multiple submissions will be returned unread. Short queries preferred: "I like to see someone say in ten sentences what they're going to do and how they're going to do it." If you will be doing interviews, give names in your query: "There may be people on the list we *wouldn't* be interested in."

Crisp stresses: "Writers *must* realize that when they send a query, the only thing I know about that writer is what's in front of me. Poorly presented queries won't succeed; neither will arrogant presentations. I also don't like queries that start out like a press release, something like: 'Wouldn't it be wonderful if you had two more hours each day? Well, you can! Two women in Massachusetts . . .' Just talk to me in a regular way."

Include one or two clips, "something similar to what we publish." But remember the clip policy already mentioned (no clips from competitive publications). And "never, never send pictures. And don't tell me: 'By the way, my neighbor is an artist and she would be willing to illustrate my story. . . .'"

REJECTIONS: A more personalized letter is sent to contributors who are on the right track; otherwise a standard rejection letter is used. But Crisp adds: "The smart writer encloses a postcard that the magazine can use for a reply."

SCIENTIFIC AMERICAN

415 Madison Avenue
New York, NY 10017
(212) 754-0550

No free-lance material is accepted. Articles are written by scientists reporting on their findings.

SELF

Condé Nast Publications
350 Madison Avenue
New York, NY 10017
(212) 880-8800

SOURCE: Valorie Griffith Weaver, managing editor

IN SHORT: Limited possibilities for beginning writers.

ABOUT THE MAGAZINE: Monthly; 50% free-lance–written. *Self* is a women's magazine with a special emphasis: health and fitness of body and mind. Fashion, food, and money issues are covered but the concentration is on general fitness—which includes exercise, health and medical topics, beauty and good looks, nutrition, sexual and emotional health, psychological "think" pieces, relationships. Says Valorie Griffith Weaver: "Our reader is fitness-oriented; she's very active about her life and she wants to *do*. She doesn't just flip through the pages; she wants information she can use." Average reader age is 29. Most readers have some college, a very high percentage work, about half are married, and more than one-third are parents. *Circulation:* One million. *Estimated readership:* 3 million. *Areas open to free-lancers:* Articles. (Fashion, beauty, decorating, fitness, "Money Watch," "Health Watch," and "Food Watch" are written in-house.) *Rates:* Articles: $600–$1200, and higher. *Payment:* On acceptance. *Expenses:* Pays reasonable expenses. *Kill fee:* 20%. *Rights:* Buys first North American rights, by written contract. *Number of submissions received weekly:* 150. *Reply time to queries:* "Usually a couple of weeks." *Advance dates:* Lead time is three months. Issues are planned three to six months in advance.

FREE-LANCE POSSIBILITIES: Apart from good ideas and good writing skills, what's required at *Self* is most often excellent research skills. Explains Valorie Weaver: "We often handle material that's quite sophisticated; the trick for the writer is to be able to present the information in a simple, readable way. It's the kind of work that generally requires real experience."

The editors rely on a few regular writers but would be happy to have more. A new writer does tend to appear every issue, but they usually have good clips to show and a lot of experience. For the beginning writer, possibilities at *Self* are limited; beginners break in rarely.

Health and nutrition, psychological issues (particularly in the love/sex/relationships area), money and career are all possibilities. One writer recently broke in with a diet/calorie quiz Weaver described as "very clever"; another successful query was on how to plan a financial wardrobe—"it was an interesting way to approach money." A doctor sold *Self* a piece on the need for emotional care when someone in the family is very ill physically. Weaver cautions, however, that writers querying in the health and nutrition areas should be specialists, and that psychological articles are even harder to pull off: "You need the background for these pieces." Generalists should try for less specialized areas. But forget about imparting to others, through *Self*, how your life has changed through jogging: "I must get ten of those a week!"

Weaver's advice? "Study the magazine before you query. The worst overall mistake writers make here is not paying attention to the market we're aiming at. We get queries on pet stories, which is completely inappropriate. And we get personal reminiscences, subjects like 'The Last Day I Spent with My Grandfather.' That may be nice for another magazine, but it's wrong for *Self*."

Work is done on assignment here. Occasionally work on spec will be requested from the beginner. If the idea you submit isn't quite right but your credentials and clips are good, the editors *will* keep you on file; you may end up getting a call. And writers are used more than once if they handle the first story well and another comes up that would suit their skills.

HOW TO SUBMIT: Photocopied manuscripts are accepted. Of multiple submissions Weaver says: "We don't encourage them; the writer *must* inform us. We buy only exclusive rights." Include in your query a rundown of the specialists/experts you'll be talking to for your information, where you've been published, any particular expertise. It's not necessary to enclose many clips at query stage, although one or two may be helpful; if there's interest in the idea, further clips will be requested. At that time it's a good idea to send a range of clips, not just one or two, and if a published piece has been heavily edited, *Self* would prefer to see the unedited manuscript instead. Weaver notes: "If I get newspaper or trade clips I read them only for style. But writers should be aware that there's a big jump from newspaper reporting to magazine writing, especially pieces that require the kind of research ours do."

REJECTIONS: Standard forms are used. Personalized notes occasionally are sent "if the idea is right or the writer looks right; if it's an idea that's good but not quite correctly focused; or if it's a wonderful query that just provokes a personal response."

SEVENTEEN

850 Third Avenue
New York, NY 10022
(212) 759-8100

SOURCE: Karen Larson, articles editor

IN SHORT: Open to new writers.

ABOUT THE MAGAZINE: Monthly. *Seventeen* is a magazine for young women aged 12–20; the average reader is a little younger than 17. The magazine combines beauty and fashion, food, decorating and crafts, celebrity interviews, movie and record reviews, with articles of interest to teen readers. *Circulation:* Just under 2 million. *Areas open to free-lancers:* All articles and "Mini Mag." "Your Words" is open to teen writers. (The following areas are staff-written: beauty, fashion, food, decorating crafts, entertainment—includes celebrity profiles.) *Rates:* Articles: $500–$2000. "Your Words": $150. "Mini Mag": $50–$175. *Payment:* On acceptance. *Expenses:* Phone calls and certain travel costs. *Kill fee:* 25%. *Rights:* Buys all rights from teen writers, first North American rights from professional writers. By written contract. *Number of submissions received weekly:* 50. *Reply time to queries:* A few days. *Advance dates:* Lead time is four months. Issues are planned six months in advance.

FREE-LANCE POSSIBILITIES: Part of the philosophy at *Seventeen* is to provide ample opportunity for the teen readers to have their say. Teen writers contribute many of the short articles and viewpoint pieces published monthly. *All* the major articles, and a good percentage of "Mini Mag," are written by free-lancers. The editors want good story ideas; it's definitely worth trying to break in here and it's very possible to do so via a major piece.

What's important here is keeping in mind the magazine's very specialized market: teens. Says Karen Larson: "We're geared toward helping the teenager cope with what's going on around her. In articles we try to get information from a range of ages; we like our authors to talk to young women for their information, as well as to counselors, psychologists, etc. if the piece calls for it.

"We emphasize how-to. If we were to do a story on breaking up, there would be an emphasis on *how to* go about that. Relationship stories about boyfriends, friends, parents, siblings are also important. We're especially on the lookout for fresh ways of approaching the two most popular subjects: boys and friends. We'll also tackle issues that are significant to teens; we've done pieces on birth control, teenage alcoholism, teen suicide."

Most of *Seventeen*'s readers are still in high school and live with their parents in middle-class homes. Articles for too affluent a market won't work. An article on tennis camps was published, for instance, while one on summer camps in Europe was rejected. "We felt the summer-camps story was way over line, price-wise. But we felt there would be enough readers in a spending category for most of the tennis camps."

Many of the teen readers have part-time jobs, so articles in this area have included: how to get summer jobs, jobs in fast food, 25 best career opportunities for women.

Two ideas that came in over-the-transom: a piece on black/white friendships, by Mac Margolis, in the March '82 issue; in the May '82 issue, "So You Flip for Your Girlfriend's Guy," by Cynthia Elflein.

Of the 50-odd article submissions received weekly, only "a couple" are pulled for consideration and only a few end up as major pieces in the magazine. Nevertheless the door *is* open and there's no bias against little published or unpublished writers. Says Karen Larson: "Most of the article ideas come from us. But we're always interested in ideas from free-lancers. Often, if it's a really good idea, we'll give a go-ahead to someone who may not have even written much before. We don't have contributing editors; though we do have people we call on frequently for assignments. But we're always looking for writers who can become regulars; we want good writing from people we can rely on."

One area where it may be easier to break in is "Mini Mag." This section runs around nine pages each issue and consists of several small pieces. Some published examples: a high school cave-exploring club in Illinois, how to send away for wall charts on hairstyling and running, news of an upcoming art exhibition touring the country, a miniature horse farm in Pennsylvania, the fears of graduation, how to run a meeting, tips on what to do/what not to do when visiting a friend in the hospital, more tips on "keeping your cool while leaving a burning building," how to find information for a research paper. "Mini Mag" runs a lot of material monthly, making the odds of breaking in somewhat better than in main articles.

On general articles, if you're not extensively published, you will probably be asked to work on spec. But if this happens, it means that the editors think enough of your idea to want you to go ahead with it. "We'll only ask someone to do a piece on spec if it's a pretty strong idea and we're really hoping it will work out." And if it does, it's likely you'll be hearing from the magazine again.

Editing varies, but rewriting is done by the author, time permitting. Galleys will be shown if the author requests it.

HOW TO SUBMIT: Send queries to Karen Larson for articles; to Jan Cherubin, "Mini Mag" editor, for that department. Completed mss. are read (original copies preferred), but if the story is not already written, queries are preferred. Says Karen Larson: "A page is really enough to give us an idea, unless the writer really feels a longer query is necessary. If you have a working title, tell us; it shows you have a focus. A title, by the way, reflects a specific angle. 'How to Get Out of a Bad Relationship' is a title; 'Bad Relationships' is a subject, not a title."

A query letter that presents a fresh story idea, *written* well, is what will bring a favorable response at *Seventeen*. Details about your background are not really necessary; include them only if they're relevant to the idea you're presenting. If you have been published elsewhere, say so; including one or two clips is a good idea, but not a requirement. If you're a very new writer, send a well-written query with a good idea and you'll have equal chance.

REJECTIONS: A standard rejection form is used; personalized replies go to writers who have taken some trouble with their query, or to writers the editors would like to encourage.

SIGNATURE

880 Third Avenue
New York, NY 10022
(212) 888-9450

SOURCE: Barbara Coats, senior editor (articles)
Susan Shipman, senior editor (columns)

IN SHORT: Ideas welcomed, but assignments given only to writers with strong clips.

ABOUT THE MAGAZINE: Monthly; 90% free-lance–written. *Signature* is a magazine of travel and stylish living; offered by subscription to holders of Diners Club and Carte Blanche cards. Articles are geared to a sophisticated, spending audience. Among readers, 82% are men; 74% are married; 64% are in professional or managerial occupations—29% are in top management. Median age: early 40s. Median total household income (in 1980): $52,000. *Circulation:* 690,000. *Estimated readership:* 1.9 million. *Sample copy:* $1.50. *Areas open to free-lancers:* Everything except "Sports Story," "City in the Spotlight," and certain regular columns (food, travel, book reviews, photography, "The Selective Buyer"). *Rates:* Articles (1200–2500 words): $700–$2000. *Payment:* On acceptance. *Expenses:* Pays limited expenses on travel stories. *Kill fee:* 25%. *Rights:* Buys first North American rights (lasting 60 days after publication), by written contract. Rights purchase also includes an option for one-time publication in *Signature*'s foreign editions. *Number of submissions received weekly:* 30–40. *Reply time to queries:* Generally no longer than six weeks. *Advance dates:* Lead time is 4½ months. Issues are planned six to seven months in advance.

FREE-LANCE POSSIBILITIES: *Signature* runs a lot of travel articles; however, you do not have to be a specialist travel writer to be published here. And appropriate general-interest article ideas would be welcomed with open arms. In other words, there's a good deal of scope at this magazine. There are not, however, a lot of possibilities for a beginning writer. While it's editorial policy to use a lot of different writers and not the same old faces every issue, to be considered at *Signature* you have to have good clips. Without them, probably the only way to break in is by submitting something independently on spec; no assignments are given if impressive clips aren't forthcoming, and *asking* writers to work on spec (which doesn't happen too often) is not taken lightly. Says Barbara Coats: "We wouldn't ask anyone to work on spec unless we had serious designs on the story." She adds a further comment: "When a magazine gives an unknown writer an assignment, the editor is going out on a limb for that person. I hate seeing someone work really hard on a piece that turns out to be unacceptable. When you have a kill fee policy, there can be good bit of money involved if the story doesn't work out. We all have budgets and we have to be careful."

Even if you're an established writer, *Signature* is an attractive, well-paying market—but not a complete shoo-in. Your clips will have to include published articles that are similar to the kinds of pieces *Signature* uses. Of the 30 or 40 queries received weekly, only one or two are passed on for consideration. Of all the article ideas that come over-the-transom from writers unknown at the magazine, only about three a year materialize into articles.

How to peg an idea that's right? You've got to study the magazine carefully. Travel articles, for instance, *have* to contain an unusual slant. Barbara Coats hints: "The writer probably should *know* the particular place he's suggesting. Thinking, 'Ah-ha! This is the way to go on vaction!' is not going to work." Think angles and think uniqueness. "Writers will say they want to do a story on Rio de Janeiro. While I'm sold on Rio as a place, I'm not sure it's worth a story—unless you can come up with a new and different angle." An associate editor who does the initial scanning of unsolicited submissions and decides whether or not queries should be passed on, commented: "Often a story idea will be too narrow ('the small hotels of Vancouver') or too broad ('the beauty of Ireland'), or the story's topic will be the writer's personal experience of a place, not the place itself. We also see a fair number of travel articles slanted exclusively toward service: where to eat, sleep or shop, how to get around, what to tip, etc. There's no sense of a place's flavor in such writing, no enticement to visit. We prefer a mixture of both the personal and the objective—presented in a light, literary style."

This editor explained the kind of stories that are likely to be passed on: "Subjects we haven't covered lately, particularly interesting destinations, with an interesting premise or a news

peg. Novel article ideas about good food and drink, from a connoisseur's point of view rather than a cook's. Sports articles that
would be of interest to more than just the avid sports fan."

Don't bother sending your bio and clips in the hope of getting
an assignment. The editors want *ideas*. If your query isn't quite
right but your samples are impressive you'll be filed for the
future.

Editing tends to be light. Galleys are shown.

HOW TO SUBMIT: Queries are much preferred here. Says Barbara
Coats: "We would prefer not to see manuscripts." Address your
query to Horace Sutton, editor. Most queries go into an "unsolicited pile" and are perused by an associate editor. Senior editors
then receive only the more likely possibilities. The associate
editor explained the sorting-through process: "If a proposal or
story seems well written, if clips show the work of a talented
writer, if the tone and style of the prose seem well matched to
the magazine, and if the subject of the proposed article is appropriate, we will show the idea to the articles editors. If they don't
meet these criteria, we return them to the author."

Barbara Coats prefers to see a one-page query, in which you
get to the point *fast* (explaining, as well, how you would approach the piece—the beginning, the middle, and the end).
"State your idea right up at the top of the query; we're all working on deadlines." Enclose one clip, preferably one that's similar
to the kind of story you're suggesting. If your idea is accepted,
you'll be asked to send more clips at a later stage. Skip personal
details; where you've been published is what's important. Watch
spelling and grammar: "Your query letter should be neat and
clean and double-spaced. Something that's readable is so important." Put some time and effort into the query: "Some people
will just dash off a query that shows us nothing of their writing
ability."

Don't bombard the editors with *lots* of ideas. Says Coats:
"Often writers will send us a query on ten destinations. They'll
say: 'I'd like to do stories on Prague, St. Louis . . .' and eight
other cities. An editor can't tell anything from that. We want one
good idea, carefully developed, rather than six moderately developed ideas."

Barbara Coats's last word: "It's not easy to get into *Signature*,
but there's always room for a good writer with a good idea and a

hot typewriter. This is a magazine to read, not just flip through and consult."

REJECTIONS: Standard forms are used. Personalized replies are sent if the contributor has been referred to the editors or if they are impressed by the idea or clips submitted.

SKI

Times Mirror Magazines
380 Madison Avenue
New York, NY 10017
(212) 687-3000

SOURCE: Steve Cohen, managing editor

IN SHORT: Difficult to sell; worthwhile only if you know the sport.

ABOUT THE MAGAZINE: Published seven times a year, monthly September through March; 15% free-lance–written. *Ski* is a magazine for those who take skiing seriously (most readers are intermediate-to-advanced-level skiers). The emphasis is on the how-to (through articles on instruction, technique, and equipment) and the where-to (go skiing, that is). *Readership:* median age: 26; 24% college grads; median household income: $28,000. *Circulation:* 413,000. *Estimated readership:* 1.8 million. *Sample copy:* Free. *Areas open to free-lancers:* All. *Rates:* Full-length features: around $600. Shorter features: $300–around $500. "Ski Life": $50–$100. Regional reports: $90. *Payment:* On acceptance. *Expenses:* Pays reasonable expenses. *Kill fee:* Negotiable. *Rights:* Buys first North American serial rights, by written contract. *Number of submissions received weekly:* Four. *Reply time to queries:* Four to six weeks. *Advance dates:* Lead time is three months. Most assignments are made by December; all queries should arrive September through early December.

FREE-LANCE POSSIBILITIES: If you're a writer who's also a ski enthusiast, there may be possibilities at *Ski*. Otherwise, forget it because the challenge to come up with a salable idea will not be worth the effort involved. The magazine is planned well in advance; and it has a sizable staff of editors, contributing editors, and stringers whose lives revolve around the sport.

The easiest way to break in is with a small piece (300 words max.) for the "Ski Life" potpourri section, and you'll have the best chance if you're reporting on something offbeat. It is possible to break in with a feature; unknown writers manage to do that two or three times a year; again, however, the key is the offbeat angle. Steve Cohen advises: "Give us unique stories we can't get on our own." Where to find them? Possibly the lesser-known resorts and ski areas. Steering away from the predictable may also work; unknown writers broke in with these ideas, for instance: the steepest trails in Vermont; ski hostels (which was used as a sidebar to a larger feature on how to ski on the cheap); the first person to ski down Tuckerman Ravine (which fitted in with a planned feature on the ravine itself). Humor is a definite possibility. The regional sections can also provide an "in": the East, Midwest, and West are covered in each issue and 300–400-word reports on regional where-to-ski areas are invited (but query first).

The editors advise against submitting profiles. If the subjects are worth writing about, chances are the editors know about them. Cohen also advises against competition stories ("We rarely cover competitions and when we do we assign") and travel queries. "It has to be a very unusual travel angle," he explains. "I often get queries from writers who are off to Europe and want to do a ski travel piece while they're there. But those kind of travel pieces are staff-written; it's not worth querying on them."

Cohen also has these complaints about many of the queries that pass over his desk: "You have to read the magazine and know what we're doing; often the queries are way off. I also see a good deal of lack of knowledge about the sport. Not to mention the misspelled words in query letters!"

Most writers work at *Ski* on assignment; if your idea is acceptable and you're an experienced writer, it's unlikely you'll be asked to work on spec. But you'll only become a regular writer by regularly coming up with ideas. "We ask even our own writers to put together story-idea packages," Cohen comments.

Editing varies. Galleys are shown.

HOW TO SUBMIT: Mss. are read, but queries are preferred. Photocopied mss., multiply-submitted mss., and queries are okay. Query Steve Cohen on articles; Catherine Williams, national regional editor, on regional reports. Cohen encourages short queries: "Just give me the point of the article. I don't want people to spend hours writing a query letter. If we're interested, we'll call you and talk about it some more." Include in your query your qualifications both as a writer and a skier. Clips are required before assignments are given, but no need to send them with the query. If you can take photos as well, it's worth mentioning with regard to a package offering.

REJECTIONS: A standard rejection form is used, "but if time permits, we'll send a personalized note."

SKIING

Ziff-Davis Publishing
One Park Avenue
New York, NY 10016
(212) 725-3969

SOURCE: Alfred H. Greenberg, editor-in-chief

IN SHORT: Not easy to sell. Skiing knowledge required, and only manuscripts accepted.

ABOUT THE MAGAZINE: Published seven times a year, monthly September through March. Mostly written by staff and stringers. *Skiing* is a magazine for the Alpine skier, although some cross-country coverage is also included. Readers are mainly low intermediate through advanced skiers. The magazine tells where-to and how-to around the world; it also covers ski equipment (tested by the magazine) and clothing. Racing results and analyses are also included "to inform the spectator, to learn how the best skiers ski." *Circulation:* 430,000. *Areas open to free-lancers:* All. *Rates:* Features: up to 50 cents a word. Regionals: 10–25 cents a word. *Payment:* On acceptance. *Expenses:* Pays all incidentals. *Kill fee:* One-third. *Rights:* Buys first North American magazine rights, by written contract. *Number of submissions received weekly:* Ten. *Reply time to queries:* Can range from a few days to two months (in the busy period from June 1–November 30). But when reply time will be lengthy, postcards acknowledging arrival of manuscript are sent to all contributors. *Advance dates:* Lead time is two months. Issues are planned a year in advance.

FREE-LANCE POSSIBILITIES: "Our first requirement is that the writer be a skier," says Alfred H. Greenberg. That said, the way into *Skiing* is with a well-written manuscript (no queries accepted) on a topic that is unusual or offbeat; this magazine has an editorial staff of 12 and another half-dozen stringers throughout the country. That means a lot of topics are already well covered. How-to-ski articles are done mostly by professional instructors; racing analysis is generally staff-written. Where-to-ski is also a difficult area for the free-lancer. "If it's a new place to ski, chances are we will have heard of it." But Greenberg qualifies this: "Occasionally we will buy a piece on an exotic place to ski; I once bought a piece from a writer who had skied in Bolivia. But this piece was bought because of the quality of the writing. Our editors have been to, and covered, most of the exotic places."

In the Spring '82 issue, "Terror on Triple O" by Cheryl May (an account of an avalanche and a race against time), and "Alive, Well, and Over 40 in Aspen" by Joy Dalton (an amusing account of what it's like to be newly divorced and on the slopes) came in over-the-transom. These are typical of the kinds of pieces free-lancers can write to break into *Skiing;* either stories the staff/ contributing editors might not know about, or else personal experience accounts. For the latter category Greenberg advises: "A 'My First Time on Skis' really would be of no interest to us or our readers. 'My First Time in a Race' could work if it were different and well written; that could be amusing to our readers. But mostly the humor pieces that come in aren't really that funny. Humor *has* to be good."

Three different regional sections (East, Midwest, and West) run in the back of the book, and could be one of the best areas for free-lancers. The focus is on smaller local areas, and editorial space ranges from 4–32 pages. This is the place for local interest pieces that are not general enough for the front of the magazine.

Good writing is extremely important at *Skiing.* Greenberg has high standards in this area, and he also has a policy on submissions. He will consider only completed mss. "My standard reply to anyone who sends in a query is that we will gladly look at it in manuscript form, on speculation." He can't guarantee the free-lancer a swift reply every time, but if he accepts one piece, it's your "in" to *Skiing* (most of the regular free-lancers originally came in over-the-transom). Greenberg also justifies the "manuscript only" policy by pointing out that a manuscript submission is fair to *all* writers. It gives the unpublished writer an equal chance. Dr. Gerhart Drucker, an M.D. in his 80s, sent in a piece about skiing at an elderly age that was bought immediately.

Here are the odds: Only one or two over-the-transom pieces are bought per issue.

HOW TO SUBMIT: Send completed manuscript. Photocopies and multiple submissions discouraged. Include a basic cover letter, briefly outlining your background. Clips not necessary. It's best to send submissions in late fall to early spring; summer is the busiest period at the magazine and reply time can lag.

REJECTIONS: A standard rejection slip is usually used. Sometimes an encouraging personalized note will be sent.

(DELTA) SKY

Halsey Publishing
12955 Biscayne Boulevard
North Miami, FL 33181
(305) 893-1520

SOURCE: Donna Dupuy, editor

IN SHORT: Very limited possibilities because of "stable system."

ABOUT THE MAGAZINE: Monthly; 100% free-lance–written. *Delta Sky* is the in-flight magazine of Delta Airlines. It is a general-interest publication, with at least half the editorial emphasis on business and industry, finance and management, and economic matters. The magazine also covers sports and recreation, culture and entertainment, life-style/trend stories, contemporary technology, and some travel. *Readership:* 83% of readers are male, mostly college-educated; 73% of readers are professional/managerial, middle to high income. Most readers live in the Northeast, Southeast, or Midwest. *Circulation:* 3 million. *Sample copy:* $3. *Areas open to free-lancers:* Everything except "Sky-Lines," and the following regular columns: puzzles, psychology/human behavior series, book reviews, the business column. *Rates:* $300–$400 for columns; $400–$600 for features. *Payment:* On publication, with some exceptions. *Expenses:* Pays reasonable expenses (with prior approval; receipts must be provided). *Kill fee:* 50–100%. *Rights:* Buys first American rights only, by letter of agreement. (Magazine takes no fee on reprints.) *Number of submissions received weekly:* 10–15 queries; 5–10 manuscripts. *Reply time to queries:* "We try to answer within 60–90 days, but do not always make it." No replies without SASE. *Advance dates:* Lead time is 1½ months. Issues are planned six months in advance.

FREE-LANCE POSSIBILITIES: Although *Sky* is all free-lance–written, there is no great need either for story ideas or new writers. There are about 25 regular writers, with another 25 or so (writers Donna Dupuy calls "the second team") doing occasional articles, once or twice a year.

About eight features are run per issue. One of these is a destination piece, another a company CEO profile (queries are not accepted in either of these areas) and another a psychology piece (written by a regular contributor). This leaves about five chances per issue—for the unknown free-lancer perhaps not even one slot after regular writers' articles have been included.

Dupuy is receiving around 300 article ideas monthly; of articles published, 80% of the ideas come from staff and airline requests, 15% from regulars, and 5% from the outside (but this also includes PR companies and similar contacts). "Only about one in 200 over-the-transom ideas works out, and then it's simply a matter of luck and timing," she says. *Sky* is publishing experienced, but not necessarily name, writers, and Dupuy comments: "A good writer is a good writer. We're not afraid to take calculated risks with promising new talent." But she adds: "Our 'stable system' *does* limit opportunities."

Sky's articles fall into the following categories (in order of priority). Business and finance: industry in general, the economy, management/manufacturing techniques and methods, corporate trends and investments. Life-style: leisure, architecture, recreation, personal health and appearance, entertaining. Sports and recreation: pro sports (in season), major amateur and collegiate events, offbeat and individual sports activities and fitness. Culture and entertainment: film, theater, music, TV, art, dance. Contemporary technology: computers, modern technology, space travel, astronomy, general research and development, ecology. CEO Profile Series: no submissions accepted. Travel: determined by the airline; focuses on Delta destinations.

The February '83 issue included: "Coffee and the New Connoisseur"—coffee has risen to gourmet heights; a piece on jealousy, "The Green-Eyed Monster"; "Alternative Abodes," an article on dome homes, log cabins, and other less traditional housing concepts; a behind-the-scenes look at what it takes to be successful in the music industry. The September '83 lineup included: "Who's Training the Great Chefs of America?"— American cooking schools are!; teaching children via "Computers in the Classroom"; a piece on the serious business of professional bass fishing; an article on meditation and how it can help the harassed businessperson; "Big Beautiful Boats," a look at the poshest pleasure boats afloat.

The magazine also holds an inventory of "expansion," or timeless stories—articles that can be slotted in at any time. Free-lancers who can come up with text/color photo packages have the best chances; 12–20 expansion stories are used each year.

Sky does not publish light humor, reprints, religious, or first-person experience material, restaurant/hotel/events listings, or "down" stories like disease, disaster, crime, life problems. Says Dupuy: "We don't want to see any more queries on psychology/human behavior, book/movie/music reviews, food/beverage articles, travel articles, celebrity profiles, financial how-to pieces, management/personnel theory, fashion/grooming."

An associate editor reviews the unsolicited material, passing on any promising submissions to Dupuy. The writer is then contacted for a further discussion, then a group of proposals is presented to the airline for approval/comment/response. A favorable reply results in an assignment. Writers are not asked to work on spec, and are often not required to show clips. Assignments depend on the idea, the proposal, and format approval.

If revision involves "more than a paragraph or two," the manuscript is given back to the writer. Editing varies, but Dupuy adds: "We *have* been told we're very considerate." Galleys are shown on request.

HOW TO SUBMIT: Completed manuscripts are considered (photocopies okay), but queries are preferred. Multiple submissions are accepted. Phone calls are accepted, but not collect calls. Preferred query length is 75–150 words. Include working title, general concept of story, approximate length, details of any available color photography. Adds Dupuy: "We rarely find personal information useful or persuasive, even when it's credentials; someone might be perfect for XYZ magazine but not suited to us. The query or manuscript says a lot more of what we need to hear." Clips not necessary at query stage. But SASEs are; no replies without them. "The importance of SASEs cannot be overemphasized, especially when slides/prints are enclosed. About a third of all submissions we receive do not have SASEs —a sure way to get ignored."

REJECTIONS: A standard form is sent. This includes several reasons for rejection, which the editor will check off. Dupuy sometimes will also recommend other possible markets.

SMITHSONIAN

900 Jefferson Drive, S.W.
Washington, DC 20560
(202) 357-2600

SOURCE: Marlane A. Liddell, articles editor

IN SHORT: Specialized market; fairly difficult to sell.

ABOUT THE MAGAZINE: Monthly. Most articles are free-lance–
written. *Smithsonian* is the magazine of the Smithsonian Insti-
tution. It covers not only Smithsonian exhibitions and events but
also general-interest articles in the fields of art, natural history,
the sciences, and culture, both in the U.S. and abroad. Adds
Marlane Liddell: "We're not an investigative magazine and we
don't cover political or news events or controversial issues."
Readership: male/female ratio split; median age: 42; half are
college grads and higher; income level is high. (Magazine subscription rate—$17—is never discounted.) *Circulation:* just
under 2 million. *Estimated readership:* 4.5 million. *Sample
copy:* $1.25 to subscription department. *Areas open to free-lan-
cers:* All features. ("Phenomena, comments and notes," "Around
the Mall and beyond," and "Highlights" are staff/contributor-
written.) *Rates:* Back-page humor column (750 words): $500.
Features (3000–4000 words): $1500 minimum (for first-time con-
tributor). *Payment:* On acceptance. *Expenses:* Pays all incidentals. *Kill fee:* One-third. *Rights:* Buys first North American rights,
by letter of agreement. *Number of submissions received weekly:*
200 minimum. *Reply time to queries:* Immediately to up to six
weeks (if idea is being considered). Inquiry calls accepted, "but
give us two to three weeks." *Advance dates:* Lead time is two
months. Issues are planned three months in advance.

FREE-LANCE POSSIBILITIES: Competition is stiff at *Smithsonian*;
articles are specialized, writing standards are high, and there are
30–40 regular contributors. But Marlane Liddell is willing to
work with enthusiastic writers: "That first article is the most
difficult one to get in. But once you're in, it becomes easier."
    One or two new by-lines, usually from magazine-experienced
writers, appear per issue. A beginning writer breaks in only two
or three times a year; it happens when the subject matter is
particularly appealing, and often when the idea is offbeat. Like

the nostalgia piece on song slides John W. Ripley wrote from a query over-the-transom; it appeared as the cover story of the March '82 issue.

In the May '82 issue, Thomas A. Bass broke in with a piece on the Rocky Mountain Biological Lab. Comments Marlane Liddell: "Tom wrote a very good query. The Lab. isn't a new story, but he proposed spending a good deal of time there, at minimal expense, to see how viable the research is. The piece turned out to be very people-oriented, which we like. We want stories that are lively and colorful and anecdotal."

The free-lancer's best chances—presuming you do not have a particular specialty that would fit the magazine's range of interests—are in offbeat, unusual subjects; historical (well-researched) pieces; and profiles.

Profiles run around 2500 words. "We profile people here or abroad who are making a difference in our lives. We like lots of anecdotes, finding out what makes these people special. It's a good area for free-lancers. No question-and-answer profiles, though." Published examples: the new director of the Smithsonian Astrophysical Observatory in Boston, a scientist who is an expert at restoring streams.

Historical pieces are a fertile area for the free-lancer, but Liddell cautions: "These are difficult to do, because of the research involved. And they have to be illustratable, either with photographs or existing prints." (It's worth noting here that visual/illustration possibilities are very important in general. An idea won't be considered if it cannot be adequately illustrated; *Smithsonian* either assigns its own photographers or buys from stock agencies or specialized sources).

The back-page humor column is a real possibility. "We're always looking for material for this column," Liddell says. Writers are requested to send manuscripts, however, not a query.

Because there are regular contributors overseas, the magazine rarely sends American writers out of the country. But Liddell comments: "On the positive side, if you plan to go overseas and have an idea that's different, we'll happily consider it." An article on tea (by Jill Jonnes, February '82), and another on the Thames Barrier and saving London from an impending threat of flood (by Jane Wholey, August '82), were done this way. Articles on art are not good possibilities. Most art stories are done to coincide with new exhibitions and are assigned to writers in the field. Over-the-transom suggestions here have a very slim chance.

Writers generally work on assignment because they tend to be experienced and seasoned magazine writers. Full-length magazine clips are preferred here. Without impressive clips, your idea might be rejected if it would be an expensive or time-consuming project. "I don't like to ask writers to work on spec under those circumstances," Marlane Liddell comments. On less complex pieces she *may* ask you to work on spec, and adds: "Writers with few credits should be willing to work on spec—till we see what they can do. Just because you have only newspaper clips doesn't mean you won't be considered; I'll judge you by your proposal."

Liddell sees all but the immediate rejections: poetry, short features, how-tos. She will direct specific-area queries to the appropriate editor; on general queries she'll either make a decision, or else confer with the editor if an idea seems a possibility. Of the 200-odd submissions received weekly, she's likely to put aside 25–30 for further consideration. Most of these won't make it into the magazine, but half of the writers probably will be encouraged to try and come up with more ideas. "I've been working with one writer on ideas; he originally came in over-the-transom. It has taken him four years, but now he's come up with the right idea for us. I'll try and encourage writers as often as I can because I consider that an investment in the future."

Heavy fact checking is done here. "Every word is verified in every article. Writers have to have sources. Generally a researcher works very closely with the writer. Editing is not heavy generally. It's our goal to have a variety of writing styles in a given issue. Often articles have to be cut for space, though." Galleys "will be shown to the writer, if there's time. But we'll always tell you about any changes."

HOW TO SUBMIT: Mss. are read (photocopied mss. okay), but queries are preferred. Multiple submissions are accepted "on timely stories, when a dated event is involved. Queries should be one-page minimum, two pages maximum. The queries I pay attention to are the ones that are presented with this magazine in mind. I want to know how the writer is going to treat the story. If there are anecdotes or new information, I want to know about them in the proposal. I want to see and feel the writer's enthusiasm for the subject he's presenting." Include clips; a résumé is also helpful. "Don't just give me the names of the magazines where you've been published, or dates. We want to see actual samples."

REJECTIONS: A standard rejection form is used, "but if the reply is in any way personalized, that's a positive."

SOAP OPERA DIGEST

254 West 31st Street
New York, NY 10001
(212) 947-6300

SOURCE: Meredith Brown, editor

IN SHORT: Good market for writers with knowledge of the day-time TV industry.

ABOUT THE MAGAZINE: Bi-weekly; 40% free-lance–written. *Soap Opera Digest* is a digest-sized magazine for soap opera enthusiasts; it carries synopses of all the major network shows as well as interviews with the stars, "behind-the-scenes" stories, and information on the daytime industry at large. *Readership:* aged 18–40. They're mostly women, with high school and some college education, middle income. Distributed nationally, as well as in Canada. *Circulation:* 650,000. *Estimated readership:* 1.6 million. *Areas open to free-lancers:* Everything except "Reel to Real," "New York News," "Hollywood Happenings," and the show synopses. *Rates:* $150–$250 ("We do pay higher depending on writer and assignment"). *Payment:* On acceptance. *Expenses:* Pays reasonable expenses. *Kill fee:* One-third. *Rights:* Buys all rights whenever possible, by verbal contract. *Number of submissions received weekly:* Four. *Reply time to queries:* Two weeks maximum. *Advance dates:* Lead time is 2½ months. Issues are planned four months in advance.

FREE-LANCE POSSIBILITIES: New writers are appearing in *Soap Opera Digest* roughly every other issue. Says editor Meredith Brown: "We do want well-established writers; we are actively looking for new writers who *know* daytime TV. We are also interested in new talent and in helping develop that talent."

One or two decent clips will be enough to get your foot in the door, provided they are accompanying an appealing story idea. The following stories originally came in as over-the-transom queries: An "open letter" to network executives, complaining—in a humorous way—about the viewer's anger when a favorite show is temporarily halted for "news"; "Why Men Watch Soaps"; an interview with an actor on "Guiding Light" (whom the writer knew personally).

The outside free-lancer must come up with "new ideas for

stories or else new angles that are thought provoking." Brown adds: "We are interested in viewer-oriented stories. Aside from those mentioned, we've recently done features on 'Working Women and the Soaps,' 'Do soap characters suffer from the Cinderella Complex?' "

It is more difficult to break in with a profile. The magazine's sizable staff of editors and stringers have covered just about every actor, and they have their collective fingers on the pulse of the daytime TV world. Chances are *they* will know first who's debuting, who's leaving, and the gossip on and off screen. "We'll consider a profile idea if a writer has a *new* slant on an actor, or a contact with a hard-to-get-in-touch-with actor."

Regular contributors get assignments here, but they may also be given to unknown writers if clips are satisfactory and if the magazine *needs* the story.

The amount of editing done "depends on the writer. We have a group of wonderful editors who work *with* writers." Galleys are not shown.

HOW TO SUBMIT: Prefers not to accept manuscript submissions (and will not accept photocopied manuscripts). Query with a writing sample (one or two clips is enough), and include your writing experience. "We're only interested in people who have some experience."

REJECTIONS: A standard form is used. A personalized reply is sent "if the piece is very good but we can't use it; if the writer shows promise."

SPORT

119 West 40th Street
New York, NY 10018
(212) 869-4700

SOURCE: Neil Cohen, managing editor

IN SHORT: Good free-lance market; editors looking for good magazine writers.

ABOUT THE MAGAZINE: Monthly; 90%–95% free-lance–written. *Sport* is a magazine for the sports enthusiast—the kind of sports lover who attends games several times a year, is a keen TV spectator, and who is "looking for the unusual, offbeat sports stories and for *interpretations* of the facts." Adds Neil Cohen: "We are an original kind of magazine, sort of a Whole Sports Catalog: forward looking, irreverent, analytical, entertaining, but informative in a sharply written, sharply focused format, with sidebars and boxes aplenty." *Readership*: largely male; the highest percentage fall into the 18–34 age group, although they really run the spectrum in age and income level, everyone from teenagers to blue-collar workers to doctors and lawyers. Only the major spectator sports are covered (pro and college baseball, boxing, hockey, and pro and college football and basketball). Tennis, golf, and track and field are covered only occasionally—in season, and when the story is geared to a specific major event. *Circulation*: around 900,000. *Estimated readership:* 3 million. *Areas open to free-lancers:* All. *Rates:* Payment starts at $100 for short pieces. Features: $1000–$1500. (Average article fee is $1000.) *Payment:* On acceptance. *Expenses:* All reasonable expenses. *Kill fee:* 25%. *Rights:* Buys first North American rights, by written contract. *Number of submissions received weekly:* 10–15. *Reply time to queries:* Two weeks. *Advance dates:* Lead time is one month. Issues are planned three months in advance.

FREE-LANCE POSSIBILITIES: A good 90%–95% of *Sport* is written by free-lancers—half of them regulars and half of them writers contacted by the editors. And while about 75% of the article ideas are staff-generated, Neil Cohen says, "We would like to get more input from the outside." A good idea from a writer unknown at the magazine has a good chance of making it. Says Cohen: "We always feel proud of ourselves when we find someone good who comes in over-the-transom." And most stories are done on assignment, rather than on spec.

Some points to consider: "Story ideas should show a little imagination. If it's a profile suggestion, it should have an unusual angle, a special focus. We're not interested in straight profiles. We cover only high-visibility sports personalities: players and managers for 'Interview'; obscure people aren't going to make it, unless they have something outstanding to say. We want clear-cut ideas and it's much better if the writer has made the contact; don't just give us something obvious like a sportsman's name or just the subject matter; that's not something we haven't thought of ourselves." A humor piece won't work, but a humorous approach to an article just might.

A good place to break in may be either with an item for "Sport Talk" (a potpourri of small items—includes newsy snippets, points of view, lists, stats; as long as it hasn't appeared elsewhere) or with a smallish piece that could work as a sidebar to a major feature. Sidebars and boxes generally run 500–600 words (payment is 50 cents a word); to the editors they represent a low-risk investment if you're unknown. Breaking in via a major feature, though, is not out of the question and you don't *have* to be a specialist sports writer; Joe Flower, who wrote "The Five Most Powerful Men in Sports" in the July '82 issue, is a business writer. The story was the result of an unsolicited query. The key is to try and come up with an idea that's *clever*.

"We're actively looking for new writers," Neil Cohen comments. "But we don't want first-time writers. We want people who can handle magazine-length stories. We will consider newspaper writers, but only if they can show us they've written articles of 1500–2000 words. We are a top-flight magazine, and we just don't have the luxury of time to work with inexperienced writers."

Don't be surprised if your first piece for *Sport* ends up heavily edited. Explains Cohen: "We try to present articles that are chock full of information; you have to be able to squeeze 3000 words' worth of information into a 1500-word space. And our pieces are written in a lively style, not upbeat but more good, clever, concise writing." The editors try to show galleys whenever possible, "when time permits, and on request."

HOW TO SUBMIT: Sending a completed manuscript is a waste of

time here and, according to Neil Cohen, one of the biggest mistakes contributors make. "A manuscript probably has less than a 1% chance of making it here," he says. And sending a photocopied manuscript could lessen your chances even more. So send a written query and include "as much detail as possible. Don't just give us the name of someone; let us see what we're going to get. Give us as much advance research information as you can: supportive data, statistics, that kind of information. Give us your plan of operation; we want to see that you've given the idea some thought and that you'll be able to handle the piece." Include two or three clips, magazine-length pieces if possible; writers who don't send clips with the initial query are, Cohen feels, doing themselves a disservice: "If you don't include clips, the moment could be lost!" For "Sport Talk," send queries to Barry Shapiro, associate editor.

REJECTIONS: Standard forms are sent; personalized replies often go to contributors the editors would like to encourage.

SPORTS AFIELD

250 West 55th Street
New York, NY 10019
(212) 262-8835

SOURCE: Lois Wilde, associate editor

IN SHORT: Very open, to both experienced and beginning writers. Prefers manuscript submissions.

ABOUT THE MAGAZINE: Monthly; 60% free-lance–written. *Sports Afield* is a high-quality, outdoors magazine that emphasizes hunting and fishing. Circulation is over the half-million mark; its subscribers, according to reader surveys, tend to hold on to each issue and refer back to it often. These are outdoors enthusiasts who take their hunting and fishing seriously; they are most typically high school graduates or with some college, with the highest percentage in the 25–40 age group (plus a good number of retirees). The magazine also publishes six additional "annual" issues each year devoted to "Fishing" (published in mid-January), "Bass" (early March), "Fishing Secrets" (late March), "Hunting Hotspots" (mid-July), "Hunting"(late August), "Deer" (mid-September). *Areas open to free-lancers:* All features, "Wideworld," "Hunter and Angler," and "Almanac." *Rates:* Articles: $650–$1500. Average fee for article/photo package: $800. "Almanac": $10 per published inch. Annuals: $300 and up. *Payment:* Features: on acceptance. "Almanac" and "Worldwides": on publication. *Expenses:* Pays reasonable expenses. *Kill fee:* $100–$300. *Rights:* Articles: Buys first North American rights, by check endorsement. "Almanac" and "Worldwides": buys all rights, by written contract. *Number of submissions received weekly:* 25–75. *Reply time to queries:* Two to three weeks. *Advance dates:* Lead time is three months. Issues are planned at least four months in advance. Annuals are planned six to nine months in advance.

FREE-LANCE POSSIBILITIES: To be published in *Sports Afield* you need experience outdoors and experience as a writer. Says Lois Wilde: "I don't care who the person is or where they've been published as long as they can write well. But writing about the outdoors *does* require some experience in the field." New/unknown writers break in with features eight or ten times a year, so if the outdoors is an interest, this is a market that's—if you can bear the pun—definitely worth a shot!

The magazine has a collection of contributing editors who cover the different outdoors topics: angling, hunting, camping, shooting, nature, boats, recreational vehicles, etc. So the way into the magazine is *not* with a suggestion that would be covered by these editors. Once you study the magazine and see how these columns are written each month, your next move should be to try and come up with an idea—or ideally for *Sports Afield*'s editors, a manuscript—that's a story of personal experience, adventure, humor, how-to, or where-to-go. It must always have a hunting or fishing connection. Says Lois Wilde: "We get lots of camping and hiking and canoeing material, but they don't combine hunting and fishing as well so they have to be rejected; we really want to keep this a hunting and fishing magazine." Humor is welcomed. My-first-experience-in-the-outdoors stories are out, though, "unless it's something that's absolutely hilarious." The magazine does not cover conservation issues heavily. But adventure and articles about new places to go hunting and fishing are sought. (Examples: the fishing canyon in the Idaho Rockies Andrew Slough wrote about in the June '82 issue. "Going after North Woods Salmon" in the same issue.) Keep in mind, though, that this is a *national* magazine with no regional inserts, so where-tos have to be accessible. Women-in-the-outdoors stories may be a possibility: "We know we have women readers and we *would* like to find more women writers in the field."

The "Worldwide" pages highlight only *new* places to go—worldwide. "Almanac" is a collection of newsy/human-interest shorts. Both sections welcome free-lance contributions.

Your chances are definitely better with a completed ms. here. The editors want to see up front what they're getting, and because they're so open to new and unknown writers they want to *see* how you can write. A query may save only time; work is rarely done on assignment here. If you're planning a hunting/fishing trip and want to know if the magazine would be interested in your report, you will only be asked to submit on spec. Explains Wilde: "We'll just tell you: 'Let's see what you have when you come back.'" And even after you've been published in the magazine, your next piece will still be on spec—that's the policy. Editing varies. Galleys are usually not shown.

HOW TO SUBMIT: By query or, preferably, send a manuscript—the original (there's a "bias against" policy here on photocopies). It's not necessary to send clips. The magazine is well organized with submissions: as soon as a query or ms. is received, a green slip is clipped to it. It's then passed around to different editors who write their comments.

PHOTOGRAPHY: The magazine prefers to buy copy/photo packages, so if you can take good photos yourself or have access to appropriate photography, say so in your query, or better still, include the photography with your submission. For general features, color is preferred (slides only); preferably Kodachrome 64. You must send originals, not dupes. For annuals, b/w is preferred. For both also include a caption sheet. Go for interesting, preferably action, shots (no dead animal portraits, please). And think covers; a cover shot pays $1000. But remember: This is a lavish production and photography must be high standard. So much so that good photos could make all the difference.

REJECTIONS: A personalized, but standard form letter is used mostly. If you receive a rejection that's encouraging, particularly one that suggests trying again at another time, it could mean that only your timing was off; it would be worth a resubmission.

SPORTS ILLUSTRATED

Time/Life Building
1271 Avenue of the Americas
New York, NY 10020
(212) 586-1212

SOURCE: Myra Gelban, articles editor
        Constance Tubbs, assistant articles editor

IN SHORT: Difficult market. All free-lance work done on spec.

ABOUT THE MAGAZINE: Weekly. Almost all staff-written. *Sports Illustrated* is a sports news magazine, covering professional, amateur, and recreational sports and issues surrounding them. Eighty percent of readers are male. Age group ranges from 18–49, but readership core is 18–34. Almost half of readers have attended college, they are middle income, and they're active in sports, both as participants and spectators. *Circulation:* Around 2.5 million. *Estimated readership:* 17 million weekly. *Areas open to free-lancers:* Features and regionals (all news stories are staff-written). *Rates:* Features: $2500 maximum. Regionals: front-of-the-book $400; back-of-the-book $750. *Payment:* On acceptance. *Expenses:* None. *Kill fee:* Not applicable. *Rights:* Features: buys first North American rights, by written contract. Regionals: buys all rights. *Number of submissions received weekly:* 100. *Reply time to queries:* Three to four weeks. *Advance dates:* Lead time varies and is affected by news-breaking stories. Regionals close three to four weeks ahead of other copy. Feature suggestions should be submitted *at least* two months in advance.

FREE-LANCE POSSIBILITIES: *Sports Illustrated* is a staff-written magazine; in an average issue probably only one piece is free-lance–written and it's very unlikely it would be a feature. Where free-lancers do have a chance is with "regionals," a somewhat confusing term that actually refers only to advertising. All stories should be written for a national audience. Regionals appear in different parts of the magazine and different criteria apply: The front regionals are the ones that appear before "Scorecard"; they range from 400–1000 words but preferred length is either 400 or 800 words (accurate word length is important to fit into the regional one- or two-column format; editing is often heavy as a result). Payment is a standard $400 for all lengths. Front regionals fall into one of these categories: "Shopwalk" (shopping pieces about unique clothes or equipment); "Footloose" (sports-oriented travel pieces); "Viewpoint"; "Sideline" (a general sports observation, interview, or service piece); "On Deck" (profiles of up-and-coming young athletes); "Spotlight" (stories on excellent athletes in less well covered sports); "Hot Stove" (off-season analysis of and information on any sport); "Sports Prescription" (shorts on what's new in sports medicine); "Replay" (short pieces on a particularly memorable pre-1970 play); "Update" (what are they doing now; follow-ups on former athletes); "Stats" (points or positions based on notable, newsworthy numbers).

Back-of-the-book regionals appear after the main features. The preferred length is 1100–1500 words; payment is a standard $750. Categories: "Yesterday" (nostalgic recreations of some sporting scene or moment, pre-1954. Query first for this category); "First Person," "Nostalgia," and "Reminiscence" (first-person accounts of unusual sporting events); "On the Scene," "Perspective" (an opinion about a sports-related incident or subject, not necessarily first-person; should be current and timely).

It's not only the presence of staff writers that makes *Sports Illustrated* a hard market to sell. All free-lancers must work on spec (even after you've been published once or twice in the magazine); assignments are never given to anyone but staff and regular contributors. Explains Myra Gelband: "Queries on main features don't fare as well as regionals might because we run only three to four major features an issue and we can't give up that kind of space to someone working on spec."

Nevertheless all submissions are read and considered, and Gelband is encouraging: "I don't think good writing can slip through the cracks here. Good writing won't be overlooked or get lost in a pile of bad writing."

Another encouraging point is the fact that you don't have to be a sports specialist to publish here. "We don't care where you've been published," Gelband says. "We judge on the merit of the particular query or manuscript in hand."

Still, only one or two queries work out weekly—and that's in a good week. Most often submissions are rejected because of the writing quality. Often, too, ideas are too *timely* from a news point of view. That kind of story is in the staffers' realm; the free-lancer's best approach is with an idea that's either timeless, or else tied to a season but not a specific date. And where geographic proximity may give a writer an edge elsewhere, here it's no advantage; *Sports Illustrated*'s staffers travel all over.

HOW TO SUBMIT: Send all submissions to Myra Gelband; she sees all over-the-transom material. Both queries and mss. will be considered. Keep queries short—"one page is plenty." Enclose SASE. Clips not necessary because of on-spec policy. And Gelband asks: "Please be patient in waiting to hear from us." (If you want to know if the manuscript has arrived, enclose a stamped return postcard.)

REJECTIONS: Rejections are hard to interpret here. If you're on the right track, you may get a personalized note. But because Gelband and Tubbs make an effort to reply personally as often as possible, a personal note without a specific suggestion to try again merely reflects courtesy.

SPRING

Rodale Press
33 East Minor Street
Emmaus, PA 18049
(215) 967-5171

SOURCE: Emrika Padus, executive editor

IN SHORT: Receptive to free-lancers, although space is limited.

ABOUT THE MAGAZINE: Monthly; 20% free-lance–written. *Spring* debuted in April 1982. Its publisher also puts out *Prevention*. *Spring* is a women's magazine that believes beauty starts with inner health and there is a no-nonsense approach across the board: whether it be food (recipes consist of all fresh, wholesome ingredients, no salt, sugar, or alchohol); consumer causes ("Smart Small Cars," "Health Gadgets We Like," "Creative Interiors You Can Build That Save Fuel Dollars"); health ("A Shopper's Guide to Gynecologists—And Their Alternatives," "Vitamin B6: God's Gift to Women," "How to Exercise When You're Hurt"); beauty ("Firm Answers for Fat Thighs," "Which Soap Is Best for Your Skin?"); fashion (the emphasis is on quality apparel, not fad fashion); and emotional well-being ("How TV Affects Your Energy, Sex and Creativity," "Power Thinking!", "Improve Your Learning Ability—with Music!"). The magazine is aimed at women 20–40, not necessarily career women but "women who are busy and active, who are interested in self-fulfillment and self-sufficiency. We emphasize practical and functional approaches to life." *Circulation:* 400,000. *Areas open to free-lancers:* All articles. *Rates:* For columns and sidebars: $150. For features: $250–$1500. *Payment:* On acceptance. *Expenses:* All reasonable expenses. *Kill fee:* 20%. *Rights:* Buys all rights, by written contract. Negotiable. *Number of submissions received weekly:* 50. *Reply time to queries:* Three weeks to three months. (Outright rejections receive fastest replies.) Inquire by mail, not phone. *Advance dates:* Lead time is three months. Issues are planned four to five months in advance.

FREE-LANCE POSSIBILITIES: Article ideas at *Spring* are mostly staff-generated, and Emrika Padus points out: "It's difficult for the free-lancer because non-staffers can't know the kinds of issues we're planning." Space is faily limited, and articles are not bought for inventory. Still, this is a young magazine and one that does use free-lancers. "We're looking for new people to add to our regular writers," Padus says. "And when we find someone we like, we hope to develop them into regulars."

Studying the magazine is the key. Service pieces are always backed up with some kind of solid research and/or authority. Rodale Press is very big on product testing, if relevant, and fact checking. "We have a large research department—more researchers than editors—and the researchers have a very important say. They document painstakingly; the fact checkers go back directly to the source." Two areas already covered in the magazine have been home gyms and home security alarm systems. All products mentioned in the articles were tested extensively by Rodale's product-testing center.

A new writer coming over-the-transom breaks in to the magazine only about once per issue. Chances are better with smaller, catchy pieces. Something like "The Great Stocking Runoff" (April '82) which tested several home remedies for strengthening panty hose. "We're always looking for the unusual. We're really very open at this point. We're looking for fresh ideas all the time."

Exercise and fitness is a good category. So are health bulletins for "Natural Healing Network," as long as they can be substantiated and don't present potentially harmful ideas. Relationship articles can be well worth the try, if they contain "good solid information. We don't want 'ten ways to keep your husband' or '65 ways to seduce your lover.' We think women are sick of the whole sexual hype. Being a woman to us isn't all glitter and plunging necklines; it's being healthy."

Humor is a possibility if it's related to an issue that could be of service to readers (send manuscripts, not queries, on this kind of piece). Personality pieces are needed—less straight celebrity though and more the interesting success stories. Travel is covered occasionally, but here articles must appeal, somehow, to the sense of fulfillment. Some of the travel topics covered: cruising up the coast of Maine, bicycling in Vermont (this one came in over-the-transom), clown workshops, a hotel restoration weekend on the Jersey shore. Currently there's a need for "short weekend breaks."

What works best for all articles is "a light, chatty style—tight and light, not wooden. We love catchy first sentences; hook the reader in the first sentence." (The "Smart Small Cars" survey had this lead: "Buying a car is like getting married. It's a major decision, it says something about your values, and a good choice can result in a long-standing emotional attachment.") Editing can tend to be heavy, particularly on story leads. Says Padus: "We think it's important the magazine has a tone of its own. But at the same time we do want variety. We try to be lively and entertaining and yet very quickly accessible to the reader." What won't work at *Spring:* "Clichéd ideas and pedestrian writing styles."

Assignments are general, although without good clips you will probably have to work on spec. "We would never give an assignment blind," Padus says. However, asking writers to work on spec is taken seriously here, "and we try not to do it very often," she adds.

HOW TO SUBMIT: Send completed manuscript (photocopied manuscripts okay), or query. Queries should be kept short: "an informal paragraph or two. The idea is what's most important." Include clips with your query. "Without including clips you might as well not write. They don't have to be published clips necessarily; in fact unpublished—a copy of the unedited manuscript—is often better. Just send us something that gives us an idea of how you can write. We'll be looking for compactness, liveliness, clarity of thought, organization."

REJECTIONS: A standard form letter is used here. A personalized reply should be taken as a sign of encouragement.

THE STAR

730 Third Avenue
New York, NY 10017
(212) 557-9200

SOURCE: Jock Veitch, editorial administrator
Christina Kirk, associate editor

IN SHORT: Very open; one of the best markets for free-lancers.

ABOUT THE PUBLICATION: Weekly; 50% free-lance–written. *The Star* is a celebrity/gossip/news mass-market tabloid, sold mainly in supermarkets. Readers are mostly women; average age: 35–40. *Circulation:* 3.9 million. *Estimated readership:* 16.5 million. *Areas open to free-lancers:* All. *Rates:* Fillers pay $25 and up. "Star People": lead $350, item $50. Other articles: page lead $250–$350. Plus the following system of bonuses: right-hand page lead front-of-book or main spread story: $350; left-hand lead front-of-book or second lead-on spread: $200; back-of-book lead: $100. Further bonus if story makes main headline and/or main photo on cover: $500; further bonus if story is "plugged" elsewhere on cover: $150. *Payment:* On acceptance. *Expenses:* Pays all incidentals. *Kill fee:* Negotiable. *Rights:* Buys first North American rights, verbally. *Number of submissions received weekly:* 200–300. *Reply time:* Immediate. *Advance dates:* Lead time is four to five days. National edition: ten days. Issues are planned up to deadline.

FREE-LANCE POSSIBILITIES: *The Star* is one of the most open — and profitable—markets around. Free-lancers supply a good half of the material used. You do not need a published track record. What's required is simply the right kind of story to fit into the weekly's format. Says Jock Veitch: "We don't care about what you've written before. All we care about is the story you're offering us."

The big bonus-paying stories are generally celebrity-connected, as many of *The Star*'s articles are; this is probably the most difficult way in, however, because there are a number of established stringers throughout the country covering the celebrity/gossip circuit.

Best bets for free-lancers trying to break in are stories in the following areas: Medical (breakthroughs, new advances, illness survival, medical dramas, unusual operations. Here, though, the story will probably have to have local origins. Says Christina Kirk: "I get all the major medical journals and the wire service reports"); how-to (new solutions for old problems; example: "ten tips to get the best of your refrigerator"); true adventure/survival stories (published examples: the mother who snatched her child from the claws of a grizzly bear; how four Poles escaped to freedom by helicopter); good human-interest ("Often local newspapers are a good source for these." Example: the 13-year-old boy who scared off burglars with his cowboys-and-Indians bow and arrow); diets (says Kirk: "We run one a week; we're always interested in them. We have found, though, that our readers respond best if you can promise them X amount of pounds lost in X amount of weeks." Any questionable diet is checked by a nutritionist. Weight-loss stories are also a possibility); food (money-saving food ideas and quick and easy recipes); health (vitamins are a popular topic; any new angle in this area would be welcomed); fashion (dressing for less, how to disguise figure faults); child raising (how to keep your kids healthy); psychological research findings ("Often these get reported locally, not nationally. Local universities are a good source"); personality quizzes (these require the assistance of a psychologist for questions and scoring). Of course, even though celebrity stories (news, features, or roundups) are difficult for the free-lancer to do, any new angles *are* welcomed. Probably it's easier to break in with a filler, but it's certainly not essential.

For all *Star* material, it should be noted: "We check everything, information and quotes. With celebrity stories, we go back to the celebrity to check if we can use their name. We conduct regular research focus groups and what shows up strongly is *The Star*'s credibility. That's something we're not going to blow. And if there's any legal doubt, we send the copy straight to our lawyers." Any service/how-to articles must contain quotes from a recognized authority. (Says Christina Kirk: "I have to reject so many pieces that are just essays. They're not backed up by any named authority.") Seasonal stories should be submitted about two months in advance.

What *won't* work at *The Star?* Poetry, personal reminiscences, first-person articles, stories about "interesting local" people, new-product pieces, depressing stories. Adds Veitch: "We also get dozens of offers saying: 'In a month I can give you a 3000-

word article.' That just shows the writer hasn't read *The Star.* Our stories rarely run longer than 800 words. And ours is a news publication. If your story happened three months ago it will be too late for us. We're looking for news, written by good news writers. That's why we're so open; when we find a good new writer, it's a total joy. And we're constantly looking for good local stringers. If you're a good *Star*-style writer living in a small town, you've got it made."

Newcomers are generally asked to work on spec for the first couple of articles. Clips won't open the door. "Just because you've been published in a leading newspaper or a major consumer magazine doesn't necessarily mean you can write for us. We have a very hard, economic style. But we're also happy to help you along with your story." Submissions *can* be heavily edited here, due to the publication's particular style. "If we rewrite, we'll tell the writer. But we don't send galleys because of the volume of our material and the deadlines."

HOW TO SUBMIT: For urgent news stories, query by phone (toll free 1-800-223-6806) Jock Veitch or the News Desk. For features, phone the regular number or send written query or ms. to Veitch. Photocopied mss. are okay; no multiple submissions. Keep queries as succinct as possible; it is not necessary to include personal details or clips.

REJECTIONS: Because of the volume of material received over-the-transom, standard rejection letters are generally used.

SUNDAY WOMAN

King Features Syndicate
235 East 45th Street
New York, NY 10017
(212) 682-5600

SOURCE: Merry Clark, editor

IN SHORT: Good market; very open.

ABOUT THE MAGAZINE: Weekly. All free-lance–written. *Sunday Woman* is a Sunday newspaper supplement. It's general-interest, with entertainment and service information—but all oriented to women readers. It appears in 65 newspapers nationwide. *Estimated circulation:* 3.5 million. *Sample copy:* Free. *Areas open to free-lancers:* All (except for regular columns). *Rates:* Reprints: $50 flat rate. Original material: $50–$500. *Payment:* On acceptance. *Expenses:* Phone calls. *Kill fee:* Negotiable. *Rights:* Buys first North American rights, verbally. *Number of submissions received weekly:* "Hundreds." *Reply time to queries:* "Generally a week, but may be longer." *Advance dates:* Lead time is six to eight weeks. Issues are planned several months in advance.

FREE-LANCE POSSIBILITIES: Five percent of *Sunday Woman* consists of reprints; the rest is original material, done on assignment. There are about 40 free-lancers writing regularly here, but there's room for more. "If I had 200 good writers I'd be happy," says Merry Clark, adding: "Any writer who successfully suggests and completes a story will have the opportunity to work with me on a regular basis. I love working with talented writers and enjoy having a 'stable' of writers I can depend upon."

Clark runs *Sunday Woman*. She contacts writers, makes assignments, does the editing. There is little time for handholding; consequently most of the writers published are experienced (generally in newspaper feature writing, the style that's required here). She needs to see clips. Less experienced writers appear only "occasionally," but Clark will take a chance. She will either assign or request the piece on spec, depending on the story. She says: "Making a good first impression—on paper—is most important. A professional approach is the key. I consider myself a professional and I expect the same from free-lance writers. I enjoy dealing with positive, talented people. I love finding new writers. And I've found that not all *good* writers are located in New York City; I like using writers not located on the East or West Coast. But I don't want to worry about a story, that it will have to be rewritten/reworked; I just don't have the time."

Clark mentions two writers who originally approached *Sunday Woman* over-the-transom. "A free-lance writer in Sacramento queried me on a story on drunken drivers. It ran as 'Killers Loose on the Highway' and was a marvelous, comprehensive story. The same writer then proposed and finished another story for me on 'Women in Sales: Stalking the Big Bucks.' Another writer in Austin, Texas, suggested 'The Rebirth of Homebirth.' It ran and then she proposed another: 'Correspondence Courses: Upgrading Your Education.' "

Sunday Woman does buy reprints. Maximum length is 2000 words; ideally the story should have appeared in a small magazine or newspaper rather than a well-known national publication. Newspaper-style features have the best chances.

What won't work at *Sunday Woman?* "I get queries from writers who are not familiar with the publication; they make inappropriate suggestions. Writers spell my name wrong, the name of the publication will be incorrect (like, *Sunday's Woman*), they'll give me typos and sloppy letters. If a writer isn't neat and accurate in a story query, she's not going to be in an article! Also, if a writer is difficult—misses deadlines, etc.—I don't deal with them again. Because there are so many outstanding and cooperative, easy-to-work-with writers that I *enjoy* working with."

Clark does minor editing; rewrites are done by the author. Galleys are not shown.

HOW TO SUBMIT: For reprints, send published clip and include name of publication and issue date. For original material, send either a completed manuscript, with cover letter (photocopied manuscripts okay), or query. Keep queries short, giving story outline and possible information sources. "I like short, direct queries and *clean* copy," Merry Clark says. She adds: "I don't mind a résumé. I like to know where you've free-lanced—what publications. And I want to see your writing style, so including clips is a good idea. With clips I'm looking for good reportorial pieces."

REJECTIONS: A standard form rejection is sent but Clark says she usually tries to add a personal note to each.

TEEN

8490 Sunset Boulevard
Los Angeles, CA 90069
(213) 657-5100

All articles are staff-written; no nonfiction free-lance contributions accepted.

TENNIS

495 Westport Avenue
Norwalk, CT 06856
(203) 847-5811

SOURCE: Shepherd Campbell, editor

IN SHORT: Open, but very little space available for free-lance contributions.

ABOUT THE MAGAZINE: Monthly; 10% free-lance–written, at the most. *Tennis* is a magazine for tennis enthusiasts who have been playing tennis several years, and who are on the courts two to three times a week. Says Shepherd Campbell: "We're trying to help them play the game better and enjoy it more, and we do that with instructional articles, advice on equipment, features about tennis and the players, and articles about the mental aspects of the game. The tennis-playing boom of the seventies has tapered off now, but the spectator end of it hasn't, so we've added a lot of material on the pro-circuit side, at the expense of some of the lighter features we used to run." The average age of readers is 31; 75% are college grads; average income is $43,000. *Circulation:* 465,000. *Estimated readership:* 1.7 million. *Areas open to free-lancers:* Articles, travel, "Player to Watch," "People in Tennis," and "Passing Shots." *Rates:* $100–$750. *Payment:* Generally on publication, "unless there's going to be a long time lag till publication." *Expenses:* Pays reasonable expenses to regular/known writers. *Kill fee:* Negotiable. ("But we've only paid one kill fee in the past ten years.") *Rights:* Buys all rights, by check endorsement. Not negotiable. (The magazine has reciprocal agreements with sports publications in other countries; any resale fees are split with the author.) *Number of submissions received weekly:* 12. *Reply time:* Replies to queries in one week; mss. can take several weeks. *Advance dates:* Lead time is five to six weeks. Issues are planned up to a year in advance.

FREE-LANCE POSSIBILITIES: Despite a refreshingly open policy to *all* tennis enthusiasts—"so that the magazine doesn't become predictable, static"—chances of getting published here are "unfortunately, becoming less and less." Very little free-lance material is used—a turnaround from the magazine's earlier years in business. Explains Shepherd Campbell: "As tennis has gotten more popular and the magazine has grown, we now have quite a large staff and a stable of contributing editors, both professional players and tennis writers. I wish I could say the chances for free-lancers are better than they are. We don't have a lot of space, and dateless pieces (the area where chances are best for the free-lancer) can often take a long time to get in." (The average time is six months to a year, but it *can* take longer than that —the record is 4½ years!)

Still, Campbell does admit: "If the quality of the material coming in from the outside were higher, if people were a little more intelligent about the subjects they choose to write about, we *would* use more. The problem with a lot of the unsolicited material is redundancy—pieces like 'My Week at Tennis Camp' or 'Why I Admire Jimmy Connors.' Or else you get everyone wanting to interview Bjorn Borg. Instead, writers should concentrate on the areas of the game that are unique to their location or themselves."

Campbell mentions several pieces that came in over-the-transom, were good, were unusual, and were bought: "A woman sent us a story on trying to play tennis with a toddler in tow. It was humorous and it was terrific. Another sent us a piece that discussed being single and trying to find a tennis game when you're traveling. A writer sent us a piece on a high school team in California that was extraordinarily good; we didn't know about them. Someone else sent in a delightful piece about a group of truckers who played tennis on concrete behind a diner in New Jersey. Then, some years ago, someone sent us a piece suggesting the best thing to happen to tennis would be to abolish the second serve. It was well written and well reasoned; of course this guy obviously knew his tennis. But the one I'll never forget was the 12th grader from a small town in Texas who sent us a piece one year on 'The Night Before Christmas,' which she had adapted to a Wimbledon setting. It was wonderful; we used it in our Christmas issue."

The area where free-lance contributions are used most often is "People in Tennis." "Unfortunately this is also the column that gets dropped most often when we're squeezed for space. But when we do run it, it consists of three profiles, about 100 lines each, and anybody is fair game for this department, as long as they're interesting people doing something interesting in tennis." Possibilities are celebrities, teaching pros, people behind-the-scenes—but not pro players. This department has run pieces on Luciano Pavarotti and Lionel Richie—both avid tennis players. Payment here: $200–$500.

Campbell describes travel as "one of the more available areas for free-lancers." He elaborates: "If you're going to be taking a tennis trip somewhere, we could be interested in a travel story. We have covered most of the tennis vacation spots, but something exotic could work. One of the things we do try and do with travel is present fantasy. It doesn't have to be a practical, let's go-to-Florida piece. The location can be off-the-beaten-track."

The "Player to Watch" page is open. Here Campbell's guidelines are: "It has to be about a relatively new player; someone who is just becoming a factor on the pro circuit. The piece should talk about the player's emergence, how he or she got there, what their hopes are."

Major profiles are difficult for the free-lancer; these are always done by a staffer or contributing editor. Campbell *does* recall an exception however. "A free-lancer once sent us a profile of Rosie Casals. We ran it because this woman had such unusual perceptions and views on Casals. It was very compelling reading; very refreshing."

Tennis does run three special sections yearly, and all are open to free-lance contributions. "We do two on women's tennis, and I don't like to fill them just with material on the pros. A free-lancer sent us a piece once on the 'killer instinct' in tennis—is it feminine? We used it in this section." (Women's tennis sections appear in March and April; submissions required by the preceding fall.) The other special section, run in the winter, covers the other racquet sports—specifically, racquetball, squash, and platform tennis. "If anybody has any stories in this area that would be of interest to tennis players, we'll gladly consider them." (Submissions required by the end of July.)

In all areas, Campbell is happy to consider both mss. and queries. In the case of completed manuscripts, he asks all staff editors to read them, a policy that can lead to a delay in getting back to the writer if certain editors are out of the office. But he adds: "I really feel it's worth the delay; I don't want anything worthwhile to slip by. I want to be sure." If you send a query, chances are Campbell will request the manuscript on spec. "I don't turn down queries if I see any possibility in them," he says. "Unless I know there's just no way I'm going to use the particular topic, I'll encourage you to send in the manuscript." Of marginal topics Campbell says: "There are some stories where the chances of our being able to use them immediately are remote. In that case, I'll probably urge the writer to submit the piece elsewhere and to send it back to us if it doesn't work out anywhere else. I don't accept manuscripts that I'm just going to have around as a security blanket."

If you're not a known, specialized tennis writer, you will be asked to work on spec—at least for the first story or two. Campbell does not place much faith in clips; they won't get you an assignment here.

Editing varies, "but, yes, we tend to edit fairly heavily." Rewriting is done by the author. Galleys are shown "only if there's been a substantial amount of editing done."

HOW TO SUBMIT: Mss. are read but photocopies are discouraged. ("We tend to be suspicious of them.") Brief queries are preferred; "the contributor should outline the story and their credentials for doing it." Include a list of writing credits, but not clips.

REJECTIONS: One of several relevant form letters is sent to most contributors. Adds Campbell: "I really do try and be honest with people." Personalized notes are sent to encourage more submissions.

TIME

Time, Inc.
1271 Avenue of the Americas
New York, NY 10020
(212) 586-1212

Time is completely staff-written; no free-lance queries or contributions are accepted.

TOWN & COUNTRY

The Hearst Corporation
1700 Broadway
New York, NY 10019
(212) 903-5000

SOURCE: Kathryn Livingston, executive editor

IN SHORT: Surprisingly open—looking for ideas and style.

ABOUT THE MAGAZINE: Monthly. *Town & Country* has always been *the* high society magazine, combining articles on exotic travel, lavish entertaining, and the affluent life-style, with picture reports on society weddings and functions throughout the country. But now its readers also include the upwardly mobile executive, and editorially, the magazine now aims to include the kind of information needed to successfully "live the good life." Among readers, 42% are men; median reader age: 45; highest percentage of readers are managerial/administrative; minimum household income: $50,000. These are the people who belong to private clubs, own expensive homes, travel and entertain. *Circulation:* 320,000. *Estimated readership:* One million. *Areas open to free-lancers:* All. *Rates:* Essays: $300 minimum. Articles: $750–$3500. Average article fee: $1750–$2500. *Payment:* On acceptance. *Expenses:* All. *Kill fee:* One-third. *Rights:* Buys first North American rights, by written contract. *Number of submissions received weekly:* 15–20. *Reply time to queries:* Up to six weeks for queries; up to four months for mss. *Advance dates:* Lead time is four months. Issues are planned six months in advance.

FREE-LANCE POSSIBILITIES: There *are* possibilities here for the free-lance writer. One-third of the article ideas come in unsolicited, and Kathryn Livingston says: "We're pretty responsive and for a good idea I think we go a lot further than a lot of other magazines will. We're always looking for new writers and a lot of our regular writers first came to us over-the-transom."

The key is an idea that's a mix of style and timeliness, a trend story or something offbeat that also has a touch of stylish eccentricity to it. A writer from Detroit sent in a piece on Cuba; the slant was specific: in search of Hemingway, hijackers, and baseball. It struck the right chord. So did an over-the-transom piece on China, again one with an unusual angle: basically, what it's like to travel with a group of wealthy companions. A trend piece on the return to manners was bought from the slush pile. So was a piece asking "Whatever happened to the Iranian royal jewels?" (That one Livingston remembers as "exotic and timely, it had a lot of lore and legend in it, and it was a very knowledgeable piece.") A piece on Frisbees, another on amusement parks, and another on antique merry-go-rounds all came in unsolicited. All these articles were originally submitted in ms. form, probably the best approach if it's a large piece. But Livingston admits that it probably is easier to break in with a smaller piece. "We're less likely to commit ourselves to a major piece that would require a lot of costly photography." And a smaller piece "may just lock into one of our theme issues."

Good break-in areas are: health ("that could be a big area for free-lancers"); articles aimed at men ("we're really making an aggressive effort in this area because of the increasing number of male readers"); money management ("but only on a very high level").

Personality profiles may be a possibility, with these guidelines: "We like important people who are not overexposed. People in business (who are also doing other things that are interesting—hobbies or something altruistic), politics, or someone who is doing something culturally significant." Profiles generally run around 3000 words.

Unusual trend pieces are good: "something like polo playing in the West. That's a local story with national social implications. We're always interested in insider's stories and information."

Travel pieces must be "highly original and highly specific," and are one of the most difficult ways to break in. Grand-tour travel stories (with or without restaurant reviews) are definitely out, and approaching the magazine with a free travel package all lined up "is the worst thing to do; we can easily see through those." Travel and the big social stories are, by and large, covered by staffers and contributing editors.

It's also worth noting: "The writing should be upbeat, informative, and the more detailed and closely focused-in the better. We focus on the best. Also the quirky, the eccentric, the exotic, and the adventuresome. And we've really broadened our scope in the how-to area."

It's a highly unlikely market for the first-time writer, unless you submit a completed ms., or unless you're an expert writing in a particularly specialized field. But if you have some clips to show, and if *Town & Country* really wants your idea, assignment chances are good. Assignments are made "if the timing and topic is right." The only time a published writer may be asked to work on spec is if he is planning to take a trip anyway, and he suggests a travel piece. The editors may then ask him to submit the article on spec, giving them extra time to consider the idea.

Only about one in 40 queries works out here. "Writers just want to travel. Or they're not looking at the needs of the magazine. Or the ideas are not specific, or social, or exotic enough. Ideas are a dime a dozen; it's how you carry them off; that's what we respond to."

Rewriting "varies. But I think we probably do more than people realize," Livingston says.

HOW TO SUBMIT: Mss. are read ("but we're forced to take our time with them; they're not our number-one priority"). Photocopied mss. are okay. Queries are preferred. These should be "short, concise, no more than a page—but detailed." Include a brief rundown of writing experience, and one or two clips. Also include a rundown of the people you would propose interviewing. "We have to have some assurance that you can pull off the story, that you've done more than just think about it."

TRAVEL & LEISURE

American Express Publishing Corporation
1120 Avenue of the Americas
New York, NY 10036
(212) 382-5600

SOURCE: Charles Monaghan, managing editor
(Mr. Monaghan has since left the magazine.)

IN SHORT: Very difficult to sell. Only writers with strong clips considered.

ABOUT THE MAGAZINE: Monthly: 80% free-lance–written. *Travel & Leisure* is a travel magazine aimed at sophisticated readers who travel frequently (as opposed to the armchair traveler) and go first class in all aspects of their life. "We aim to be definitive in the matter of service, and stylish in our subject matter and its presentation." *Readership:* median age is 42; 65% have attended/graduated college; 38% are in professional/managerial jobs. *Circulation:* 950,000. *Estimated readership:* About 3 million. *Areas open to free-lancers:* All. *Rates:* Middle-of-the-book articles: $1000–$2000. Regionals (2000 words): $600, with extra fees if piece is published in other regional sections. Black-and-whites: payment depends on length; 400-word piece: $300; pieces of 2000 words and up: up to $1000. *Payment:* On acceptance. *Expenses:* Pays reasonable expenses. *Kill fee:* 25%. *Rights:* Buys one-time American and British rights, by assignment letter. *Number of submissions received weekly:* 50–75. *Reply time to queries:* Within two weeks. *Advance dates:* Issues are planned up to a year in advance.

FREE-LANCE POSSIBILITIES: Forget *Travel & Leisure* unless you are an experienced writer with impressive credits and specialized experience in travel or travel-related areas (sports, food and wine, leisure activities). There are about 200 regular contributors here; a writer without such credentials breaks in rarely. Writers appearing in *Travel & Leisure* come to the magazine mainly through contacts or reputation, or are found in other publications. "These are writers who know our magazine well, who understand our needs, and who are able to come up with ideas that are sharply defined just for our market," Monaghan said.

"Those with the requisite background should approach us with queries, not with manuscripts."

The main article area —the features in the middle of the book —is, technically, open to free-lancers. But for over-the-transom purposes, it should not be attempted. "We generate a good 90% of the main article ideas and we virtually conceive of them with a specific writer in mind. Chances of breaking in here over-the-transom are infinitesimal."

There are four possible break-in areas: black-and-whites, regionals, "On Course," and "Taking Off!"

The most open area is regionals. There are seven different regional sections: Eastern, New York Metro, Midwestern, Chicago Metro, Western, California, and Southern. Local-interest pieces for this section are best if not tied to a specific date; the size of each regional section carried per issue is determined by the amount of advertising and a regional article will have a better chance if it's something that can be used at the last minute when extra pages become available. The subject matter can range from profiles of small towns to regional museums.

The black-and-white sections (these are smaller pieces with accompanying photography that is black-and-white, not color) run both front and back of the magazine, and are carried nationally. They tend to cover travel-related subjects, rather than destinations, and can be either non-American or else pieces of national interest about America. (Examples from November '82 issue: "Pick of the Prep Schools—a Tour of Phillips Academy, Exeter, Groton and Deerfield"; "Travel and Stress"; "Ode to the Sleeper Seat.")

Then there are the two smaller sections, both printed on brown craft paper. "Taking Off!" consists of 100–150 word news items and is a good place to get started. Subjects could include new, interesting hotels; outstanding restaurants, changes in passport or customs regulations, etc; and offbeat shorts, like the rent-a-car company in Beverly Hills that stocks dream cars for hire. "On Course" generally consists of three to four longer articles (1200–1500 words) with a heavy service orientation: how to prevent tropical diseases, travel for the handicapped, how to keep your home secure while you're away, walking tours around the world's major cities.

To succeed, ideas *must* be perfectly targeted and fit into the magazine's needs. "The angling and the point of view is what's wrong with so many of the submissions we get," Charles Monaghan said. Editors here work with writers only on assignment; if the writer seems unsure of an idea, or if strong clips aren't forthcoming from the writer, they'll drop the proposal. And it probably will not be worthwhile asking to work on spec. "We'll either assign or we're not interested."

Rewriting is always done by the author; half of the manuscripts that come in are returned for revisions. But editing does tend to be light once the author has reworked the article, with detailed editorial guidance. Galleys are shown.

Worth noting: "We are not interested in photojournalism. We assign our own photographers."

And the last word: "Beginning writers shouldn't approach us, but *should* keep us in mind as a goal. They should try and build up credits in our areas of interest —travel, restaurants, hotels— in consumer magazines, trade publications, city magazines. Then they can present some kind of evidence that they've grappled with our kind of writing."

HOW TO SUBMIT: Send regionals to Lisa Higgins, senior editor; black-and-whites and "Taking Off!" to Kitty Mackey, senior editor; "On Course" to Monique Burns, associate editor. Completed mss. discouraged. "We glance at them only," said Charles Monaghan, adding: "It's really a mistake to send us a manuscript. The chances of it working out are virtually nil. We can only work with queries." Queries should be three to four paragraphs. Don't include clips at query stage. These will be requested if there is interest in the idea.

REJECTIONS: A standard form is sent. Personalized replies go to "contributors with professional standing and those writers we feel may have potential."

TV GUIDE

Triangle Publications
100 Matsonford Road
Radnor, PA 19088
(215) 293-8500

SOURCE: Andrew Mills, assistant managing editor

IN SHORT: Virtually closed market.

ABOUT THE MAGAZINE: Weekly. Mostly staff-written. Andrew Mills says of this digest-sized publication: "It's a popular magazine for people who are interested in television. We want to keep them informed about what's going on in television and to entertain them. We try not to bore them with overlengthy pieces." The magazine runs five or six articles per issue as well as several regular columns. *Circulation:* 17 million. *Estimated readership:* 40 million. *Areas open to free-lancers:* All articles. *Rates:* $750–$1250. Average article fee: $1000. *Payment:* On acceptance. *Expenses:* Pays all incidentals. *Kill fee:* $300. *Rights:* Buys first U.S. rights, by written contract. *Number of submissions received weekly:* 30. *Reply time:* Replies to queries in two to three weeks. Mss. take longer. *Advance dates:* Lead time is two months. Issues are planned about three months in advance.

FREE-LANCE POSSIBILITIES: *TV Guide* is heavily staff-written, by writers in New York and Los Angeles bureaus and by regulars throughout the country. Andrew Mills gives the bottom line: "For a free-lancer—someone we don't know—to sell to us, the chances are extremely small. Although we do read and consider all queries and manuscripts, we really don't encourage freelance submissions at all." The magazine receives about 30 submissions a week, and most weeks none of them works out. "To say we buy three free-lance pieces a year would be a generous estimate," Mills says. (And what *is* bought is always on spec, never on assignment.)

The way into *TV Guide* could be with an idea that fits this format: "An idea has to have a pretty clear and simple point to make it for us. We're always interested in, and in need of, short humor pieces." (First-person pieces are okay.) "Or perhaps you might come across something that's interesting and unusual, offbeat or bizarre going on in television somewhere in the country.

But to approach us with a suggestion to profile Robin Williams or Victoria Principal is just a waste of time. If it's either important or obvious, chances are we've done it or plan to do it."

What's going to sell your piece is personal experience, particular personal knowledge or access to sources—"access our writers wouldn't have." Terri Even's unsolicited piece ("Confessions of a Collegiate TV-Watcher," April 25, '81) is an example of "personal experience" that could make it. Written while she was a college student, it was a piece about "TV snobbery"; she detailed the reaction of her college friends when she told them she watched TV soap operas. Explains Mills: "It was lighthearted and amusing, with a touch of irony." Submissions are generally rejected for one of the following reasons: "They're not promising, or we've already done them, or else they're too boring or too scholarly."

HOW TO SUBMIT: Send a short query of 1–1½ pages. "The query should be clear and should quickly tell us your angle." Include any unique qualifications, if relevant. Also include a clip if you wish, "one sample of something that's recent and good." If sending a manuscript, submit the original, not a photocopy.

REJECTIONS: A standard rejection form is used; occasionally a more personal, encouraging note will be sent—"but it's rare."

TWA AMBASSADOR

The Webb Company
1999 Shepard Road
St. Paul, MN 55116
(612) 690-7295

In-flight magazine; 95% free-lance—written, but by regular writers. Editor: David Martin. Declined to participate.

UNITED

East/West Network
34 East 51st Street
New York, NY 10022
(212) 888-5900

SOURCE: Laura Manske, associate editor

IN SHORT: Open and encouraging, but not easy to sell.

ABOUT THE MAGAZINE: Monthly; 90% free-lance–written. *United* is the in-flight magazine of United Airlines. Laura Manske explains the editorial content: "*United* features trends of national significance and profiles of the people who influence America. Regular features include an interview with a chief executive of a major corporation, a timely portfolio of art or photography, and travel destination and service features." The magazine is geared to a sophisticated audience with slightly more male than female readers; median age is 40; middle to high income; 46% are in professional/managerial jobs. *Circulation:* 350,000. Each copy is read by six travelers, on the average. *Sample copy:* Free on United Airlines flights, and in Westin Hotels. Or send $2 to the magazine (this includes postage). *Areas open to free-lancers:* Everything except "Communiqué" (an information column for executive travelers). *Rates:* Columns: around $300. Features: $500–$1200 (average article fee: $600–$700). *Payment:* On acceptance. *Expenses:* Phone calls, travel. *Kill fee:* Generally 50%. *Rights:* Buys first North American rights, by written contract. *Number of submissions received weekly:* 50. *Reply time to queries:* Within a month. *Advance dates:* Lead time is three months. Issues are planned at least three months in advance.

FREE-LANCE POSSIBILITIES: *United* magazine, like most of the in-flight publications, is, potentially, an excellent market; most of the magazine is written by free-lancers, and in terms of showcase and exposure, the credit's a good one. However, over the course of an average year, only one or two over-the-transom queries materialize into articles, reflecting a lack of *good* article ideas from free-lancers. Says Laura Manske: "You must be previously published and you must send us clips. We do have our trusted stable of free-lancers; however we're always interested in hearing from other writers."

Assignments are the norm. "We never ask people to work on spec"—but the magazine also does not make a habit of paying kill fees. So, if you're unpublished, your chances of breaking into print through *United* would be slim, even if you have a terrific idea. The editors would probably even be reluctant to allow the unpublished writer to work on spec; "the odds are really against the inexperienced writer." But if you have a few clips, this is a magazine definitely worth trying. "We never assign without seeing clips," Laura Manske says. But newspaper or trade/small magazine clips are okay. "If you're a good writer, it's going to show, no matter where you've been published."

The editors welcome queries for profiles. Subjects can come from almost any area: education, business, entertainment, government, the arts. But keep in mind that they must be *leading* Americans who are somehow influencing our lives. Published examples: Pulitzer Prize–winning playwright Charles Fuller, discussing racial issues in the theater; David Lloyd Kreeger, entrepreneur and avid art collector; Martha and Andy Stewart, publisher and gourmet cook/author husband-and-wife team.

Thematic pieces are also worth trying, but keep in mind that a broad focus is needed. For instance, a rundown on new-technology typewriters would be too narrow but a piece on the office of the future, perhaps, would work. Some other examples: an art exhibit that is touring the country, an aspect of a business boom, new trends in architecture in big cities.

Service pieces are generally directed at the executive traveler. They've included a piece on what the executive is wearing during business hours and a style piece on shaving equipment for the executive man. Travel is *not* a good area for the free-lancer. Writers are considered (see "Portfolios and Positive Thinking," pages 7–9) but actual story ideas are not needed; travel stories are generated in-house.

Some don'ts: bad grammar and misspelled words in queries. Missing deadlines on assigned articles. Not getting all the facts; quoting studies or statistics that don't exist (they *will* be checked out). Arguing with the editors if they reject your idea.

Laura Manske's last word: "I can't emphasize enough—*know* the magazine before you contact us."

HOW TO SUBMIT: Send submissions to David Breul, the editor. Although mss. will be read, the editors prefer written queries.

Don't send photocopied mss. or queries. "I reject them right off," Laura Manske says, explaining, "I don't know where else they've been and I don't think it's very professional." In other words, no simultaneous submissions.

Keep queries short (one page tops). Forget personal details, but if you have worked at a publication, say so, and if you have been published elsewhere, list credits. Send copies of recent, relevant clips (two tops). And don't forget SASE, one of Manske's pet peeves.

REJECTIONS: Most submissions receive form rejection slips.

US

Peters Publishing
215 Lexington Avenue
New York, NY 10016
(212) 340-7500

SOURCE: Richard Sanders, senior articles editor

IN SHORT: Very open to new writers and ideas; good possibilities.

ABOUT THE MAGAZINE: Bi-weekly; 30% free-lance–written. *Us* is a magazine that carries celebrity interviews and reports on the latest trends; the mix is 60% entertainment pieces, 40% nonentertainment (offbeat and human-interest). The magazine is distributed to supermarkets as well as newsstands. *Readership:* 60% female, 40% male; aged between 15–30 (males) and 18–40 (females); over half have some college; middle income. *Circulation:* 1.1 million. *Estimated readership:* 4.5 million. *Areas open to free-lancers:* "Front Runners" and all features. (Reviews are written in-house.) *Rates:* $400–$1000. Average article fee: $500. *Payment:* On publication. *Expenses:* Pays all incidentals. *Kill fee:* 25–50%. *Rights:* Buys all rights, verbally. Negotiable. *Number of submissions received weekly:* 100. *Reply time to queries:* Two to three weeks. *Advance dates:* Lead time is six weeks. Issues are planned two to three months in advance.

FREE-LANCE POSSIBILITIES: Richard Sanders estimates there is at least one piece written by a new writer (unpublished or little-published) in every other issue. Each story idea is considered according to *its* merit; if the story idea appeals to Sanders and the writer looks competent enough, assignment chances are excellent.

There are catches: This brand of slick "star" writing is not as easy as it may appear: "It requires a really sharp focus and takes quite a bit of practice," Sanders explains. "As a result, we do tend to edit heavily." And half the battle is in coming up with an idea that hasn't been done or isn't in the works. There are 15 staff members and Sanders has a stable of regular free-lancers; all these people are monitoring the country via ears, eyes, TV, and print. "We try to be as topical and as trendy as possible," Sanders says. "It's hard to come up with something suitable that we don't know about."

Celebrity profiles must follow a formula: "They have to be someone with a product out now, or in the very near future. The product has to be selling well and the artist has to have some personal story to go with it." These are not a good bet, however, because the regular writers have the entertainment business blanketed.

Where are the best possibilities? In "Front Runners," or in the features that report on the offbeat or are *strong* human-interest stories. "Front Runners," the front-of-the-book short pieces, run 200–300 words. About 20–25% of the ideas come in over-the-transom; good subjects are new products, new inventions, new medical breakthroughs, and anything oddball.

Features run 800–1500 words (1200 on the average), and word length is important. "When I ask for 1200 words, I mean 1200 words because that's the way our format works," Sanders explains.

Tom Viola broke in with a piece (April 13, '82) on Charles Cochrane, the New York City police sergeant who publicly admitted his homosexuality and who has been active in the push for a New York City gay rights bill. For the August 3, '82 issue, Andrew McCarthy interviewed sewer engineer John Flaherty and wrote a piece pondering the existence of alligators in Manhattan's sewers. Jeffrey Jolson-Colburn, a journalism student, published a piece in the May 11, '82 issue; it was an eyewitness account of the last party John Belushi attended and included the report of an interview the author had originally intended for his college music magazine. In the July 6, '82 issue, Annette Kornblum wrote about master cockroach exterminator Alvin Burger. All four authors reached Sanders over-the-transom.

"You need a very sharp focus," Sanders says. "Your idea has to be something that's new, preferably something *you've* never heard about before. Or it has to be *really strong* human-interest. Often people send us ideas that are just too local; something extraordinary in Wichita could easily be commonplace in Florida, for instance."

HOW TO SUBMIT: Mss. are read (no photocopies please), but queries are preferred. Submit feature ideas to Richard Sanders; "Front Runners" to Rochelle Chadakoff, senior editor. Multiple submissions are not encouraged. Phone queries are accepted, "but only if it's an urgent idea." In query letters Sanders prefers "a good lead paragraph, something that tells me immediately 'here's the story.' One of the common mistakes writers make here is submitting poorly written query letters. I hate having to wade through three pages to get to the point." Clips are "helpful, but they don't mean too much. It's nice to know the person has been published elsewhere, but I look at the story idea and I either go with that, or I don't."

REJECTIONS: *Us* uses a standard rejection letter, but Sanders adds: "If I think there's definite promise, I really do try and write a personal note."

USAIR

East/West Network
34 East 51st Street
New York, 10022
(212) 888-5900

SOURCE: Richard Busch, editor

IN SHORT: Good general-interest market for experienced writers.

ABOUT THE MAGAZINE: Monthly; 95% free-lance—written. *USAir* is the in-flight magazine of USAir, which, like all the airline magazines, caters to an across-the-board audience but gears itself to the intelligent, sophisticated reader. *Circulation:* 140,000. *Estimated readership:* 965,000. *Sample copy:* $2. *Areas open to free-lancers:* Everything except "Airwaves." *Rates:* Articles (1500–3000 words): $400–$750. *Payment:* On acceptance. *Expenses:* Pays modest expenses. *Kill fee:* 25%. *Rights:* Buys first North American rights, by written contract. *Number of submissions received weekly:* 40. *Reply time to queries:* Two weeks. *Advance dates:* Issues are planned six months in advance.

FREE-LANCE POSSIBILITIES: The in-flight magazines are not only nice showcases, they're also one of the few markets left for general-interest topics. "We're trying for a combination. . . . we're trying to be interesting and informative as well as entertaining," says Richard Busch. "So we're not dealing with weighty or controversial subjects; don't send us a 5000-word tome on some vast subject like, say, electronics. But at the same time we're not trying to be a gossipy magazine full of short takes. We're trying to be a real general-interest magazine."

What *has* worked here are articles on collecting art, quilting as part of the American heritage, lightning, canoeing, rodeos, maple syruping—the kinds of atmosphere pieces that are, as Busch coined it, entertaining and informative as well. His advice is: "The best way to break in here is by hitting us with an idea that's irresistible."

Only about one query in 40 works out (some weeks none do), a low percentage considering the scope of this market. Here's what contributors are doing wrong: "Often the suggestion is completely inappropriate for our magazine. For instance, we'll get a query on traveling in Great Britain. Obviously we're not going to be interested in a travel piece on a place the airline doesn't fly to. Other queries are so sloppily done I wouldn't touch 'em! Then there are ideas we've done before, which isn't necessarily the fault of the writer, who may not get to see the magazine on a regular basis. And ideas that just don't ring a bell."

The magazine runs 8–12 travel features a year, either on a specific city or the surrounding area—but all are USAir destinations. "Travel is one of the least likely areas for the free-lancer," Busch comments. "The reason is that we do profiles of cities— the kind of piece that says 'This is Houston'—at the specific request of the airline whose marketing department usually makes the decision. A free-lance writer suggesting a travel piece may have a very good idea, but it's unlikely to coincide with our plans."

Suggestions for personality profiles also are not a good idea. "We don't do them very often, mainly because so many other magazines do." (When profiles are run they're generally pegged to a news angle.) Health and money are good areas, but only if you're a specialist. "We would want to see your track record in either field first, because from our experience, when a generalist tries to tackle a specialized area it often becomes a problem."

The best idea is to try for a general-interest subject. In the July '82 issue, free-lancer Jack Waugh wrote a piece on professional lumberjacking (after submitting a query). The article highlighted two of the sport's champs within the context of the sport itself. That's the kind of idea that can lead to an assignment.

Richard Busch doesn't believe in asking people to work on spec. He only gives assignments, but to get one you have to have the right idea and be able to show some professional published work. This means that if you're a new writer, or if you have an article idea that's really out of the ordinary, you might consider approaching the magazine with a ms. "We've had some oddball manuscripts come in and we've used them; if they'd come in as a query we probably wouldn't have made an assignment."

This is a visually pleasing magazine; it's no surpirse to hear that Busch was previously an editor at both *Life* and *Popular Photography*. "The writer should always consider the illustration possibilities as well. A subject that can be illustrated well is more likely to make it here."

Editing varies. If a rewrite is needed, the piece is returned to the author, with directions. A copy of the edited manuscript is shown to all writers.

HOW TO SUBMIT: Query or send ms. (photocopied ms. okay; so are simultaneous submissions). Queries should be short: "If writers can't explain what they're going to do and how they're going to do it in the length of a page, they have a problem." Including one or two clips is "a good idea," although "the quality of the idea and how it's presented is at *least* as important as sending clips."

REJECTIONS: A standard form rejection is used. Busch adds: "Whenever I can I'll write a note, mainly to encourage more submissions, and most often right on the query they've sent me."

U.S. NEWS & WORLD REPORT

2300 N Street, N.W.
Washington, DC 20037
(202) 861-2242

U.S. News & World Report is almost entirely staff-written; no free-lance queries/contributions accepted.

VANITY FAIR

Condé Nast Publications
350 Madison Avenue
New York, NY 10017
(212) 880-8800

Vanity Fair is described as "a magazine of literature and the arts, politics and popular culture." When we went to press, the magazine had published only its first couple of issues. The editors felt it was too early to discuss free-lance submissions—the kinds of article topics considered and the form of query required.

While the first issues contained articles by name writers, the editors stressed they were hoping to use outside submissions, and that all over-the-transom material would be considered. Both completed manuscripts and queries are accepted; clips should be included with queries. All submissions, with SASE included, should be sent to Leo Lerman, editor-in-chief.

Studying back issues of the magazine is recommended.

VOGUE

Condé Nast Publications
350 Madison Avenue
New York, NY 10017
(212) 880-8800

Monthly. Declined to participate.

WEIGHT WATCHERS MAGAZINE

575 Lexington Avenue
New York, NY 10022
(212) 888-9166

SOURCE: Trisha Thompson, associate editor

IN SHORT: Good opportunities; first article always on spec.

ABOUT THE MAGAZINE: Monthly; 30% free-lance–written. You don't have to be a member of Weight Watchers to get this magazine; it's available on the newsstand. According to Trisha Thompson, the magazine's audience consists mostly of people who are on diets or who have already lost weight but are interested in maintaining their weight loss. The magazine runs 20–30 staff-written recipes each month. Before-and-after-weight-loss stories are regular features, as are articles dealing with the psychological aspects of losing weight. *Readership:* mostly women, in their middle to late 30s. More than half have attended college; most readers work, more than half of them at full-time jobs (but only a small percentage are in professional or managerial positions). A high percentage are married. Average weight loss is about 20 pounds; the goal is to fit into a size 10 dress (they're around size 14 now). *Circulation:* 800,000. *Areas open to free-lancers:* All articles (two to three main features of 1200–1500 words used each month); the "Body/Wise" health feature; "New Profiles" (one to two used per issue). *Rates:* "New Profiles": $300. Feature articles: $300–$600. *Payment:* On acceptance. *Expenses:* Pays limited expenses. *Kill fee:* 25%. *Rights:* Buys first North American rights, by written contract. Magazine retains rights for reprint use in English and Italian editions of the magazine and in the book, *The Best of Weight Watchers Magazine. Number of submissions received weekly:* 50. *Reply time to queries:* Two to four weeks. *Advance dates:* Lead time is three months. Issues are planned four to five months in advance.

FREE-LANCE POSSIBILITIES: Only about half of *Weight Watchers Magazine* articles are generated in-house, so the editors constantly look for, and welcome, ideas from free-lancers. New writers have an excellent chance here. "What counts is that you have a good idea and the reporting and writing skills to back it up," says Trisha Thompson. A newcomer appears about every three issues on the average. The magazine has a standard policy of asking all writers to do their first story on spec. If the story is bought, all future work will be on assignment.

Writers can break in through any of the *three* areas open to free-lancers: feature articles, "New Profiles," or "Body/Wise." Among features, some recent subjects have included dieting with your spouse, why life's little hassles make you overeat, how your dieting affects your child. Psychological self-help pieces are sought. Although humor is definitely considered, very few humor pieces are bought.

Writing a "New Profile" is probably the easiest way to break in. Stories for this department can be autobiographical, or about someone else who has managed to lose weight and whose story has an interesting slant. And it doesn't *have* to be a weight loss of monumental proportions. "While it's interesting to read about people who have lost a lot of weight, we like to balance these with stories about people who have lost only 10 or 15 pounds. Profiles that show the reader the importance of any weight loss, small or large, are our objective." (The dieter does not have to have been on the Weight Watchers Program, but he or she does have to be involved in a sensible diet program.) Trisha Thompson adds a tip here: "The weight loss is not so important in a 'New Profile'; rather the writer should concentrate on the problems the person had prior to losing weight and the ways in which weight loss has affected the person's life." Before-and-after photos are a requirement when you submit to this department.

Some recent "Body/Wise" topics have included back problems, medical checkups, yoga, posture, diabetes. Come up with a new slant on a health/medical topic; it will work best at *Weight Watchers Magazine* if the topic ties in somehow with weight loss.

Editing varies here. Writers are not shown galleys.

HOW TO SUBMIT: Query Linda Konner, managing editor, on feature articles, Trisha Thompson on "New Profiles." Manuscripts are read (no photocopies), but queries are preferred. Short queries are best; include a list of the experts you plan to interview and their credentials. Clips are not required, but they are welcomed. Include SASE.

What leads to rejection? "Not knowing what's right for the

magazine, repeating ideas that we've covered recently, having only a very vague article idea, and poor spelling and grammar."

REJECTIONS: A standard rejection form is sent to contributors who send in poetry (which is never run). Other contributors receive a polite letter, usually with guidelines sheet included.

WESTERN'S WORLD

East/West Network
5900 Wilshire Boulevard
Los Angeles, CA 90036
(213) 937-5810

SOURCE: Ed Dwyer, editor

IN SHORT: Open, but mostly publishes experienced writers.

ABOUT THE MAGAZINE: Monthly; 90% free-lance–written. *Western's World* is the in-flight magazine of Western Airlines. Ed Dwyer explains the editorial focus: "General-interest for the American West—its business climate, environment, life-styles, and outdoors." *Readership:* age group 30–50; college-educated; most are professionals or own their own businesses. *Circulation:* 110,000. *Estimated readership:* One million. *Sample copy:* $2 to Dottie Hogan, Reader Service, East/West Network. *Areas open to free-lancers:* All. *Rates:* Departments: $300. Features: $600. *Payment:* On acceptance. *Expenses:* Pays reasonable expenses, to about 10% of fee. *Kill fee:* 10%. *Rights:* Buys first North American rights, by written contract. *Number of submissions received weekly:* 25. *Reply time to queries:* Three weeks. *Advance dates:* Lead time is three months. Issues are planned four months in advance.

FREE-LANCE POSSIBILITIES: "One of the biggest mistakes contributors make here is in assuming that *Western's World* is a travel magazine," says editor Ed Dwyer. "We're a general-interest magazine. We don't want travel queries. We want to see suggestions for general stories, and articles about people involved in business or endeavors that are typically western, either in a western town or in something that is having an impact on the West."

In the former category, general articles, *Western's World* has run stories ranging from industrial espionage in the West, to smart (i.e. intelligent) jocks, cattle rustling, a tongue-in-cheek look at secession movements in America, to how the "cute" concept is marketed. There are no specific guidelines; the idea must catch the editors' fancy. The magazine rarely runs articles that would focus on, say, a health/medical topic. But this area could work with a general-interest perspective. For instance, a piece was run on the new trends in medical care. The story included information on the new paramedical systems, new private medical groups, etc.

"People" stories generally come from these two groups, as Dwyer explains: "They're either the movers and shakers, or they're people who have a life-style in a Western Airlines destination locality that epitomizes all the charms and excitement of that area." Examples: a lawyer in Phoenix and his wife who collect Hopi dolls, an architect in Seattle who lives on a yacht and sails the Puget Sound, a lawyer in Houston who flies by private plane to his ranch.

Of the approximately 25 submissions received weekly over-the-transom, Dwyer estimates one or two would work out. Those that don't are rejected mainly because the writers "are not aware of our needs. You have to get hold of the magazine and *see* what we do."

Dwyer sees all submissions. On any with promise, he generally will call the writer to discuss the story in more detail; he will also ask to see clips. If this follow-up pans out, an assignment will be made. He does not ask people to work on spec. If the writer does not have good clips—either consumer magazine or good newspaper clips—he is unlikely to take a chance. He *does* buy ideas.

As a result, most writers appearing here are experienced; they have clips from other magazines, or as is more often the case, they're known at East/West Network.

The beginning writer, then, has two choices: either to send the complete ms. or to try this magazine when he's amassed some impressive clips.

Editing tends to be light-handed here; the staff is small and there is rarely time or people to go to work on a manuscript. Says Dwyer: "It's another reason why I try to make sure all the parameters are set beforehand—that the story is clear and that the writer is competent." If a rewrite is needed, he will return the ms. to the writer, if there's time. Galleys are not shown; writers are not informed of changes.

HOW TO SUBMIT: Mss. are read (photocopies okay), but queries are preferred. Multiple submissions are accepted on queries, but not on mss. Brief queries are preferred. Include any background/

experience that is relevant to the query. Clips are not required at query stage.

REJECTIONS: A standard rejection slip is usually used, but Dwyer adds: "Sometimes I'll write a personal note on the bottom, just to tell the writer the query wasn't a lost cause."

WOMAN

Harris Publications
79 Madison Avenue
New York, NY 10016
(212) 686-4121

SOURCE: Sherry Amatenstein, editor

IN SHORT: Good for reprints; less so for original material.

ABOUT THE MAGAZINE: Published nine times a year; 15% free-lance–written. *Woman* is a women's service magazine; articles on work and relationships have a psychological emphasis, but there are also articles that give practical money-saving information on beauty and fashion, finances, health, legal matters. Also an emphasis on both well- and lesser-known women who have achieved success or come through some obstacle. Eighty-five percent of the magazine is reprinted, mostly from other women's magazines. Says Sherry Amatenstein: "We see ourselves as a self-help bible, telling women how to better themselves in all areas." *Readership:* The magazine is aimed at women in their 20s through 50s, both working and at home, single as well as married. Focus is on the woman as an individual. *Circulation:* 400,000. *Estimated readership:* 1.2 million. *Areas open to free-lancers:* Theoretically, all the magazine is open, but the use of reprints restricts opportunities. *Rates:* $75–$125 (same for reprints). *Payment:* On acceptance. *Expenses:* None. *Kill fee:* Negotiable; "only when we're familiar with the writer." *Rights:* Buys all rights, by written contract. Negotiable. *Number of submissions received weekly:* 30. *Reply time:* Up to three weeks. *Advance dates:* Lead time is two months. Issues are planned two to three months in advance.

FREE-LANCE POSSIBILITIES: This is a good market for reprint sales, and the magazine welcomes published clips from writers for possible reprinting. But chances of selling an original article are slim. The number of reprints used leaves very little space for original material. Explains Sherry Amatenstein: "A free-lancer has to come up with an angle on a story that's really different; because there are so many books and published articles around, chances are it's easier for us to buy a reprint—rather than having to have discussions with the writer and to do the editing and everything else an original piece entails."

There are, however, a couple of areas where Amatenstein *wants* more material:

Short (300–800-word) interviews with women who are successful—either by starting their own business, working in a unique field, or having overcome some kind of obstacle. "Preferably we're interested in women who are not famous, but who have a good story to tell." A recent example: a woman who overcame polio and is now a top saleswoman.

The other area is the personal experience piece: "one which will touch a chord in the reader." Preferred length: 1000–1500 words. "The writing style should be personal and chatty." A recent example: a piece that probed the emotions of a writer about whether she could feel fulfilled without having a child.

Short humor pieces are possibilities and so, of course, are articles for the regular service areas. But there is less chance than in the two areas mentioned. Amatenstein adds a thought here: "Our readers are most interested in relationships and how to better them. So this is always a good area. But the angle *has* to be different, not just the same old 'Ten Ways to Say I Love You.'"

Writers mostly work on spec here; clips won't necessarily get you an assignment. "I'll only assign someone whose work I really know," Amatenstein says. Editing varies but Amatenstein says she tries to keep it to a minimum. "I'm a free-lancer, too, and I've had some horrendous things done to me by editors, so I really try to do as little as possible." Galleys will be shown in most cases if the writer requests them.

HOW TO SUBMIT: For original material, phone queries are accepted. Manuscripts are read (photocopies okay), but queries are preferred. "If you've written the piece, just drop us a line telling us the topic." Simultaneous submissions are accepted if Amatenstein is informed. Keep queries short. Clips are not necessary, but are "helpful." For reprints, send the published clip to Amatenstein. Give name of publication and issue date.

REJECTIONS: A standard form is sent "unless the query is a little bit closer to the mark"; then a personalized note will be sent.

WOMAN'S DAY

CBS Publications
1515 Broadway
New York, NY 10036
(212) 719-6000

SOURCE: Rebecca Greer, articles editor

IN SHORT: Very competitive; difficult break-in market for the less experienced writer.

ABOUT THE MAGAZINE: Published 15 times a year. Most articles free-lance–written. *Woman's Day* is described as a "women's service magazine." Articles editor Rebecca Greer adds: "Our primary interest is in helping women improve their lives in some way." The magazine covers beauty and fashion, health and fitness, food and nutrition, home decorating, sewing and crafts, family finances and relevant issues—geared to the family woman. *Woman's Day* is sold mostly in supermarkets; some newsstands. *Readership:* "Diverse and broad; a cross section of American women." *Circulation:* Between 7 and 8 million. *Estimated readership:* 17 million. *Areas open to free-lancers:* Articles. (Columns and service departments—fashion, decorating, beauty, etc.—are written by staff/regular contributors.) *Rates:* Features: "pays top rates." Back-page essay: $2000. *Payment:* On acceptance. *Expenses:* Pays all reasonable expenses. *Kill fee:* Negotiable. *Rights:* Buys first North American serial rights, by written contract. *Number of submissions received weekly:* 80 queries, 75 manuscripts. *Reply time:* For queries, three to four weeks; for manuscripts, six to eight weeks. *Advance dates:* Lead time is three to four months. Issues are planned six months in advance.

FREE-LANCE POSSIBILITIES: Any subject "of interest to women" is a possibility for articles: marriage, education, family health, child rearing, money management, relationships, life-style, careers, emotional problems, but chances are described as "very slim" for the writer coming in cold. Most articles are written by experienced magazine writers. These people are pitching ideas all the time and are also being assigned staff-generated ideas. "Very few good ideas come in over-the-transom," says Rebecca Greer. "*Very* few unsolicited manuscripts work out, and only an occasional query; a new writer breaks in only a couple of times a year."

What's lacking are story ideas right for the market. Greer lists some reasons for rejection: "Many writers seem unfamiliar with the magazine. Many ideas conflict with staff-written material (food, fashion, crafts). And we'd like to see fewer old-hat ideas. We're getting a lot of tired and trivial ideas, material that's poorly written, queries that are too vague or sketchy for us to make a decision." The less experienced writer does have a slight chance, though probably would be asked to work on spec.

An area where the editors would like to see more queries: first-person dramatic narratives, personal stories of women who've overcome some obstacle. A new feature, the back-page essay, could also be a possibility. Here the editors are looking for strong opinion pieces—either serious or humorous—but with a real point of view. Discussions of significant issues are preferred and convincing controversy is encouraged. Reader identification and relevance is the key; ideal length is 900–1200 words.

The unsolicited pile is sorted through by several staffers. The editor-in-chief makes final decision for all purchases.

A copy of the edited manuscript is sent to the writer before publication.

HOW TO SUBMIT: Completed manuscripts are accepted (no photocopies), but queries are much preferred. "The query should describe the article—including approach, point of view, sources —and indicate the writer's qualifications." Include clips only "if they are from similar markets and/or relevant to the idea being submitted."

REJECTIONS: A standard form reply is usually sent. Personalized replies go to writers known at the magazine and sometimes to encourage more submissions from an unknown writer who's on the right track.

WOMAN'S LIFE

1790 Broadway
Suite 7111
New York, NY 10019
(212) 265-7650

SOURCE: Yolanda S. Drake, editor-in-chief

IN SHORT: Open, but very little space for free-lance material.

ABOUT THE MAGAZINE: Monthly; 25% free-lance—written. *Woman's Life* is a women's magazine that highlights women of achievement in all fields: business, philanthropy, the arts, sciences, and sports. The magazine has a heavy emphasis on volunteerism, and at least one women's organization is featured monthly. Also included is a feature titled "Man Among Women" that highlights a man who is aiding the progress of women. Comments Yolanda Drake: "We thought we should try to bring women and men together again." Largest distribution is to women's groups and organizations; some supermarket sales. No traditional women's service topics are covered. *Circulation:* 300,000. *Sample copy:* Free. *Areas open to free-lancers:* All features. *Rates:* Features: $250. *Payment:* On publication. *Expenses:* All reasonable expenses. *Kill fee:* Negotiable. *Rights:* Buys first North American rights, by letter of agreement. *Number of submissions received weekly:* 80. *Reply time to queries:* Two weeks. *Advance dates:* Lead time is three months. Issues are planned six months in advance.

FREE-LANCE POSSIBILITIES: *Woman's Life,* one of the newer magazines, is different from the other women's publications. It is dedicated to achieving women; it has no traditional departments (food, fashion, how-tos). And it has an editorial advisory board and list of contributing editors who, for the most part, are not writers. They include businesswomen, attorneys and academics, and such well-knowns as Betty Friedan and Celeste Holm. The magazine uses very little free-lance; most of the articles are written by contributing editors who are expert in specific fields. Explains Yolanda Drake: "When I give an assignment to a free-lancer, it's because the story is something no one on the board can do." Assignments are given on over-the-transom suggestions only if the idea is a special one and the writer has experience enough to handle the story; writers won't be asked to work on spec.

Yolanda Drake offers these guidelines: "We're looking for unusual stories: perhaps a volunteer effort in the community, or an artistic production. We recently bought a piece from a freelancer on a museum in the South that was holding an unusual exhibition by African-American artists. We like an American flavor. Profiles of women of achievement are also a possibility. There's not a lot of space for free-lance material, but we would like to find free-lancers we can trust and use again." (See "Portfolios and Positive Thinking," pages 7–9).

Any rewriting is generally done by staff copy editors. "But we will always ask permission—usually it's to edit the style somewhat or to cut for space—and we show galleys. If the writer doesn't approve, then we'll return the story to them."

HOW TO SUBMIT: Mss. are read (photocopies preferred). Multiple submissions are okay. Queries should be short. Include your professional background, a rundown of your writing credits, and one clip. Magazine/newspaper clips are good. "We're looking for style, originality, sensitivity."

REJECTIONS: No standard form rejection is used. "We always send personal replies."

WOMAN'S WORLD

Heinrich Bauer North America, Inc.
177 North Dean Street
Englewood, NJ 07631
(201) 569-0006

SOURCE: Janel Bladow, news-features editor

IN SHORT: One of the best free-lance markets.

ABOUT THE MAGAZINE: Weekly. Articles mostly free-lance—written. *Woman's World* is a general-interest women's magazine with a strong family orientation and a traditional women's service magazine bent. It is sold mostly in supermarkets. The emphasis is on affordable, wearable fashion, thrifty recipes, commonsense health and beauty, and articles that highlight lesser-known but intriguing women, cover issues and concerns relevant to middle-class families, and entertain with escapist themes: "Polygamy Now," "Confessions of a Mafia Wife," "I Dared to Love a Younger Man." Readers are both working women and homemakers, aged 25–60. The magazine is distributed to half the nation (does not include New York City). *Circulation:* Just under one million. *Estimated readership:* 2½ million. *Sample copy:* $1. *Areas open to free-lancers:* "Opening Up," "In Real Life," "Families," *"Woman's World* Report," "Women & Crime," "American Woman," "Turning Point," "Feeling Good." *Rates:* Pays 50 cents per word for articles. (Payment is specified on agreement sheet sent to author on assignment.) Pays $250 for "Turning Point." *Payment:* On acceptance. *Expenses:* All reasonable expenses. *Kill fee:* 20%. *Rights:* Buys all rights, verbally. These revert to author six months after publication. *Number of submissions received weekly:* "Several hundred." *Reply time to queries:* Four weeks (call to inquire after this time period). *Advance dates:* Lead time is three months. Issues are planned four months in advance.

FREE-LANCE POSSIBILITIES: *Woman's World* is quite possibly the best consumer free-lance market around. This is a weekly magazine so the editors need a *lot* of material. Articles are short (1000 words is the average); subject matter is wide-ranging; and the writing style required is straightforward and commonsensical. Payment is 50 cents a word (that's $500 for four to five ms. pages) and assignments are the norm.

The editors are *very* open to ideas, from both established and new writers. They'll give assignments to writers with good credentials (see "Portfolios and Positive Thinking," pages 7–9). And this can be an excellent market for the little-published or unpublished writer. "Turning Point," a regular feature that's a dramatic, moving first-person account of a life-changing experience, often runs pieces by first-timers.

There *are* several factors to be wary of here. One is that response time to submissions can lag. But writers should feel free to call and inquire after a month. Another is that purchased articles can take months to appear; the inventory here is large. But payment *is* on acceptance. And editing can be heavy-handed and rewrites are not unusual.

Only about half of the article ideas are staff-generated. A large number of the articles come from regular writers; about 10–25% of the over-the-transom submissions from writers unknown at the magazine work out. Says Janel Bladow: "The main reasons we have to reject are because writers haven't looked at the magazine—and yet it's the same format every week—and because they just can't tell the story." If you write well and your idea is a catchy one that will fit into one of the regular feature areas, your chances here are very good.

Here's an area rundown. "Opening Up" is, in both content and style, the weekly "attention grabber." It runs on page 3, is written in an upbeat style and can be a fun piece or article about coping, or an issue piece—presenting a balanced view of the subject. (Examples: "Are We Pushing Our Kids Too Hard?", "Love at First Sight: Myth or Magic?".) "In Real Life": human-interest real-life stories—adventurous, dramatic or emotional. Can be first-person. The piece preferably should end on an upbeat note. (Examples: "Agoraphobia—I Was a Prisoner in My Own Home for 30 Years," and "Sharing a Husband with Two Other Wives.") "Families": stories of unusual families. (Examples: the family that writes the Hagar the Horrible comic strip; a circus family.) "*Woman's World* Report": an investigative report, written in a news style. Must include statistics and quotes from experts/authorities. (Examples: "Sex Offenders—Can They be Stopped?", "Video Games—Amusement or Menace?" "Women and Crime": True stories of women convicted of crimes. Must have an unusual twist ("Please, no more stories of women who've killed their husbands"). (Example: "Sandra Brown—the $10 Million Swindle.") "American Woman": profiles of uncelebrated women with an unusual, fascinating life-style or profession. (Examples: woman puppeteer; stuntwoman; Madame Wellington, diamond counterfeiter. "Please, no more women cops or district attorneys.") "Turning Point": 2500–3000 words. Reader submissions are accepted. Must be accounts of *unusual* turning points. (Examples: "I Dared to Love a Younger Man"; Becoming an actress at 60. "Please, no more coping with the death of my child, coping with alcoholism, how I went back to work.") "Feeling Good": short (600-word) how-tos. (Examples: Coping with stress; overcoming inferiority.)

Bladow adds: "We would like to see more ideas on controversial issues, and more women-surviving or women-coping stories —as long as they're unusual." Articles always contain anecdotes and quotes. *Woman's World* does not buy previously published material/reprints.

Galleys are not shown before publication. "Ours is more of a newspaper than a magazine setup," Bladow explains.

HOW TO SUBMIT: Completed mss. are read (originals preferred over photocopies), but queries are preferred. Keep queries short. "The faster you summarize and get to the angle, the better. Give us the gist of the story fast." Include a rundown of your writing experience. Clips are not required, but sending them "doesn't hurt."

REJECTIONS: Janel Bladow says: "Generally we reply to queries with a personal note, unless that week we're swamped with letters; then I'll send a form letter with a dashed note on the bottom."

WOMEN'S SPORTS

310 Town & Country Village
Palo Alto, CA 94301
(415) 321-5102

SOURCE: Amy Rennert, editor

IN SHORT: Limited possibilities because of space; best chances with shorts.

ABOUT THE MAGAZINE: Monthly; 20–25% free-lance–written. Says editor Amy Rennert: "Our logo sums us up: 'For the Active American Woman.' We're a women's magazine just as much as a sports magazine, aimed at the participant more than the sports fan. We're a magazine for women who like being active—recreational, amateur or professional—at any level." General articles on health, fitness, and nutrition included with sports stories. *Readership:* 68% are in the 18–34 age group; most are employed; 78% have some college, plus; median age is 29; median household income: $28,000. *Circulation:* 125,000. *Estimated readership:* Just under 600,000. *Areas open to free-lancers:* Articles and the following columns: "Sports Pages," "Active Woman's Almanac," "End Zone." *Rates:* Shorts: $25–$100. Features: $200–$400. *Payment:* On publication. *Expenses:* Up to 20% of fee (and occasionally to $100, higher under special circumstances). Expenses also usually paid for on-spec work specifically requested by the magazine. *Kill fee:* 20% minimum. *Rights:* Prefers to buy all rights, by letter of agreement. Negotiable. *Number of submissions received weekly:* 25–50. *Reply time to queries:* Six weeks. *Advance dates:* Lead time is six to eight weeks. Issues are planned three to four months in advance.

FREE-LANCE POSSIBILITIES: There is not a lot of space for unknown free-lancers at *Women's Sports.* A newcomer breaks in with a feature only two or three times a year. But there are several departments where writing a short can get you an "in" —namely, "Sports Pages" (news about sports, sportswomen, sports business); "Active Woman's Almanac" (mini-profiles; small health, how-to items; small informational pieces, e.g. running camps); and "End Zone" (the back-page issue/think piece —can be personal, political, controversial). Comments Amy Rennert: "Probably another three to five people will break in with a short and then go on to write a feature, say the following year."

Some general points should be kept in mind. Rennert emphasizes that this magazine is also for women who want general information related to being active in sports. "We're always interested in ideas for stories on health, fitness, nutrition; we look for service pieces that every sportswoman can relate to, no matter what her sport. Because we have staff and regular writers, what works over-the-transom are unusual angles on subjects. For instance, when the New York Marathon is coming up, I'll get six queries from people who just want to do a story on the race. We're not getting enough unusual slants.

"Profiles are a possibility, but again, we want more than just scores and results. Someone might be worth a profile not just because they won some event, but because they also did something else that was interesting. We like ideas on the more popular sports—less on the offbeat ones. And we don't want to see any more first-person running stories—unless the angle is really unusual."

The following *Women's Sports* articles originally came in over-the-transom: a piece on the junior Olympics in volleyball; article on master swimming—what's going on for older people in swimming and how to get involved in a masters program; a humor piece by a man whose wife is a runner—and he isn't.

Free-lancers generally work on spec here—after the editors have seen and are satisfied with clips. (These should be included with the query.) Unlike most magazines, *Women's Sports* will pay expenses for on-spec work if the piece has been requested and expenses discussed.

Editing varies "from changing two sentences to a total rewrite." Rewrites are done by the author if there's time; if not, and a real overhaul is needed, the piece is more likely to be killed. Galleys are shown on request.

HOW TO SUBMIT: Send feature submissions to Amy Rennert, editor or Susan Brenneman; "Sports Pages" to Liz Schmidt; "Almanac" to Karen Kotoske; "Mixed Media" and "End Zone" to Pamela Feinsilber. Send completed mss. (photocopies discouraged) or queries. Simultaneous submissions accepted on queries, discouraged on mss.; in both cases, editor *must* be informed. Short queries are preferred. One page is best, with the story lead if possible. Include two or three clips, "particularly any that would relate to the story being presented."

REJECTIONS: A standard rejection letter is usually used; this, however, gives a choice of five different reasons for rejection which the editor will check. Personalized notes are sent to encourage more submissions.

WORKING MOTHER

230 Park Avenue
New York, NY 10169
(212) 551-9412

SOURCE: Mary McLaughlin, managing editor

IN SHORT: Good possibilities with targeted ideas.

ABOUT THE MAGAZINE: Monthly; 60% free-lance–written. *Working Mother* is a magazine for working mothers, that is published under the McCall's flagship. It is geared to younger mothers (those with children under about age 18). It's a service magazine; the emphasis in every article is on support and encouragement; the articles let women know they're not alone with the many problems of juggling careers inside and outside the home. Article emphasis is on relationships, child raising, home organization, and coping with a job outside the home. Humorous articles are included; less for comic relief, however, and more as a helping hand. Food, home furnishings, beauty, and fashion are also included. *Circulation:* 400,000. *Areas open to free-lancers:* Everything except "Bulletin Board." *Rates:* Articles (2000–2500 words): around $500. *Payment:* On acceptance. *Expenses:* Pays basic expenses. *Kill fee:* 20%. *Rights:* Buys all rights, or first North American rights, by written contract. *Number of submissions received weekly:* Unable to estimate. *Reply time to queries:* "Our reply can take a very long time. Our staff is small and we get backed up."

FREE-LANCE POSSIBILITIES: The staff at *Working Mother* is small, and only half to two-thirds of the articles published monthly come from staff-generated ideas. But this market is not as easy a sell as it may sound. This magazine is very different from, say, *Family Circle* or *Woman's Day* or *Good Housekeeping*, which cover so many varied areas of interest to women. *Working Mother* articles must speak about the specific problems working mothers experience.

New writers have a good chance here—with two conditions. You have to be able to prove you can write well and can handle a magazine article, and you have to be able to come up with an idea that hasn't been done before. "We're always looking for new writers," Mary McLaughlin says. "But what we're really after are people who can bring a fresh view and a new voice to the magazine. And what I don't want to see are story ideas that have been treated in the other magazines." A piece in the January '83 issue on kids and computers, discussing whether computers are beneficial, came in over-the-transom as a query. The author wrote the piece on spec and it worked out.

The query letter is very important here; it should include not just your idea but also an explanation of how you would carry through the assignment, how the topic would be treated. A letter asking: "Would you like an article on working from home?" is not enough.

Show the editors that you have an interesting slant and advice that is not predictable, that you can write, and that you've thought through the idea from beginning to end, and you may just get an assignment—even if you're a beginning writer. If the editors like your idea, but it's not very clear how you will go about it, you'll probably be asked to work on spec. Also, you will probably be asked to work on spec if your idea depends on particular style and tone as opposed to a straight research and reporting job.

One published story in *Working Mother* will not make you a regular. You'll still have to come up with ideas to get published again. "We have to get used to writers, see what kind of stories they can handle best."

However, virtually all the magazine is open to free-lancers, even the food section and fashion (if you can come up with a new idea and offer it as a package). Child-psychology pieces are not a good bet, not even if you have several experts in the field lined up and ready to be quoted. The magazine feels there is a real responsibility attached to this kind of piece and is "very reluctant to assign them to an unknown writer." The same goes for articles on money matters or medicine; chances are slim unless you're an established writer specializing in these areas. The magazine can always use ideas for stories relating to ways in which to increase wage earning, particularly if flexibility is offered as well. Past examples have included: commission sales, door-to-door selling.

Editing varies here. The editors prefer not to show galleys, but will on request.

HOW TO SUBMIT: Send ms. (photocopies okay) or query. Multiple submissions are discouraged. Note importance of query letter, just discussed. Sending clips with the query is not a must, but it's a good idea if the clips are good ones (small magazines, trades, and newspapers are okay). "If a writer sends me good clips, I would certainly be more encouraged to assign the story," Mary McLaughlin says. But she also adds: "I don't like a lot of clips. One or two good clips is sufficient." And if you have them, send clips that are related to the query—that really helps. Details on your personal background? Include them only if the information is relevant to the query in hand. Be sure to include a SASE with your query, or ms. It's important here.

REJECTIONS: A standard rejection form is usually sent.

WORKING WOMAN

1180 Avenue of the Americas
New York, NY 10036
(212) 944-5250

SOURCE: Julia Kagan, articles editor

IN SHORT: Needs well-targeted, *new* ideas.

ABOUT THE MAGAZINE: Monthly; 85% free-lance–written. *Working Woman* was the first magazine of its kind, bowing in 1976 and aiming itself at all working women. It has since changed its focus. After discovering that the bulk of readers were in managerial/professional positions, the magazine began to focus on the professional and executive women. Says Julia Kagan: "Most of our readers are not beginning their careers; they don't need to be told how to get started. We are a service magazine—there is a lot of how-to included—but we also discuss issues relevant to our readers." Feature topics include: business, personal finance, profiles, trends, psychology, politics. The majority of readers are college-educated, over half are married, over half are mothers. *Circulation:* 550,000. *Estimated readership:* 2,350,000. *Areas open to free-lancers:* All areas except those written by regular columnists. *Rates:* Features (around 2500 words): $500. Columns (1500 words): $300. Shorts ("Memoranda," "MBA"): $50–$300. *Payment:* On acceptance. *Expenses:* Pays reasonable expenses. *Kill fee:* 20%. *Rights:* Buys all rights, by written contract. Author receives 50% of any reprint fees. *Number of submissions received weekly:* 100. *Reply time to queries:* Two days to six weeks. Outright rejections receive a quick response. Those submissions put under consideration are acknowledged with a postcard to that effect. *Advance dates:* Lead time is three to four months. Issues are planned four months in advance.

FREE-LANCE POSSIBILITIES: *Working Woman* can be a good market, but only for the published writer. The magazine's pages have been increasing and the article scope is wide. Most ideas do come from staff and regular writers, but with the number of pages to be filled there is always a need for fresh ideas.

No assignments are given without satisfactory clips. Magazine clips are preferred. "Clips from newspapers or trade magazines may not show off a person's writing style as well. But of course

I will read them," Julia Kagan says. Kagan sees all submissions that pass the first screening; she will then ask to see clips before recommending the query to other editors. But if you're unpublished or low on magazine clips, there *is* a way in. Suggest a small piece; the smaller the story, the less risk there is for the magazine. Or send a completed manuscript; stories *have* been bought out of the slush pile. (An example: the April '81 issue ran an article on a woman in Charlotte, North Carolina, who runs a baseball team. The author *did* have to revise the original article she sent in, but she has since gone on to write more pieces for *Working Woman.*)

The following subject areas could all be possibilities: profiles, trends, business, consumer, careers, education, health, automotive, entrepreneurs. Check the masthead; columns with a contributing editor's by-line will generally not be open to freelancers.

"Memoranda" is the section highlighting new products, new strides, etc. It is mostly staff-written, but it *is* open. Essays and humor are welcomed, but here, if you're unknown at the magazine, you must send a completed manuscript first. There's a particular need for articles from writers who have business or professional expertise; finding executives who can write is apparently not an easy task.

Keep in mind that readers want how-to information; a profile on a successful working woman must be informative as well and tell the reader how they, too, can be successful in their careers. Remember the readership: It's a sophisticated one. Says Kagan: "We don't want a lot of cute stuff, and we don't want to sound too adoring. We need information of a high level of expertise. Our readers are not beginners; they know what a money-market fund is. We need information that will enable them to go further in their careers and to earn more." A patronizing tone of voice won't work. Neither will ordinary ideas; the magazine has had several years to cover the field extensively. And ideas should be geared to the career woman; it should not be assumed that readers are married and/or have children. Many are, but they're not reading *Working Woman* for advice on child raising and for family-oriented pieces.

Also worth keeping in mind is that this is a national magazine and as such must appeal to readers all over the country. Regional pieces must have some kind of national appeal. Writers not liv-

ing in big cities can have a real advantage; the editors are looking for stories from different parts of the country.

All articles are carefully checked. That includes quotes. If it's
a controversial piece, you will be required to tape interviews
and provide copies of your notes. Editing varies. Writers are
informed of copy changes, however, even though galleys are
generally not shown.

HOW TO SUBMIT: Send submissions to Basia Hellwig for "MBA";
Paula Gribetz Gottlieb for "Memoranda"; Jacqueline Paris-Chi-
tanvis for "Careers" and "Consumer"; Jennifer Fortenbaugh for
"Education" and "Automotive." All other articles, query Julia
Kagan; she is happy to read either a query or a manuscript—
your choice. For queries, though, she prefers substance. "I want
an idea of how the writer is going to handle the piece. And I
want to know where writers have been published and if they
have any particular expertise relevant to the piece they're suggesting. It should be a well-thought-out query letter." Sending
one or two clips with the query is a must. Some don'ts: Don't
forget to include with any submission a phone number where
you can be reached during the day. Don't scatter the query with
misspellings: "We *do* notice typos." Don't submit a query letter
that gives only scanty information: "A lot of the queries we get
don't tell me enough about the topic, or the writer."

REJECTIONS: Immediate rejections receive a standard form reply.
If the submission gets past the first screener to an editor, the
reply will usually be a personalized one.

WORLD TENNIS

CBS Publications
1515 Broadway
New York, NY 10036
(212) 719-6000

SOURCE: Susan B. Adams, editor

IN SHORT: Difficult market.

ABOUT THE MAGAZINE: Monthly; 60% free-lance–written. *World Tennis* is the magazine of the United States Tennis Association. First published over 30 years ago as the newsletter of the Houston Tennis Association, it is now the national magazine for some 175,000 USTA members; with another 225,000 subscribers and newsstand sales, the total monthly circulation is around 400,000. Says Susan B. Adams: "Our purpose is not only to inform but to entertain as well. And we're a literate book; we pride ourselves on our writing." Published regularly are player profiles, articles on tennis vacations and pieces on the varying aspects of the big business tennis is these days, plus instructional articles. Readers range from juniors (under 18s) right on up to super seniors (the over 80s), but the basic readership core is between 24–35. Readers tend to be well educated, well-to-do, and professionals. Adds Susan Adams: "They're active, physical people. Tennis is but one link in their lives, but it's probably the strongest link too." *Areas open to free-lancers:* Everything except the instructional articles. *Rates:* Payment starts at $150 for a column or feature; $25–$50 for a spot item. *Payment:* On publication. *Expenses:* Pays reasonable expenses. *Kill fee:* Rarely paid. "Usually if we accept an idea and assign the story, we don't kill it." *Rights:* Buys first-time world rights, by written contract. *Number of submissions received weekly:* 20–40. *Reply time to queries:* Two weeks to two months. *Advance dates:* Lead time is six weeks. Issues are planned, according to tournament schedules, about a year in advance.

FREE-LANCE POSSIBILITIES: Susan Adams says she would like to be encouraging. But she doesn't mince words: "Our magazine is a tough sell."

World Tennis has a fairly large contributing staff of specialist

writers and stringers everywhere, so breaking in here *is* a difficult task. You do not have to be a tennis or sports writer (general-
interest writers are published), but you do have to fall into one
of these categories: you're a known writer; you have a unique
idea that would make for a special story; or you're in a place a
World Tennis editor, writer, or stringer can't reach.

A unique local story is probably the best bet, or a small piece
that could fit into an area like "Around the World" (photos and
"short take" reports on both the pros and amateur tennis players
doing something offbeat/worthy of note). It's possible to break
in with a major feature, but not probable. "In the eight years
I've been here," Adams notes, "it's never happened." Forget
suggestions for tennis-player profiles. "I don't want anybody
I don't know sending me a Tracy Austin profile. I have
more than enough profiles, and more than enough writers to
do them." Humor? "That's hard to pull off." Personal experience pieces? "I get tons of those; there might be one in 150 that
stands out."

All writers new to the magazine are asked to work on spec.
Assignments come "when I know the writer's work." Adams
adds: "I would still want the writer to come up with his/her own
ideas after that. But once they've proven their work, I could be
calling them for future stories."

Sometimes Adams will discuss an over-the-transom idea with
a couple of other staff editors; often she'll make a sole decision.
If there's time, the writer does any needed rewriting. But mostly
there's deadline pressure here. It's magazine policy, however,
to rewrite as little as possible. Galleys are not usually shown.

HOW TO SUBMIT: Mss. are read (no photocopies; "I just don't
know where else the writer has sent the story," Adams says).
Queries are preferred. Your idea is what's of prime importance
here. "Writing ability and knowledge of tennis will pretty much
reveal themselves in the query letter. I'm really looking for the
quality of the idea." Clips are helpful, but not a requirement;
you may never be asked to show any. But include them if you
think they will make a difference. Keep in mind that a unique or
else a hard-to-get-at idea is what will work at this magazine, and
present it so that it's "short, snappy, and enticing. Long-winded
query letters are the scourge of an editor's existence!"

REJECTIONS: Susan Adams generally replies with personal notes, giving the reason for rejection. If the idea is way off-target, however, she's likely to say something like: "Sorry, but it doesn't suit our editorial needs." If the reply encourages sending more ideas, Adams's advice is: "Definitely keep trying."

YANKEE

Dublin, NH 03444
(603) 563-8111

SOURCE: Judson D. Hale, editor

IN SHORT: Good possibilities for stories with regional slant.

ABOUT THE MAGAZINE: Monthly; 75% free-lance–written. *Yankee* is a digest-sized regional magazine that covers the New England states—the places, people, and events. It is a general-interest magazine. *Readership:* "People who are interested in the scenery, history, and culture of New England—though they may not necessarily live in the six-state region." *Circulation:* 900,000. *Estimated readership:* 3.5 million. *Sample copy:* Free. *Areas open to free-lancers:* Everything except "Plain Talk," "House for Sale," and "Books." *Rates:* Small items: $100. Articles: $450–$500 average, $1000 maximum. *Payment:* On acceptance. *Expenses:* Pays all reasonable travel and film expenses. *Kill fee:* $100–$150. *Rights:* Prefers to buy all rights, by written contract. Negotiable. *Number of submissions received weekly:* 40 queries; 50 mss. *Reply time:* Replies to queries in three weeks; replies to manuscripts in four to six weeks. *Advance dates:* Lead time is three months. Issues are planned two months in advance.

FREE-LANCE POSSIBILITIES: Only 35% of *Yankee* material is generated in-house; 50% of the articles come in as queries either from regular writers or over-the-transom, 15% as unsolicited manuscripts. It's very possible to break in with a feature and then be assigned in the future.

An editor reads all unsolicited submissions. Anything with promise is discussed at a weekly editorial meeting. If the writer is known, and the subject wanted, the piece will probably be assigned; if the writer has never written for *Yankee* before, he or she will probably be asked to work on speculation.

It's not necessary to live in New England to write for *Yankee* but it *is* necessary to know the magazine's style and kind of coverage, and to think about its readership. Coverage of events of interest must be timely and substantial, like the efforts to produce a super potato in Maine. Coverage of places must have an unusual slant; a midwesterner or Californian might be intrigued to read about Maine's rocky coastline, but the *Yankee* reader probably knows the area well. The best people stories are the ones that focus on uncelebrated residents: Dick Lucius, master falconer; Connie Small, a New England lighthouse keeper's wife for 28 years; Dick Fecteau, Boston University faculty member who was a POW in China (this story came in over-the-transom). The magazine also runs general-interest articles highlighting area people and places. Like the Connecticut Raybestos Brakettes, one of the best women's fast-pitch softball teams in the world; the students of New England's School of Mortuary Science (an over-the-transom submission).

Some guidelines before you submit: "Writers frequently attempt to 'hook' us by writing a query so information remains a mystery. It's a ploy and we don't feel it's professional. And writers could save themselves (and us, too) time by obtaining access at the library to our index and checking their proposed topic to see if we've already covered it." Editing varies. "We've done a lot of work on some manuscripts and none on others." Galleys are shown only on request.

HOW TO SUBMIT: Send all submissions to Polly Bannister, assistant editor. Completed mss. are read (photocopies okay), but brief queries are preferred. Multiple submissions are accepted on mss. but not queries. Include a rundown of your writing credits. Clips are not usually required.

REJECTIONS: A standard form rejection is sent to contributors unknown at the magazine. Personalized notes are sent to writers who have been previously published in *Yankee*.

YOUNG MISS

685 Third Avenue
New York, NY 10017
(212) 878-8700

SOURCE: Deborah Purcell, features/fiction editor

IN SHORT: Very open market, but all writers new to the magazine must work on speculation.

ABOUT THE MAGAZINE: Ten times a year; one-third free-lance–written. *Young Miss* debuted in the 1930s and was, until a couple of years ago, a digest-sized book with distribution only by subscription. It was aimed at the 8–12 age group. It's now a glossy magazine competing on the newsstand and aiming itself at teens: 12–17-year-olds (the reader core is in the 15–16 age group). This is a young woman's magazine that aims to be the reader's "second-best friend"; it covers beauty and fashion and discusses issues relevant to teens. *Circulation:* 700,000. *Areas open to free-lancers:* Everything except beauty, fashion, food, and departments. *Rates:* Fillers: $50 and up. Features (1500–2500 words): $200 and up. *Payment:* On acceptance. *Expenses:* Phone calls. *Kill fee:* 15%–25%. *Rights:* Buys first North American rights, by written contract. *Number of submissions received weekly:* 30–50. *Reply time to queries:* One to four weeks. *Advance dates:* Lead time is five months. Issues are planned at least six months in advance. Submit seasonal material at least a year in advance.

FREE-LANCE POSSIBILITIES: *Young Miss* welcomes both new and experienced writers, but everybody works on spec for the first one or two stories. This is the policy for *all* writers, published or not, experienced or raw. For the beginning writer, it means that you won't have to prove your talent with clips.

    Young Miss is upbeat and slick and it *looks* like an easy market; pieces aren't too lengthy and the subjects covered are within a generalist's range. But as Deborah Purcell points out, a real "feel" for the teen is required: "Our readers are mostly junior high and high school age; a few are college age. They're still going through a lot of doubts about themselves. They're at an awkward age in which they're worrying about such things as whether they'll ever have a date, let alone a boyfriend! Their emotions are fragile.

"Writing for teens might *seem* to be easier, but it's just as difficult as writing for adults. You have to be interested in teens, for one thing. You have to be interested in the sorts of problems they face; you have to be able to remember back, to identify and empathize with them. You don't have to know a lot of teens or talk to teens every day, but your ideas do have to be timely and important to them, and presented in a nurturing and supportive way. And you shouldn't condescend to them in your writing. Teenagers are thinking human beings with a tremendous amount of responsibility; they're not a separate breed."

Article opportunities are wide. About 25% of the article ideas come in over-the-transom, and new writers are sought. "We're growing, so we're always interested in new writers. We have a healthy inventory but we're always expanding it." Fashion and beauty are out, and health and fitness pieces are mainly written in-house. Celebrity profiles are a possibility, but the writer must approach the interviewee before querying the magazine. There will be increasing emphasis on "heavier" topics like serious depression, drug addiction, and alcoholism, but these in-depth pieces are most likely to be assigned to regulars. The teen perennials—topics like loneliness, depression, shyness—have, of course, been done but a new angle or service approach is always of interest. There's also always a need for a new focus on boy/girl topics (your summer love—will it last?; blind dates; the ideal guy; what to do if he wants to be "just friends"?; what attracts and bugs boys about girls; what to do when your best friend is dating and you're not, etc.) For all psychological-style articles, writers are asked to talk to, and quote, both experts/specialists and teens. General-interest topics that are lively, fun, and out-of-the-ordinary are possibilities, too (hot-air ballooning is an example). Says Purcell: "We'd also like to see more short pieces—we're looking for fillers—humorous pieces, and reflective first-person essays." The latter should run about 850–1000 words and be written as though you're a teen or just out of your teens (they've been done successfully by writers in their 30s who are able to think back clearly and identify!). Quizzes are also welcome, but experts should be quoted in answers if the subject's a serious one.

The simple stuff is out. "We don't want to see any more queries on 'how to write a journal' or 'why you should write a journal.' " Other don'ts: "a terrific idea, executed poorly—either the prose is too dry with no style whatever, or the writer hasn't interviewed any experts or teens, and material that's too locally oriented."

Rates might not be startling, and the editors use their red pencils earnestly. But of the writer's chances at *Young Miss*, Deborah Purcell says: "If you're a good writer with a good idea, your chances are really very good." (See "Portfolios and Positive Thinking," pages 7–9).

HOW TO SUBMIT: Query or send a manuscript (photocopied manuscripts are okay). Queries "should be short—preferably no more than three paragraphs—concise, and very interesting. They should also impart some of the flavor of the article you're proposing. It's amazing how much you can tell from a query letter." Include one or two clips. As mentioned, they won't get you an assignment, but as Deborah Purcell puts it, "they give us a sense of the kind of person the writer is."

REJECTIONS: Standard forms are usually used, but occasionally (about five times a week) Purcell will add a personal note.

Cross-Listing of Magazines by Category